THE SOUTHERN FRONTIER

THE SOUTHERN FRONTIER

Australia, Antarctica and Empire in the Southern Ocean World

ROHAN HOWITT

MELBOURNE UNIVERSITY PRESS

Melbourne University Publishing acknowledges the traditional owners of the unceded land on which we work, learn and live: the Wurundjeri Woiwurrung peoples of the Kulin Nation. We pay respect to elders past, present and future, and acknowledge the importance of Indigenous knowledge.

MELBOURNE UNIVERSITY PRESS
An imprint of Melbourne University Publishing Limited
Level 1, 715 Swanston Street, Carlton, Victoria 3053, Australia
mup-contact@unimelb.edu.au
www.mup.com.au

First published 2025

Typeset by Megan Ellis
Cover design by Alex Ross Creative
Cover image by Frank Hurley
Printed in Australia by McPherson's Printing Group

NATIONAL LIBRARY OF AUSTRALIA
A catalogue record for this book is available from the National Library of Australia

9780522880519 (paperback)
9780522880526 (ebook)

FSC www.fsc.org
MIX
Paper | Supporting responsible forestry
FSC® C001695

CONTENTS

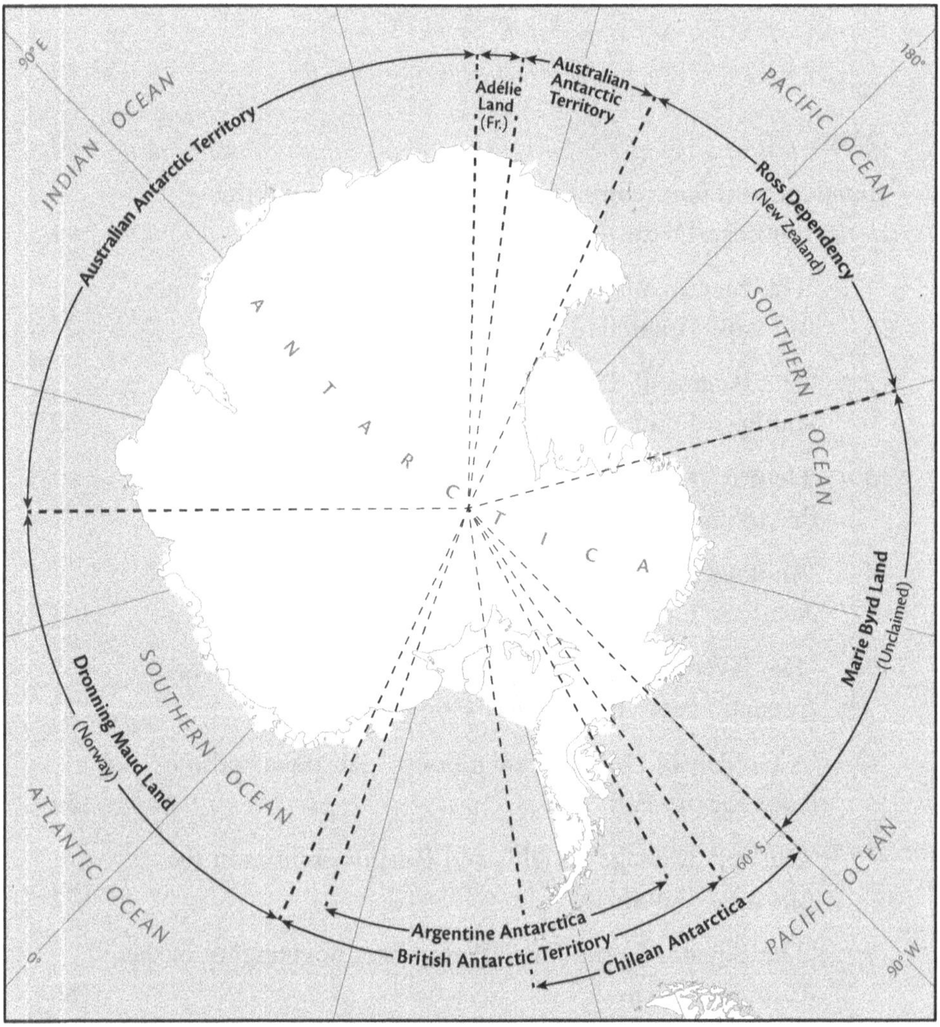

The formal territorial claims made in Antarctica as of the 1959 Antarctic Treaty. The treaty mandates that nothing that occurs while it is in force can be taken to solidify, extend or diminish any territorial claim, and that no new territorial claims can be made
Erin Greb

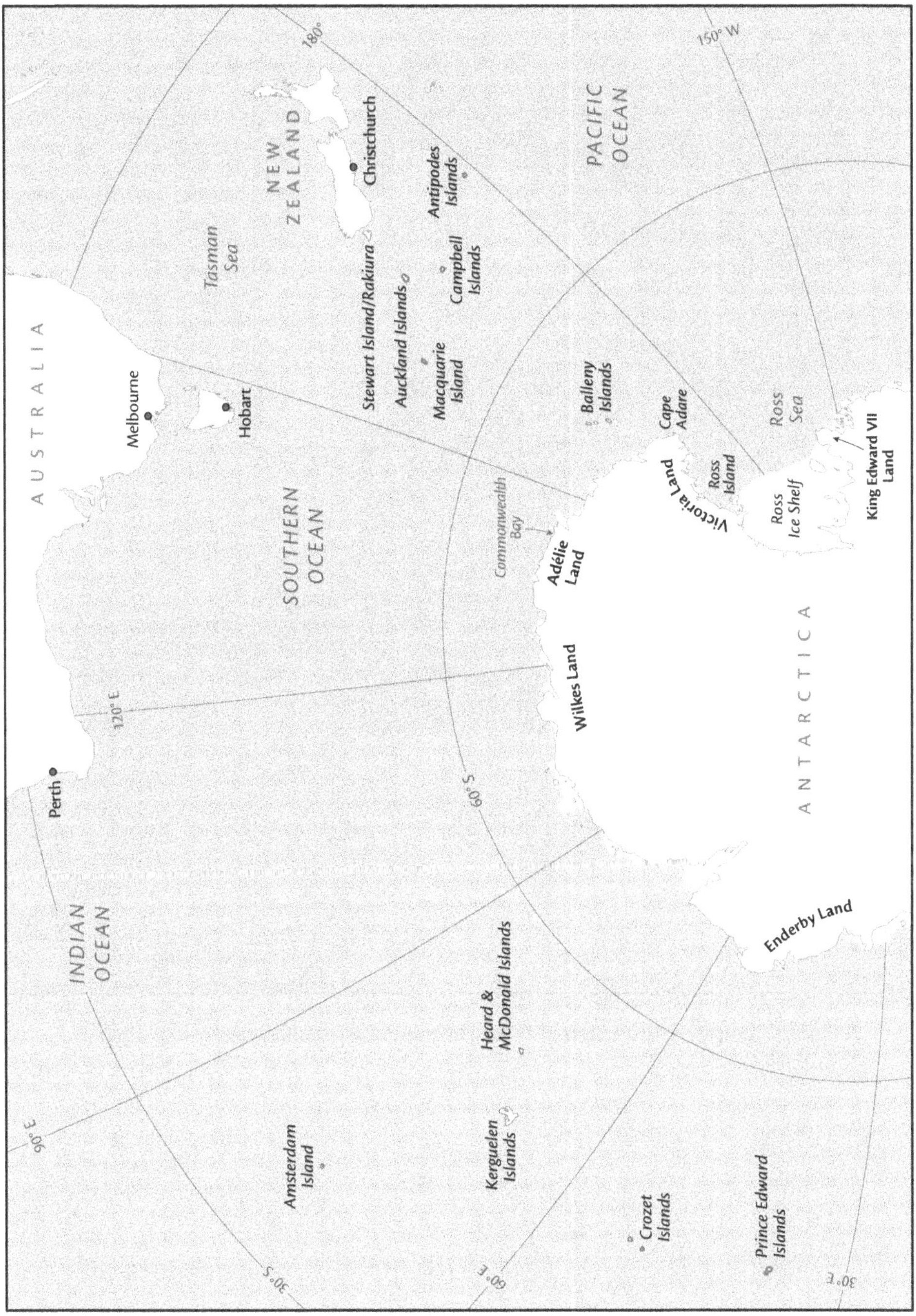

Australia's Southern Ocean world
Erin Greb

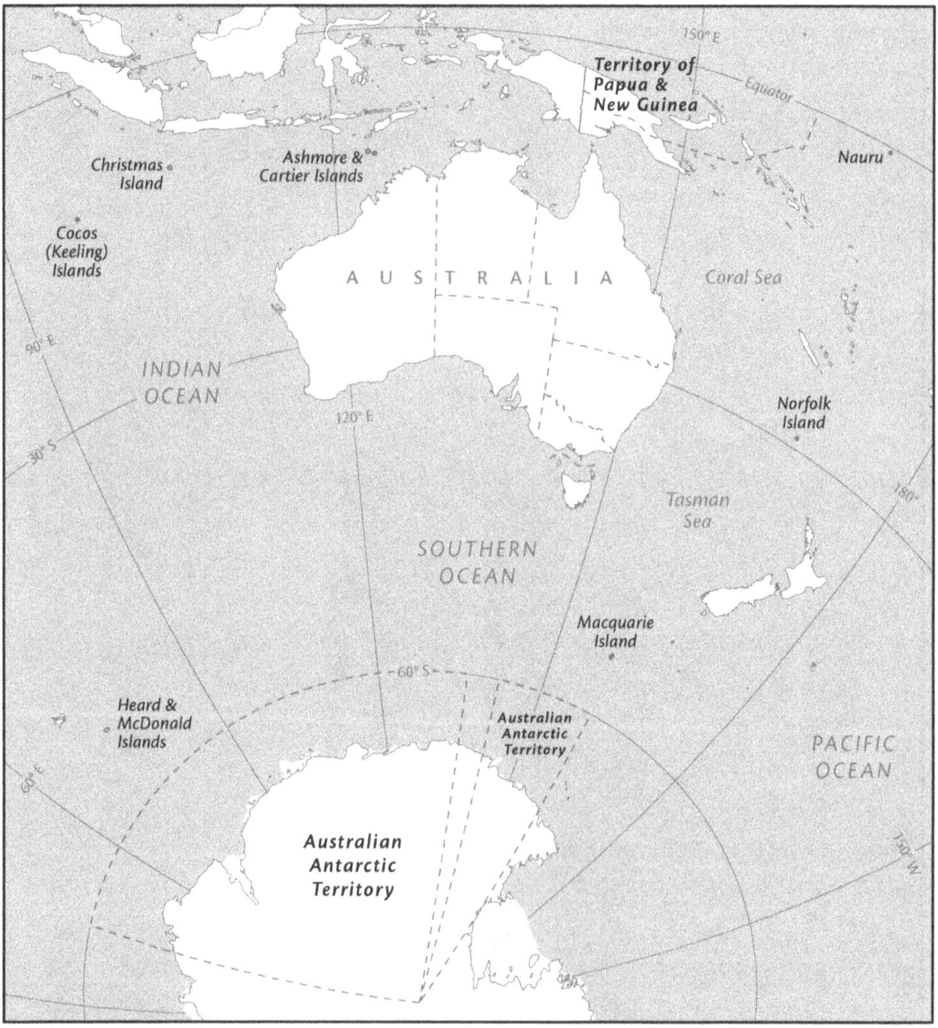

Australia's empire—the external territories under Australian control by 1958
Erin Greb

INTRODUCTION

Reorienting the Map: Australia and the Southern Ocean World

Lincoln Ellsworth sent his last wireless message at 4.15 in the afternoon. It was 22 November 1935, and Ellsworth and Canadian pilot Herbert Hollick-Kenyon were attempting to complete one of the last major 'firsts' of polar exploration: crossing the Antarctic continent. Ellsworth was far from the archetypical polar explorer of the 1930s. Unlike his contemporaries, he was neither a military man nor a university trained scientist. Instead, he was the son of an American coal magnate, a Yale dropout who, aged forty-five, had turned his attention to exploration. After using his family fortune to fund two expeditions to the Arctic, in 1925 and 1926, Ellsworth had begun looking south, beginning preparations in 1931 for the dangerous transantarctic crossing.

Ellsworth's dream of crossing Antarctica by aeroplane pushed technology and logistics to their limits. His first attempt in the austral summer of 1933–34 ended in disaster within twenty-four hours of him reaching Antarctica when a crevasse opened up beneath the expedition's only aeroplane. A second attempt the following year was thwarted by bad weather, and bad blood between expedition members. This third attempt in the summer of 1935–36 had faced an inauspicious start, too, with Ellsworth and

Hollick-Kenyon aborting their first two flights soon after take-off. It was only on 22 November—after five years of planning, three expeditions, and personal expenditure so vast that Ellsworth scarcely bothered to keep track of it—that the first transantarctic flight finally got underway from Dundee Island. Ellsworth was in good spirits, cheerfully reporting perfect flying conditions and bestowing names on newly discovered landmarks. But as the day wore on, his wireless messages became increasingly garbled. At 4.15 p.m., eight hours into the flight, these garbled messages gave way to silence.[1]

Back at the expedition's base camp on Dundee Island, on the South American side of the icy continent, Ellsworth's second-in-command was nonchalant about the lack of news. A veteran pilot and polar explorer himself, the Australian Hubert Wilkins had discussed every possible contingency with Ellsworth. Blizzards were a concern, of course, but the aviators' plan was to land on the ice and wait out any major storms. The two men had food for at least eleven weeks. They had also been bound for 'Little America', a recently abandoned American base where they knew they could find additional food and fuel. Wilkins and Ellsworth had agreed on rendezvous points for each stage of the flight, too, so Wilkins knew that he simply had to take the expedition's ship, the *Wyatt Earp*, to Little America, stopping to search each rendezvous point along the way.

Not everyone was as sanguine as Wilkins, though. While Ellsworth largely self-funded his Antarctic adventures, he had also negotiated an exclusive press rights deal with the North American Newspaper Alliance to subsidise some of his costs. Ellsworth's breezy updates from Antarctica had been widely syndicated, building a sizeable audience around the world. For those who had been following his annual quest to cross Antarctica by air, anxiety filled the silence. Had the two men crashed? Had their plane run out of fuel? Or had their wireless system simply stopped working? As the hours of silence turned into days, reports circulated around the world that Ellsworth and Hollick-Kenyon were missing somewhere in the vast, unexplored interior of the Antarctic continent.[2]

Amidst mounting concern for the missing men, Australia's federal government sprang into action. The first instinct of these politicians and public servants was to immediately send a Royal Australian Navy ship south to find the missing airmen. This bold plan was scuppered, however, by the reality that Australia simply had no ships that could safely plunge into the polar icepack. A solution was found, though, in the form of *Discovery II*, a British oceanographic research ship purpose-built for work in Antarctica and the Southern Ocean that was already en route to the Western Australian port of Fremantle. Australia's departments of Defence and External Affairs rapidly devised a plan: they would ask the British Government to borrow *Discovery II*, divert it to Melbourne to pick up a Royal Australian Air Force (RAAF) plane, and despatch it to Little America to commence an urgent aerial search for any sign of the explorers. The Australian Government pledged to bear the largest share of the costs for the hastily organised Ellsworth Relief Expedition, with the remainder covered by contributions from Britain and New Zealand.[3]

To coordinate this rescue mission, the Australian Government relied on a coterie of advisers with decades of Antarctic interest and expertise—Douglas Mawson and John King Davis, veterans of three Antarctic expeditions apiece; Raymond Priestley, veteran of two; David Orme Masson, a key organiser behind Australia's national Antarctic expeditions in 1911–14 and 1929–31, and an influential figure in Australian Antarctic policy; and Richard Casey, federal treasurer and a key player in Australia's assertion of sovereignty over the Australian Antarctic Territory (AAT). Among the first recommendations of this ad-hoc advisory committee was to recruit Eric Douglas, a RAAF pilot who had flown in Antarctica with Mawson and Davis, to take charge of the aerial search.[4] In keeping with the nostalgic spirit of the relief expedition, Mawson reportedly liberated his old Antarctic skis from the Adelaide Museum in case they were needed for the search.[5] This was a mission deeply and self-consciously rooted in Australia's Antarctic history.

Ellsworth had meticulously planned his transantarctic flight for more than five years; just thirty-one days after his transmitter fell silent, *Discovery II* was steaming south to search for him. And on 18 January, fifty-seven days after contact was lost, the Australian Government announced to the world that Ellsworth and Hollick-Kenyon were safe aboard *Discovery II.*[6] The rescue had proved to be spectacularly uneventful. The two men had been found safe and well at Little America and were thoroughly bemused by the international concern for their welfare. Their silence had been caused by the failure of the plane's wireless transmitter, not a calamitous crash in the heart of the Antarctic continent. The plane had run out of fuel 29 kilometres short of Little America, but they had landed safely, walked the rest of the way, and taken up residence in the abandoned buildings while waiting for the *Wyatt Earp* to collect them as planned. Ellsworth was bored, having inadvertently left his reading glasses in the abandoned plane, and his foot was frostbitten, but the men were well fed and otherwise in good health.[7] Indeed, the rescue was so uneventful that Australia's acting commissioner-general to the United States privately raised suspicions that Ellsworth's disappearance had been a carefully choreographed 'publicity stunt', with Australia's intervention scuppering Ellsworth's secret plan for Wilkins to find him while providing regular updates on the search to the expedition's exclusive media partners.[8]

Ellsworth vehemently denied such allegations, insisting he had ample safeguards in place to ensure Wilkins could mount a rescue if required. His published account of the expedition betrays his frustration that his pioneering flight was overshadowed by a wholly unnecessary rescue (his choice of chapter title, 'Not "Rescued"—"Aided"', is indicative).[9] Publicly, however, he was grateful for the Commonwealth's efforts, and resolved to travel to Australia with *Discovery II* while Wilkins and Hollick-Kenyon salvaged the plane and returned to the United States. On arrival in Australia, Ellsworth was feted as a hero—the RAAF arranged for planes to fly over *Discovery II* as it sailed into Melbourne, while Mawson, Masson, Priestley and Davis formed an official welcoming committee. Once he had made it ashore, Ellsworth was swept off to a reception hosted by the JC Williamson theatre company, then another by the governor of Victoria, then the Australian Club, the governor-general and finally the federal government.[10] Fox News and the Australian Broadcasting Commission teamed up to interview Ellsworth and film his return to civilisation for an international audience, while his stories of Antarctica and regular statements of gratitude were fodder for the Australian press.[11] Australian prime minister Joseph Lyons publicly labelled Ellsworth 'an inspiration to all mankind'.[12] Much of this press coverage was characterised by self-congratulatory sentiment, such as *The Sydney Morning Herald*'s claim that 'we may find especial gratification in the fact that it was the Australian Government which suggested and supported the search' and that this ensured 'we have had some share in their achievement in the Antarctic'.[13]

The Australian Government's reaction to Ellsworth's 'disappearance' in 1935, both in terms of *how* they coordinated the most rapidly organised expedition ever to sail for Antarctica and *why* they felt the need to do so, is illuminating. The relief expedition of 1935–36 was organised so quickly because it built on more than a century of interest by Australian governments, institutions and individuals in the region to Australia's south. Once Lyons had decided that the Commonwealth should take the lead in searching for Ellsworth, it was a relatively simple case of assembling an expedition out of established plans and existing resources. After all, everything from the ideal route and departure date to avoid heavy pack ice in the Ross Sea, to the rations and equipment needed to travel on foot over Antarctic ice, to the best model of aeroplane for Antarctic flying, was already known, a product of a series of Australian-led or -aided expeditions since the 1890s.

As for *why* the Commonwealth felt compelled to intervene, there was clearly a humanitarian rationale at play. Ellsworth and Hollick-Kenyon were missing in one of the most hostile environments imaginable. Indeed, one of the few descriptions of the Antarctic interior available in 1935 was Robert Scott's widely circulated remark: 'Great God! This is an awful place.'[14] Yet underpinning this humanitarian rationale was a rather more calculating idea. Ellsworth was not simply missing in Antarctica; he was presumed to be missing in either the land Australia claimed as the AAT or in New Zealand's claimed Ross Dependency. While the back-and-forth correspondence between ministers, government departments and advisers in Australia, Britain and New Zealand focused mainly on prosaic concerns—Which radio frequency was Ellsworth using? Would alterations to *Discovery II* come out of Defence's budget, or the prime minister's?—another idea was repeatedly articulated: mounting an expedition to find and rescue Ellsworth would be a 'useful demonstration of authority in both the Australian and New Zealand Antarctic Territories'.[15] By racing to rescue Ellsworth, the Commonwealth was seizing an opportunity to prove to the world that it had the capacity and the will to administer the 'Australian Antarctic'.

But why did the Commonwealth feel obliged to prove its capacity to govern the Antarctic territory it claimed as its own? Indeed, why had it claimed the AAT in the first place? Asserting this claim had required two joint Australian–British–New Zealand expeditions in 1929–30 and 1930–31—at a cost of £22,000 to the Australian Treasury—to consolidate a patchwork of older British and Australian sovereignty claims. Why devote public funds to two Antarctic expeditions of dubious scientific value during the acute social and political turmoil of the Great Depression? And why, in the context of ballooning government debt and a deepening economic crisis, did this public spending go unchallenged on the floor of parliament or in the columns of the Australian press? The answers to these questions lie in the way Australians had thought about and engaged with the region to their south over the previous century.

‹ ›

This is a book about Australia's deep entanglements with Antarctica and the islands and seas of the Southern Ocean. From the earliest years of European colonisation in Australia, individuals, institutions and governments have looked to the world beyond the continent's southern frontier. Some looked for answers to major scientific questions; others looked for an opportunity to enact fantasies of heroism and exploration. Some saw vast, untapped resources ripe for exploitation; others saw a space for strategic manoeuvring and territorial expansion. This book traces these ways of thinking about and engaging with the Southern Ocean world over time, from early bursts of scientific and commercial activity in the 1800s to assertions of sovereignty in the 1930s and 1940s. In doing so, it reconstructs a way of thinking about Antarctica and the Southern Ocean as a natural extension of Australian territory that has been largely forgotten.

Recovering this lost way of thinking is significant for two reasons. First, it provides an alternative way of viewing—and indeed writing—the history of Australia. These histories tend to be written from a particular geographical perspective almost by default, one that treats the south-eastern corner of the continent, and particularly the cities of Sydney, Melbourne and Canberra, as the natural centre of Australian history. Yet shifting away from this default perspective offers a radically different cartography for Australian history, one in which Australia ceases to be an 'island continent'. In this alternative cartography, Australia appears rather as the centre of a vast Australian archipelago, a sprawling region stretching from Christmas Island, New Guinea and Nauru in the north to Antarctica itself in the south, and from Norfolk and Macquarie islands in the east to Enderby Land and the Heard and McDonald islands in the west.

Imagining a different cartography offers a way to produce fresh perspectives and, importantly, new narratives for Australian history. As Regina Ganter, an advocate for reinterpreting Australian history from the perspective of the continent's far north, has argued, when the map is flipped upside down, 'what was at the centre is refracted to the margin, and what was barely noticed at the margin may move to the core'.[16] What becomes clear when Australian history is viewed from the south is that the expansion of settler Australia was a long-term, outward-looking, extra-continental project as much as it was an internal one. The invasion of Indigenous lands and the violent dispossession and marginalisation of First Nations associated with the expansion of the Australian colonial frontier inland from an initial bridgehead at Sydney can be understood as part of a wider, multidirectional logic of expansion. This was a logic driven by a sense of entitlement to the lands, seas and resources not only of the Australian continent but of a truly vast region in the Pacific, Southern and Indian oceans, as well as a sense of anxiety and grievance about the encroachment of foreign powers on what should rightfully be 'Australian' lands and Australian resources, whether that be German trading companies in the south-western Pacific or Norwegian whalers in Antarctic waters. Put another way, approaching Australian history from the perspective of its southern frontier reveals Australia to be not simply an outpost of British imperial expansion but the centre of a distinctly Australian imperial project in the Southern Hemisphere.

There is a second reason to try to recover Australians' forgotten way of thinking about the Southern Ocean world. While it offers a new perspective for histories of Australia, it is remarkable just how unexceptional this way of thinking was globally. Two notable global parallels can be found in Australian discussions of their rights, responsibilities and even their destiny to explore, exploit and control the world to their south. The first is that these discussions both echoed and drew on ideas about expansion that circulated in the public discourse of states that were commonly deemed imperial, such as Britain and the United States. One example that emerges in this book is the concept of an 'Australian Monroe Doctrine', an assertion of an exclusively Australian sphere of influence in the Pacific, Southern and Indian oceans that rose to prominence in the 1880s and enjoyed a resurgence during and after World War I. Australian ideas about expansion on its southern frontier can thus be usefully integrated into global histories of empire. Yet Australia is not unique in this regard. The Australian discussions this book focuses on have a second set of parallels in a cluster of states that are not normally considered major actors in the global history of empire—the likes of Argentina, Chile, New Zealand and Norway articulated their own claims to land, sea and resources in the Southern Ocean world. By taking Australian ambitions and activities in the south seriously and tracing their evolution and their influence over time, this book argues that not only did Australia have imperial aspirations, but that these aspirations were part of a wider tapestry of imperial expansion by relatively small states in relatively marginal regions at the turn of the twentieth century. Bringing this kind of small-state imperialism into conversation with more orthodox forms of expansion can bring a fresh perspective to understandings of empire in global history.

‹ ›

This book is far from the first to suggest that a reorientation of the map of Australia's history would be fruitful. Several prominent historians have shown that fundamental assumptions in Australian historiography—that the continent's settler history began with Europeans in the 1770s, for instance, or that a predominantly 'white Australia' in the nineteenth and early twentieth centuries slowly gave way to an increasingly multicultural nation in the post–World War II era—are untenable when viewed from the perspective of northern Australia's long history of economic and cultural connections with Asia, regional mobility and multiethnic communities.[17] Another scholarly effort to revise the imagined cartography of Australian history pushes the Australian continent to the south-western corner of a map centred on the Pacific, recasting Australia as one node in a wider Pacific world. Writing Australian history from this orientation forces historians to emphasise themes and factors that are usually treated as peripheral, such as Australia's history of imperialism and ecologically devastating resource extraction in the Pacific.[18] Imagining Australia and New Zealand as part of a single, interconnected 'Tasman world' offers another way of viewing and interpreting Australia's past.[19]

Writing from the other side of the continent, historians such as Charlie Fox and Ruth A Morgan have sought to reimagine Western Australia as a south-eastern corner of an Indian Ocean world.[20]

Mark McKenna has called for a multidirectional reorientation of Australian history, and has experimented with unpacking the national significance of stories that took place 'beyond the Sydney–Melbourne–Canberra axis' in the north, west and centre of the Australian continent.[21] Environmental historian Tom Griffiths has offered a similarly nuanced reimagination of the map as a 'continental cluster of bioregions'.[22] Frank Broeze, meanwhile, pushes back against the very idea of an Australian continent, imagining a very different cartography centred on sea rather than on land. Indeed, Broeze argues that Australia should be considered an 'archipelago of "islands" of settlement' rather than a single cohesive landmass.[23]

Yet one compass point is conspicuous by its absence from this drive to devise new cartographies for Australian history: south. Even McKenna's expansive, multidirectional conception of Australia extends only to the 'north, centre and far west of the continent'.[24] For a nation with such deep and enduring historical connections to the Southern Ocean, there has been remarkably little consideration of how Australian history can be approached from this perspective, or of how such a history might challenge or complicate broader narratives and open possibilities for new ones. Brigid Hains's *The Ice and the Inland*, an innovative analysis of the construction of a frontier mythology based on the overlapping careers of Douglas Mawson in Antarctica and John Flynn in central Australia, stands virtually alone in this regard.[25] Even then, it is notable that Hains's achievement in placing the Antarctic at the conceptual centre of Australian history relies on intertwining it with the history of the continent's physical centre.

This is not to suggest that historians have not written about the world to Australia's south. A vibrant literature is devoted to the history of this region. Tom Griffiths, for instance, has explored the history of human encounters with Antarctica, but while he declares his work to have 'an unashamed Australian bias', it is deliberately *not* a history of Australia or Australians in the Antarctic.[26] Joy McCann's history of the Southern Ocean, *Wild Sea*, is similarly informed by a distinctly Australian perspective but deliberately transcends national boundaries in its approach.[27] Lynette Russell has explored the stories of First Nations whalers and sealers working in the Southern Ocean, arguing that, in some cases, these industries 'offered Indigenous people the opportunity to escape the worst elements of colonial dispossession'.[28] Working at the intersection of environmental and international history, Alessandro Antonello and Emma Shortis have explored Australia's role in the development of systems of international governance and environmental protection in the Antarctic.[29] There have been detailed overviews of Australian activities in the Antarctic, notably by RA Swan, Marie Kawaja and McCann, and a collection edited by Griffiths and Marcus Haward.[30] These activities have also generated a substantial corpus of biography and memoir.[31] Another field of scholarship focuses on the legal dimensions of Australian territorial claims.[32]

Yet, aside from Hains and Russell, these works are not particularly concerned with the implications of their research for Australian history more broadly. Their significance is generally seen to lie in the light they shed on the Antarctic region and its bespoke mechanisms of international governance. The further south historians have cast their gaze, the more national boundaries and national histories fade into the background of their analysis. It is unsurprising, then, that Antarctica and the Southern Ocean remain largely on the periphery of wider narratives of Australian history. That these regions figure only fleetingly or not at all in major scholarly surveys of Australian history is indicative of their place on the historiographical margins.[33]

How would Australian history look if Antarctica and the Southern Ocean were shifted from the periphery to the centre of the map? I argue that what constitutes 'Australia' is radically larger than the familiar, continental map accounts for. A south-oriented cartography must find room for Australia's empire, for not one but two continents, for three oceans and four seas, and for a sprawling network of island territories stretching from the Antarctic coastline to just shy of the equator. The reality and the legitimacy of Australian control of particular places within this region—both overseas and within the Australian continent itself—is, of course, contestable, and varied considerably across time and place. To take just one example, the subantarctic Kerguelen archipelago, 4,200 kilometres south-west of Perth, was simply assumed to be under British or Australian control until 1892, when France unexpectedly announced that it had annexed the islands, leading to a spurt of diplomatic efforts to 'get them back'.[34] While Australian control could be dubious and contested in certain places at certain times, this perspectival shift reveals that territorial expansionism was a more ambitious, more multidirectional, and altogether more significant project in Australian history than has hitherto been acknowledged. In this south-oriented story, Australia cannot simply be seen as an outpost on the periphery of a British Empire; it must instead be understood as an expansionist polity with aspirations to be the centre of an empire of its own. This imperial aspiration was not limited to the south-western Pacific—the region in which historians have previously discussed the idea of an Australian Empire—but was central to Australian thinking about, and activities in, the lands and seas to the south. A history of Australian ways of thinking about Antarctica and the Southern Ocean is necessarily a history of an Australian empire.

This book, then, is a history of Australian empire written from the perspective of its southern frontier. This was, it must be recognised, a decidedly unusual frontier. Elsewhere in Australia, the frontier of European settlement was a zone characterised by dispossession, cultural devastation, violent conflict, massacres and First Nations resistance.[35] Antarctica and the Southern Ocean islands, by contrast, had never been permanently settled. Nonetheless, the southern frontier had much in common with its continental counterparts. It was a commodity frontier, a frontier of administration, and even at times a frontier of settlement. Like Australia's internal frontiers, it was a site of tension between expectations—that new territory could constantly be acquired, transformed and made productive—and environmental realities that constrained economic development and settlement.[36] There are other similarities, too. Both the southern and internal frontiers were spaces of hyper-masculinity, whiteness, and of stretched, unclear and often feeble law and jurisdiction.[37] Collective practices of remembering and forgetting were also crucial to the dynamics of both frontiers. Many of the people and events narrated in this book were remembered, commemorated and invoked for decades. Old wounds and grievances were frequently recalled, while other failures were quietly forgotten, allowing the same boosterish ideas to resurface.

It is reasonable to ask, of course, whether Australia's territorial expansion in the Southern Ocean world, the drive to control territory that was then undervalued but could in time become strategically or economically valuable, should be considered 'imperial'. While the concept is commonly applied to the Antarctic region, many historians would baulk at the idea that dominion over seals and penguins truly constitutes an empire.[38] Attempts at defining the concepts of empire and imperialism have tended to emphasise their human dimensions—conceiving of empires as composite polities comprised of a central, expansionist state that subjugates or controls territories and peoples beyond the state's own borders—but empire has always been about far more than simply governing human subjects.[39]

As historians working at the intersection of environmental and imperial histories have shown, every stage of imperial expansion and administration was influenced by environmental factors.[40] Natural resources, climate, soil and other environmental features were powerful pull factors that shaped patterns and processes of expansion, while other features such as diseases, topography and hydrology constrained them. Environments were central to justifications for empire; as James Beattie and Andrew Fitzmaurice argue, the idea that it was legitimate to occupy and claim lands that were not being exploited to their full potential was invoked to justify acts of imperial expansion.[41] Imperialism transformed landscapes and ecologies through processes of biological exchange, and in some cases these transformations, such as the introduction of novel pathogens, have been seen as crucial factors in facilitating expansion.[42] Environmental knowledge, too, was at the heart of imperial governance. Resources were carefully surveyed, territories mapped, plants and animals transplanted to new bioregions, novel species studied and tested, weather observed, forests and plantations planned, and irrigation systems devised. As Corey Ross puts it, 'reordering environmental relationships and altering ecosystems was an integral part of modern imperialism'.[43] Australia's southern frontier may have lacked human subjects, but in how it was imagined, discussed, studied, annexed and administered, it falls comfortably within the framework of empire.

‹ ›

Revising the default cartography of Australian history to reveal a more significant and more complex imperial history is not a uniquely Australian concern. American historian Daniel Immerwahr has similarly called for a shift in both the language and the imagined cartography of the history of the United States. For Immerwahr, using the language of the 'Greater United States' and zooming the map out to incorporate not just the contiguous states but all of the nation's overseas territories reveals the United States to be not just an imperialistic polity, as is commonly argued, but a bona fide territorial empire.[44] It is notable, however, that Immerwahr sees the failure of mainstream historical narratives to incorporate the current and former overseas territories—or to engage with the specialist historical scholarship produced in these territories—as a failing particular to the United States. In Immerwahr's telling, there was no confusion in states like Britain or France about whether there existed a British or French empire; 'it is only the United States that has suffered from chronic confusion over its own borders'.[45] Immerwahr's treatment of the history of US territorial expansionism is invaluable, but it is wrong to suggest that there is anything unique in the reluctance to see overseas empire as central to national history. As the Australian case suggests, there are still other territorial empires to be recovered, and there is much to be gained from exploring comparisons and connections between these diffuse sites of territorial expansion.

This book therefore seeks to incorporate Australia into the global history of empire. Doing so reveals two significant insights. First,

Australia's empire draws attention to a global scramble for control of marginal spaces. Histories of empire tend to focus—understandably—on the drive to control spaces with obvious economic or strategic value. Yet there were many spaces of empire that failed to live up to expectations or were of only fleeting significance. The history of Australian empire, and particularly of its southern expansion, is a history of thwarted dreams of seal farming and iceberg harvesting, of far-flung colonies and health resorts, of whaling and radium mining, as much as it is a history of actual resource extraction, boots on the ground and strategic manoeuvring. Many of these projects and expectations look absurd in retrospect—and some of them were certainly regarded as absurd by observers at the time—but even bad ideas and boosterism can profoundly influence imperial projects and leave enduring legacies.

A second insight also emerges from a renewed focus on imperialism in the earth's marginal spaces. Australia was never alone in its ambitions to transform the marginal spaces to its south into productive dependencies. In these projects, both the realistic and the eccentric, Australia was joined by a cadre of other imperial polities. Some were orthodox empires, the likes of Britain, France, Germany, Japan, Russia and the United States. Others were states that are less commonly recognised as autonomous imperial actors, such as Argentina, Chile, New Zealand and Norway. Writing a history of empire from the perspective of the far south brings these states into a common framework. Australians tended, in the late-nineteenth and early twentieth centuries, to view these states as rivals for control of territory, sea routes and resources, or else as exemplars for Australia's own expansion. Recovering this way of imagining Australia, as an aspiring empire in a world of empires, draws attention to a global phenomenon of territorial expansion in the world's marginal spaces. A global history of empire that incorporates Australia is therefore a history that must grapple with these overlapping and often intertwined stories of territorial expansion and engage seriously with the question of which states have imperial histories.

‹ ›

In the flood of press coverage that greeted the news of Lincoln Ellsworth's rescue by an Australian-organised relief expedition, one article stands out. *The Argus*, a conservative Melbourne daily, published an editorial shortly before Ellsworth was due to arrive in Melbourne in February 1936. The editorial welcomed Ellsworth's imminent arrival, noting that it would help to 'revive in the minds of Australian people an interest in the Antarctic continent that is apt to become dormant'.[46] It was *The Argus*'s view that Australians *should* be interested in the Antarctic. The Commonwealth had 'a mandate of Empire to supervise and explore the land and water stretching away to the south', and while the AAT was not yet 'utilisable in any commercial sense', there were 'many who regard the continent as a kind of treasure chest of the future'. Whaling and mining were the most likely industries to take hold, but the editorial raised the possibility that the AAT might become valuable in other ways; it was possible, for instance, that 'holiday programmes of the future may include summer cruises by air to the Antarctic'. With this in mind, *The Argus* was delighted that Ellsworth's adventures were likely to 'remind us of our privileges and responsibilities in relation to the great Antarctic continent'.

This editorial encapsulates three fundamental ideas that developed in Australia over the course of the nineteenth and early twentieth centuries about the world to the continent's south. The first is the idea that Australians naturally had a special interest in this region. That is, *The Argus*'s editorial was informed by a belief that geographical proximity both obligated Australians to take a leading role in exploring and exploiting their southern hinterland and entitled them to some degree of exclusivity in doing so. The second idea is that the Antarctic continent and the islands and seas of the Southern Ocean could reasonably be expected to become useful, productive Australian dependencies in the future. Opinions varied considerably about what that use would be, ranging from resource extraction to settlement to a strategic role in ensuring Australia's security, but *The Argus*'s attitude is indicative of this optimistic, boosterish way of thinking about what lay to Australia's south. The third idea is that Australia's natural right to control the lands and seas to its south, or at least to a kind of exclusive sphere of influence in this region, created corresponding obligations and responsibilities in relation to using and administering them. The most notable of these responsibilities was, as the Ellsworth 'rescue' indicated, that a claim to territorial control imposed an obligation to provide aid.

These three ideas—their genealogies and their influence—are the focus of this book. It is often remarked that Australia has a unique connection with Antarctica, a product of deep historical links and the nation's ongoing status as the largest Antarctic sovereignty claimant. This belief has shaped Australia's approach to the Antarctic Treaty System, the bundle of international agreements that has regulated international relations in the region since the Antarctic Treaty was signed in 1959.[47] It continues to shape Australia's Antarctic policy and is embedded in the Commonwealth's 2016 strategic plan for the region.[48] And it is a common refrain in scholarship, both historical and contemporary, on Australia's Antarctic interests.[49] Yet, despite its ubiquity, the origins and dynamics of this conception of Australia's Antarctic interests have not yet been uncovered. To truly understand Australia's role and interest in the Antarctic, past and present, it is necessary to understand the evolution and effects of these fundamental ideas about the opportunities, rights and responsibilities that lay on Australia's southern frontier.

This book, then, offers one way of writing a history of Australia—and a history of empire—from the perspective of the world's southernmost region. It is not intended to be a comprehensive account. Rather, it offers a deep investigation of the ways in which Australian people, governments, corporations and institutions thought about and engaged with the world to their south, and how these ideas shaped efforts to explore, exploit and control this space. Ultimately, *The Southern Frontier* tells the story of how people and institutions in Australia were able to imagine their nation as an expansionist polity and the Antarctic as an Australian space.

To trace these ideas, *The Southern Frontier* explores discussions of Antarctica and the Southern Ocean throughout a wide range of sources. Decades of scientific research, imperial strategy, diplomatic negotiation and attempts at economic development have produced a diverse and diffuse archive, one that includes books, pamphlets, the proceedings of scientific societies, scholarly journals, films, photographs, correspondence, memoranda, parliamentary debates, business prospectuses, contracts and receipts. While there is a handful of dedicated Antarctic collections—most notably the peerless library and archive of the Scott Polar Research Institute in Cambridge—most of these materials are scattered across various national, state and private collections. To investigate Australian interests in Antarctica and the Southern Ocean is to attempt to reconstitute an imperial archive from materials found in the national archives and national libraries of Australia, New Zealand and the United Kingdom; the state libraries of New South Wales, Victoria, Tasmania, South Australia and Western Australia; the universities of Sydney and Melbourne; the Australian, South Australian and royal maritime museums; the Royal Historical Society of Victoria; and the Royal Society and Royal Geographical Society in London. The press also played a key role in facilitating debates and disseminating ideas about science, exploration, industry and politics in Antarctica and the Southern Ocean. Approaching these press sources systematically can therefore provide unparalleled insights into the information and opinions people were exposed to, and the development and circulation of ideas over time.

Over such extended periods, interest in Antarctica and the Southern Ocean inevitably ebbed and flowed. There were long periods of mainstream ambivalence, during which only a handful of specialists, enthusiasts and speculators were involved in thinking about Australia's relationship with the region to their south, punctuated by short-lived bursts of genuine mass interest and enthusiasm. Government interest was similarly erratic, rising and falling in response to a range of events, lobbying and geopolitical imperatives. This book therefore focuses on a series of moments—from the arrival in Australian ports of three expeditions bound for Antarctica in a little over two years in 1839–41 to a hurried, ad hoc proclamation ceremony on a tiny island off the coast of Enderby Land in 1930—to trace the development, circulation and influence of key ideas. Proceeding broadly chronologically, it tells the story of the events, proposals and controversies that shaped Australian attitudes, expectations and ultimately policies about the country's southern frontier.

‹ ›

In the wake of the rescue of Lincoln Ellsworth and Herbert Hollick-Kenyon, it soon transpired that, even at the age of fifty-eight, Ellsworth craved one last polar adventure. In July 1938, he announced that he would return to Antarctica later that year, heading south from Cape Town in the *Wyatt Earp* with a new, heavily customised plane on board to conduct aerial surveys of 'the largest unknown territory anywhere in the world'.[50] Having achieved his long-held ambition of the first transantarctic flight, Ellsworth's goal for his fourth expedition was rather more commercial: 'to discover whether there are oil and mineral deposits in Enderby Land'.[51] Joining him once again was Wilkins, who hoped to use the expedition to lay the foundations for his own grand plan for a network of permanent stations in Antarctica that would improve meteorological forecasting and transform understandings of Southern Hemisphere weather and climate.[52] Land-grabbing was not on the agenda, with Ellsworth reluctantly acknowledging in a *New York Times* column that 'although no man has ever seen what we shall see, Australia already claims it by virtue of a landing on the coast'.[53]

It came as something of a surprise, then, when Ellsworth announced via a short wireless message in January 1939 that he had flown over 200,000 square kilometres of unexplored land along the 79th meridian east and claimed the entirety of it for the United States.[54] Few Australians had a clear grasp of Antarctic geography, so this announcement was initially reported as a point of interest rather than a source of concern. Yet interest rapidly gave way to consternation as it became clear that the land Ellsworth had claimed fell within the boundaries of the AAT. Publicly, Australian officials played down Ellsworth's assertion, insisting that the area he had claimed as 'the American Highland' was, in fact, part of the territory discovered and claimed by Douglas Mawson as 'Princess Elizabeth Land' in 1931.[55] Privately, External Affairs minister WM Hughes urgently cabled Ellsworth's Australian companion, Wilkins, and the Commonwealth's representative in Washington to request an explanation for Ellsworth's about-face.[56]

When Wilkins returned to Australia and submitted a report to Hughes, he had a fascinating story to tell. In Wilkins' version of events, he had been determined to advance Australia's interests, even while serving on a private expedition that sailed under a US flag. He had consulted with Australian officials before joining up with Ellsworth in Cape Town and had been 'given official status as a representative of the Commonwealth Government' and a letter from Hughes formally authorising him to 'enter upon, explore and report upon' the AAT.[57] It was only during the voyage south that Ellsworth had revealed to Wilkins that his plans had changed; the US Consul in Cape Town had shown Ellsworth a letter from the American Secretary of State intimating that 'it would be advisable for an explorer to claim for his country any territory that he actually explored, irrespective of whether it lay within an area already claimed'.[58]

Ellsworth had therefore resolved to ignore the 'sector principle', the idea that exploration and a proclamation of sovereignty along a stretch of Antarctica's coastline was sufficient to claim a slice of the continent stretching inland as far as the South Pole, and instead treat any territory more than a few kilometres inland from the coast as unclaimed. While in Cape Town, Ellsworth had obtained a small brass cylinder, into which he planned to place a US flag and a proclamation claiming the land 278 kilometres either side of his flight path. This cylinder would then be dropped at the southernmost point of his exploratory flight to formalise his claim to 200,000 square kilometres of territory for the United States.[59]

Wilkins, however, had come armed with cylinders of his own, and proceeded to subtly subvert Ellsworth's claims by performing ceremonies aimed at reaffirming Australian sovereignty. When the expedition went ashore at Rauer Island, a controversial inclusion in the AAT that had been discovered and named by Norwegians, Wilkins raised the Australian flag, deposited it and a proclamation of his own in an aluminium container, and marked the site with a cairn of stones. When the expedition ventured onto the mainland of the Australian-claimed Princess Elizabeth Land, Wilkins climbed into the Vestfold Hills and took a break from collecting geological samples to raise another flag, read another proclamation, stuff both into a container, and deposit it into a small hole in a nearby boulder. Then, his pièce de résistance: while Ellsworth was unloading his aeroplane and then conducting test flights, Wilkins climbed to the top of a nearby hill, raised yet another Australian flag, and penned a proclamation affirming that he had visited several points on the mainland and on nearby islands of a territory administered by the Commonwealth of Australia; flag and proclamation were safely stowed in a white enamel container and placed beneath a boulder.[60] To top it off, Wilkins persuaded Ellsworth not to sell his ship and polar equipment in the United States but instead to offer it to the Commonwealth Government. With the government agreeing to the sale and taking immediate ownership of the *Wyatt Earp* in 1939, Australia was on the cusp of solidifying its claim to the AAT by establishing a series of permanent research stations.[61]

Ultimately, however, Ellsworth and Wilkins' unfailingly polite battle over flags and cylinders was pointless. The Commonwealth resolved to simply ignore Ellsworth's claim until such time as the US Government followed it up with a formal assertion of sovereignty; the US Government declined to do so, leaving this dispute to fade into obscurity.[62] Nor did the purchase of the *Wyatt Earp* herald a new era of permanent occupation in the Australian Antarctic—at least, not immediately. As the threat of war loomed larger, the idea of annual expeditions to resupply permanent bases became less and less of a priority, and the *Wyatt Earp* was eventually stripped of its polar gear and pressed into service as a munitions transport for the Australian Navy.[63]

Nonetheless, this dispute over Australia's claim to the AAT on the eve of World War II is a fitting place to begin this book. This was not so much a dispute between individuals as a schism between differing visions of what the Southern Ocean world could and should be. On the one hand, Wilkins was defending an Australian vision in which national borders extended as far south as it was possible to go, crossing land, sea and ice. This was a world of straight lines and neatly defined territories, at the heart of which was a vast Australian sector stretching from the Australian coastline to the pole. In the words of the eternal booster Douglas Mawson, 'We are only a small number of people, but we are the only nation in the world whose territory extends from the Equator to the polar regions.'[64] On the other hand, Ellsworth was the agent of a competing vision that rejected the sector principle and insisted that only land that had actually been seen and mapped could be claimed. Ellsworth's was a more complicated map of Antarctica, a messy patchwork of territories that could only be painstakingly assembled through flights and sledge journeys.

The two men did agree on one thing, though. Ellsworth and Wilkins were united in a belief that theirs was important work, that these performances of sovereignty would hold their respective nations in good stead when, one day, the ice receded and Antarctica and its encircling seas became a source of immense wealth and prosperity.[65] Lincoln Ellsworth's adventures in Antarctica are a reminder, then, that the history of Australia's southern frontier is a history of ideas and performances, of competing understandings of sovereignty and natural rights, and of debates about the value of acquiring an empire of ice and islands.

1

'THE MEMORABLE FIRST OF JUNE'

The Australian Colonies and Early Antarctic Exploration

The most exciting thing that happened in Hobart in 1841 was a party held on the decks of two warships. Three hundred guests made their way down a torch-lit path to a small cove on the Derwent River. There, a series of boats had been lashed together to form the support for a bridge connecting the *Erebus* to the shore. The 32-metre Royal Navy 'bomb vessel' had been purpose-built for firing explosive shells in combat, but the reinforced wooden hull that made it so suitable for firing mortars also made it the perfect choice for peacetime work amidst Antarctic ice. Tonight, however, its deck had been cleared of its usual gear and clutter to create an enormous dancefloor, complete with temporary orchestra pits at the stern and around the mainmast. There was even a small refectory, staffed by the ships' officers, to provide the guests with lemonade and punch. A second ship, *Terror*, had been similarly cleared and refashioned into an open-air dining room, where wine, champagne and a lavish meal were served. The two warships, festooned with flowers, had been lashed together to allow guests to move seamlessly between them, while the officers' cabins had been transformed into ladies' dressing rooms for the evening.[1] The party continued until sunrise, and one Hobart paper would subsequently declare that 'nothing so good has been seen in this Colony, as the splendid entertainment given on board HM ships *Erebus* and *Terror*, on the memorable First of June'.[2]

The host of this unusual party was James Clark Ross, a charismatic naval captain who had cut his teeth in the Napoleonic Wars before participating in seven Royal Navy voyages in the Arctic between 1817 and 1836. While those expeditions failed to discover the fabled North-West Passage, Ross had gained wider recognition after becoming the first man to reach the north magnetic pole in 1831, and it was this that had led him to Hobart.

The earth's magnetic field was a subject that dominated European science in the 1830s. This international drive to obtain data, often known as the 'Magnetic Crusade', was partly for theoretical purposes—the variation of the earth's magnetic field was one of the great mysteries of physics—and partly for the data's practical applications, since a better understanding of the science of magnetism could improve the safety and reliability of navigation at sea. But while magnetic data from observatories and field surveys in the Northern Hemisphere was relatively easy to come by, there was a dearth of equivalent data from the Southern Hemisphere. The British Association for the Advancement of Science had therefore, in 1835 and again in 1838, proposed that the Royal Navy despatch an expedition to undertake magnetic observations at a number of Southern Hemisphere sites, including exploring as far south as possible to make observations in the Antarctic and search for the south magnetic pole.[3] With further backing from the Royal Society, and the enticing prospect that such an expedition could undertake dramatic feats of geographical discovery in the largely unexplored Antarctic, the government and the navy agreed to take up the scheme. Ross, with extensive experience in both Arctic exploration and magnetic observation, was chosen to command the expedition, which departed from England on 5 October 1839.[4]

Yet Ross was not the only naval officer commissioned to lead a voyage of exploration and scientific observation into the Southern Ocean in 1839, nor even the only one to spend time in the

Australian colonies. Between 1839 and 1841, the towns of Sydney and Hobart played host to three expeditions bound for Antarctic seas: Ross's British venture, a French expedition led by Jules Dumont d'Urville, and the United States Exploring Expedition commanded by Charles Wilkes. While Ross was the only one to transform his ship into a ballroom for the benefit of his hosts, all three of these expeditions excited significant local interest and became bound—for a time at least—with local society.

This chapter considers the significance of these three expeditions for how people in Australia thought about and engaged with the world that lay beyond their southern frontier. These expeditions have conventionally been interpreted as a sudden burst of international interest that petered out almost immediately. Yet, while this may be an accurate interpretation of how the Antarctic was viewed in Britain, France and the United States, it overlooks both a longer history of Australian interest in the Southern Ocean and its commercial potential, and the persistence of this interest in the decades after the expeditions concluded. I argue that this was a transformative moment. Australians responded to the visits of Ross, d'Urville and Wilkes by increasingly imagining the Southern Ocean world as a region for scientific research, not just a field for commercial efforts to benefit individuals and, by extension, the colonies. The three expeditions of 1839–41 therefore left a substantial legacy in Australia: the idea that the colonies had a significant stake in the future exploration of the Antarctic.

‹ ›

When the sun rose over Sydney Harbour on the morning of 30 November 1839, the town's residents were astonished to see two huge American warships anchored amidst the usual jam of whalers, cargo vessels and migrant ships. The *Vincennes*, flagship of the US Exploring Expedition, dwarfed every other ship in the vicinity, yet had somehow slipped into the harbour undetected overnight.[5] With addressing the sorry state of Sydney Harbour's defences having only recently been placed on the agenda in New South Wales, the manner of the Americans' arrival—and the startling vulnerability it had exposed—caused alarm.[6] But as the other two ships in the expedition's fleet arrived over the following days, and the Americans began to flood into the streets of Sydney on shore leave, a sense of mutual respect gradually developed between the expedition members and the locals.

Prior to the expedition's arrival, little had been known about it in New South Wales. There had been regular updates in the colonial press about preparations for Ross's British expedition and about the progress of its French counterpart, which had departed Toulon in September 1837.[7] But the US expedition, first mooted in 1828 but repeatedly delayed by political opposition, infighting, and a dearth of suitable ships and officers, was virtually unknown. Nothing was known of Wilkes, either. Where the British and French expeditions boasted seasoned naval explorers as commanders, the US enterprise was led by a relatively junior naval surveyor—one whose personality and leadership style had already alienated most of his officers and crew well before they reached Sydney.[8]

Given the mystery that surrounded the expedition, it is unsurprising that the fleet was deluged with visitors. These visitors had clearly been following the news of Ross and d'Urville's expeditions reasonably closely, too, for they interrogated Wilkes about the Americans' preparations and equipment for an Antarctic voyage. They wanted to know whether the ships were constructed with compartments to prevent them from sinking if they struck an iceberg, whether they had ice-saws to release the ship if it became frozen into the sea ice, and what anti-scorbutics they planned to use. Many were surprised that the Americans were attempting an Antarctic voyage in seemingly ordinary ships, and were openly astonished that they had no serious cold weather clothing and less than twelve months' worth of supplies. Several visitors stated outright they felt the expedition was underprepared and Wilkes was unwise to attempt such a dangerous undertaking. Wilkes' customary reply to this line of questioning was 'to agree that we were unwise to attempt such service in ordinary cruising vessels; but we had been ordered to go, and that was enough'.[9]

In addition to this steady stream of unsolicited advice, Wilkes and the expedition's officers and scientific staff were offered more concrete forms of assistance while in Sydney. Wilkes was offered the use of Fort Macquarie, the stone artillery tower that guarded one side of the fleet's anchorage at Sydney Cove, as a magnetic and meteorological observatory. Members of the expedition were likewise given free access to Sydney's peripatetic library and the Australian Museum throughout their stay, while the party's scientists and artists travelled widely throughout the colony. Wilkes himself accompanied governor George Gipps on a two-day trip to Parramatta, touring the town and visiting the Parramatta Observatory, which he was disappointed to discover was well equipped in terms of instruments but in a state of considerable disrepair.[10]

The Americans also found themselves drawn into various Sydney social circles throughout their stay. Wilkes was initially welcomed to the colony by James Hartwell Williams, an American merchant who had been appointed the United States's first consul in New South Wales earlier in the year, and by governor Gipps. The Australian Club, which saw itself as the social centre for Sydney's elite, organised a lavish dinner on 11 December to welcome and celebrate the expedition, connecting the Americans with the colony's wealthiest landowners, its most senior political and military figures, and its most prominent and internationally connected amateur scientist, Alexander Macleay.[11] This was followed by another event at Fort Macquarie dedicated to celebrating Anglo-American cooperation. Tents were erected outside the fort and decorated with intertwined British and American flags, American officers partnered with local women for an 'exhilarating dance', speeches commended the friendly relations that existed between colonists and explorers, and guests drank wine and conversed late into the evening. While the event was plagued by heavy rain, the colonial press was self-congratulatory, noting that 'the officers of the American Squadron will not have room to complain of a want of hospitality on the part of the elite of Sydney'.[12] This hospitality may not have been entirely altruistic; as the *Sydney Herald* noted, supporting the expedition would ensure the colony was 'brought into notice' in the United States, and would perhaps even stimulate trans-Pacific trade.[13]

After spending Christmas ashore with various friends and supporters, the Americans quietly departed Sydney early in the morning of 26 December 1839.[14] They enjoyed good weather for the first week of the voyage, but soon received a reminder of the unique difficulties associated with sailing in high southern latitudes. The smallest vessel in the fleet—the fifteen-man, 88-tonne *Flying Fish*—had been lagging behind since leaving Sydney. As the expedition reached 48°S, the wind picked up, a fog descended, and the *Flying Fish* was separated from the rest of the fleet. Wilkes attempted to search for the missing schooner, without success. The diminished fleet therefore set course for Macquarie Island, which Wilkes had nominated as the expedition's first rendezvous point before their departure from Sydney. There they could land and establish a magnetic station while waiting for the *Flying Fish*.

It transpired, however, that Macquarie Island was not nearly so suitable a rendezvous point as its location on the map suggested. With the fog continuing, the *Peacock* drifted out of sight and earshot and could not be relocated. Then, Wilkes' *Vincennes* and the smaller *Porpoise* were caught in a storm that dragged them off course, overshooting the island and missing the rendezvous completely. *Peacock* managed to battle through the storm to reach Macquarie, only to find that there was not a single sheltered harbour on the island. It took a dozen attempts before a party could land. Even then, they were forced to leave behind their magnetic instruments and wade ashore in chest-deep water. Unable to make magnetic observations, the landing party instead split up to collect biological and zoological specimens to add to the expedition's vast scientific collections, which would eventually form the basis of the Smithsonian's National Museum of Natural History.

The travails of midshipman Henry Eld are indicative of the landing party's torrid time: Eld was first attacked by a group of southern rockhopper penguins who tore his trousers and 'violently' pinched his legs, then lost his collection of penguin eggs to a pair of marauding albatrosses, and finally was swamped by a wave and thrown against the rocks when he attempted to return, losing most of the specimens he had collected and the three live penguins he had been attempting to shepherd into the boat. Based on his own difficulties in reaching Macquarie and the bleak reports from the *Peacock*, Wilkes had no hesitation in reporting that 'Macquarie Island affords no inducement for a visit'.[15]

Wilkes' second pre-allocated rendezvous point somehow proved even less suitable. Having overshot Macquarie, the *Vincennes* and *Porpoise* made for Emerald Island. Yet when they reached its recorded location roughly 300 kilometres south-east of Macquarie, they found themselves sailing over open ocean with no sign of land anywhere in the vicinity. Despite appearing on maps since its reported discovery by a sealing vessel in 1821, Emerald Island did not exist. Nothing so eloquently captures the difficulty Wilkes faced in drafting sailing instructions for the fleet—a task that required him to impose an orderly imagined geography over a poorly understood seascape—as this selection of a phantom island as a rendezvous point. Wilkes' instructions had ordered his officers to 'use every means in your power to avoid a separation'.[16] Within thirteen days of leaving Sydney, this plan was in tatters, leaving the four ships to make their separate ways south and attempt to follow Wilkes' orders to reach as high a latitude as possible before regrouping at New Zealand's Bay of Islands in March.

For all three ships, progress south was blocked by a dense belt of ice at around 66°S. There were various signs of land in the vicinity—rocks and sediment embedded in the icebergs, discoloured water, and sightings of seals and penguins—and on 16 January 1840 came the first reported glimpse of a range of mountains beyond the ice that barred their path. The *Porpoise* and *Peacock* soon made their way back north, the latter having lost its rudder to a collision with an iceberg, but the *Vincennes* continued westwards. Ignoring the threat posed by drifting ice and the pleas of his own surgeons to end the voyage and allow the crew to recover, Wilkes skirted the ice pack until 21 February, charting the distant stretches of land that were just visible on the horizon.[17]

The *Vincennes* returned to Sydney on 11 March, having made a rather more conventional entrance on this occasion by engaging a harbour pilot. The returning explorers were warmly received, with Wilkes claiming in his published account of the expedition that the people of Sydney 'appeared to rejoice in our success as if we had been their countrymen'.[18] They had certainly shown plenty of support for the crew of the battered and rudderless *Peacock*, which had limped into the harbour three weeks earlier and benefited from the support of the colonial authorities to carry out urgent repairs at a quite spot on the harbour's north shore. And as had been the case during their previous spell in Sydney, the American officers were deluged with social invitations.[19]

But while relations were warm between the Americans and Sydney's upper classes, the explorers initially remained tight-lipped about their discoveries. There was no shortage of gripping tales for them to tell; after all, the *Peacock* had endured a harrowing ordeal amidst the ice, and the voyage of the *Vincennes* had been an astonishing feat of exploration. Wilkes had taken an unmodified wooden vessel beyond the Antarctic Circle, sighted new land, and skirted the coastline for 2,778 kilometres. Yet for all the drama of the southern voyage, Wilkes' orders obliged him to keep tight control over information about the expedition.[20] The *Peacock*'s captain and crew had scrupulously avoided revealing any details during their stay in Sydney, while Wilkes avoided any public statements.[21] The arrival of the *Vincennes* in Sydney, however, had coincided with the first reports from Hobart that the French expedition had sighted land in the same area as the Americans and charted it for approximately 280 kilometres. Anxious to ensure due recognition for his achievements, Wilkes found a loophole in his instructions, sharing information with the Sydney press without speaking on the record. Thus, the 13 March edition of the *Sydney Herald* led with an announcement that both the American and French expeditions had discovered the long searched for Antarctic continent.[22]

Wilkes' approach drew some criticism for presenting an account 'in an uncertain and mutilated unsatisfactory way', but others in Sydney were impressed by the expedition's work, even with only the general contours of the voyage known.[23] Indeed, Wilkes' 2,778-kilometre cruise along the Antarctic coast was enough for one prominent colonial landowner, William Oldrey, to declare of Wilkes that 'on him had fallen the mantle of Cook'.[24] Linking Wilkes to as revered a British navigator as James Cook was a significant statement: Oldrey undoubtedly sought to flatter Wilkes, but the linkage nonetheless provides some insight into how the American expedition was perceived and received on its return in 1840.

Wilkes left Sydney a week later, bound for northern New Zealand's Bay of Islands to rendezvous with the rest of the fleet. The *Porpoise* and *Flying Fish* had endured gruelling southern voyages of their own, albeit with little in the way of geographical discoveries to show for it, before heading for New Zealand. Yet even after his departure, Wilkes and his discoveries remained a topic of considerable interest and discussion. Details of the Antarctic voyage finally began to reach the colonies in December 1840. This news came initially in the form of accounts from the US press that paid tribute to an expedition that that had 'covered itself in glory' by proving the existence of an Antarctic continent.[25] By the end of the month, Wilkes' official report—originally sent from Sydney in March—was available, published in full by some papers and syndicated and discussed even more widely.[26] This moment, however, proved to be the high point for Wilkes' reputation for the next seventy years. The US Exploring Expedition became mired in controversy and ignominy on its return. A bitter disagreement between Wilkes and James Clark Ross played out in public, the veracity of Wilkes' discoveries and his behaviour as commander of the expedition were questioned, and Wilkes was court-martialled. As these controversies unfolded overseas, Wilkes' claims were dissected in the pages of the Australian colonial press.[27] The man who had once been compared to Cook was instead accused of having orchestrated 'a capital specimen of Yankee hoaxing'.[28]

The controversy that engulfed Wilkes ultimately stemmed from the presence of two other expeditions similarly seeking to locate the south magnetic pole and discover new lands in the Antarctic. Only two weeks after the *Vincennes* shocked Sydneysiders by appearing in the harbour overnight, two small French warships made their way up the Derwent River to the town of Hobart. In command of the *Astrolabe* and *Zélée* was 49-year-old Jules Dumont d'Urville, already famous for his work on two scientific expeditions in the South Pacific in the 1820s. Yet while he was an enthusiastic booster of French scientific exploration and colonial expansion in the Pacific, d'Urville was a reluctant Antarctic explorer. He had proposed leading another Pacific voyage but had been ordered to combine this with an attempt to locate the south magnetic pole and reach as high a southern latitude as possible. Accordingly, the French expedition had departed the port of Toulon in September and made for what is today known as the Weddell Sea.[29]

Until 1823, the farthest south humans had ever travelled was 71°10'S, a record achieved by James Cook in February 1774. Cook's progress was blocked by ice, which he supposed continued all the way to the South Pole, with any land that might exist permanently covered by it.[30] This belief held sway until 1823, when Scottish sealer James Weddell departed the South Shetland Islands in search of new sealing grounds and was surprised to find open sea before him. There was remarkably little sea ice on the South American side of the Antarctic in the summer of 1822–23, a fact that allowed Weddell to reach 74°15'S. With instructions to sail as far south as possible, d'Urville opted to follow Weddell's route but lacked the environmental advantages the sealer had enjoyed fifteen years earlier. Where Weddell found a seemingly endless stretch of open water, the French expedition faced a dense icefield that even the *Astrolabe* and *Zélée*—modified for these conditions—could not penetrate. After spending the better part of two months trying to find a way through the ice, d'Urville took his ships to briefly investigate the poorly charted Antarctic Peninsula before retreating north to Chile. From there, he commenced a yearlong voyage across the Pacific with a view to mounting a second attempt to break the farthest south record in the summer of 1839–40.

Much of this story was already known to the people of Hobart when two battered French ships entered the Derwent on 12 December 1839. In January of that year, several colonial newspapers had erroneously reported that d'Urville had discovered a new continent south of the South Shetlands.[31] While these reports were subsequently corrected to say that he had actually discovered a new island, they ensured that—unlike the unheralded appearance of the US Exploring Expedition—d'Urville's arrival in Hobart was keenly anticipated.[32] Yet when the *Astrolabe* and *Zélée* did arrive, their crews did not entirely live up to the image of heroic polar explorers.[33] Regular waves of illness had cast a shadow over the expedition throughout its duration, and twenty seamen were ill with dysentery when they reached Hobart. Lieutenant-governor John Franklin, himself a renowned veteran of three British naval expeditions to the Arctic, was away from Hobart, so d'Urville and his second-in-command, Honoré Jacquinot, were welcomed by William Elliot, the senior military official in the colony. Elliot immediately arranged for an empty building on Harrington Street to be turned over to the expedition for use as a hospital. When Franklin returned a week later, he granted the explorers access to fresh fruits and vegetables from his private garden to assist their recovery.

Illness cast a pall over the expedition's stay in Hobart. D'Urville spent much of his time—when he wasn't struck down by gout himself—visiting the sick, and seven members of the crew died in the makeshift hospital on shore. The colony's vicar-general was another regular visitor to the hospital, and organised requiem masses, Catholic burials, and the construction of a memorial to the expedition's dead. Yet while loss and illness dominated the expedition's time in Van Diemen's Land, the French explorers were nonetheless still drawn into the social life of the colony in comparable fashion to their American counterparts in Sydney. Franklin took a great interest in the expedition, hosting d'Urville and his officers at Government House and visiting the French ships in turn. Elliott hosted a reception of his own on behalf of Hobart's garrison, while Lady Jane Franklin organised a New Year's Eve ball to farewell the expedition. Many of these social events did double duty as preparation for the imminent southern voyage; D'Urville's meetings with Franklin and with John Biscoe, a whaling captain who had discovered the stretch of Antarctic coast known as Enderby Land in 1831, provided valuable opportunities to glean information about polar exploration.[34]

The expedition was already strained to its limits by the time it reached Hobart, but d'Urville was committed to attempting a second Antarctic voyage. After toying with the idea of taking only one ship south, d'Urville settled on a plan to recruit a dozen seamen—some local, others from a French whaler then in Hobart—and outfit both vessels with enough livestock and lime juice to mitigate the risk of scurvy.[35] Leaving the sick behind, the *Astrolabe* and *Zélée* departed in the early hours of 2 January 1840. D'Urville's plan was straightforward: to sail almost directly south from Hobart towards the approximate location of the south magnetic pole. This was to be a short, concentrated effort to reach the magnetic pole, in contrast to the complex sailing instructions and far more expansive survey Wilkes was embarking on that same summer.

Aside from enduring the ferocious gales typical of the Southern Ocean, the French explorers enjoyed a relatively uneventful voyage. They encountered icebergs from around 60°S and celebrated crossing the Antarctic Circle (approximately 66°33'S) on 20 January. Later that day, land was spotted in the distance. The next two days were devoted to investigating the coastline of what d'Urville named Adélie Land, after his wife, but ice prevented a landing. Instead, a party went ashore on a small, rocky islet, where they collected geological samples, took magnetic observations, and held a ceremony to formally claim possession of the nearby islands and mainland for France. Following this, d'Urville took both ships westward, where they lost sight of land but did, on 30 January, perceive a ship emerging from the fog.[36]

The mystery ship was the *Porpoise*, which had lost contact with the larger ships of the US Exploring Expedition a week earlier and was now engaged in a cruise along the pack ice searching for signs of land. The chance encounter between the *Porpoise* and the two French ships would subsequently become one of many points of contention between d'Urville and Wilkes. Wilkes, drawing on the report of the *Porpoise*'s commander, publicly accused d'Urville of setting his sails to get away from the US ship; d'Urville claimed he had been trying to increase his speed to keep up with the *Porpoise*, and accused the entire US expedition of operating under an unseemly veil of secrecy.[37] It is impossible to know precisely what transpired, but after this brief encounter the *Porpoise* continue its fruitless cruise along the ice pack before heading for the rendezvous point in New Zealand. The French ships, meanwhile, continued westward, spotting what they thought to be land the next day. D'Urville named this ice-covered stretch of land the Clarie Coast, after Jacquinot's wife, but did not linger. Instead, on 1 February 1840, having discovered previously unknown land, collected geological samples that provided evidence for its likely continental origin, and made magnetic observations, d'Urville called an end to the southern voyage and returned to Van Diemen's Land.

The expedition was once again a subject of great interest when the *Astrolabe* and *Zélée* arrived back in Hobart on 18 February.[38] D'Urville was invited to Government House to give a personal account of the voyage to the Franklins, while he and Jacquinot were both elected members of the Tasmanian Society. The society, a generalist scientific institution inspired by England's Royal Society, was a pet project of Franklin's, established to stimulate the intellectual life of the colony.[39] Franklin's administration also assisted in refitting, resupplying and repainting the ships, and moved two seamen who were still too sick to rejoin the ships to the government hospital. In turn, the expedition members were eager to demonstrate their gratitude for the various kinds of support they had enjoyed in Hobart.[40] Notably, when the expedition's officers raised funds for the construction of a small memorial to those members who had died, the surplus raised was presented to the vicar-general to be used to help the colony's Catholic poor.[41]

Perhaps the clearest demonstration of the expedition's gratitude, though, came in the form of a detailed account of the southern voyage presented by d'Urville to the Hobart press. It would have been easy for d'Urville to be vague and general in his dealings with the press to ensure his king and countrymen would be the first to learn of his discoveries, just as Wilkes had been in Sydney. D'Urville likely had one eye on shaping the narrative, of course, sharing news to claim credit for his discoveries before Wilkes could. Nonetheless, his decision to be so open was a significant one, making Vandemonians the first people in the world to learn of the discovery of land 'of considerable extent' directly south of Australia.[42] This helped ensure Antarctic exploration remained a topic of palpable interest in Van Diemen's Land well after the *Astrolabe* and *Zélée* departed for New Zealand, via the subantarctic Auckland Islands, on 25 February 1840. D'Urville's account would be referenced, syndicated and summarised in newspapers throughout the colonies in the following months, generating interest in the prospect of future exploration as well as discussion of the commercial possibilities for sealing and whaling in Antarctic waters.[43]

‹ ›

It was into this surging interest in Antarctic exploration that the third expedition of 1839–41 arrived. The British expedition was, by some distance, the best prepared and most ambitious of the three. If Wilkes was underqualified and d'Urville unenthusiastic, James Clark Ross was uniquely suited to command of a naval expedition dedicated to magnetic data collection and geographical exploration in the Southern Ocean. Ross was, by 1839, one of the world's most experienced Arctic explorers, having both located the north magnetic pole in 1831 and been part of the expedition that set a new farthest north record in 1827. Yet, as well as polar experience, Ross was also enthusiastic about science and had spent much of the period since 1835 working on a magnetic survey of Britain and Ireland orchestrated by Edward Sabine and the Royal Society.[44]

These dual qualifications held Ross in good stead. His instructions required him to not only search for the magnetic pole but also address the Southern Hemisphere–shaped gap in the world's magnetic data. Ross was ordered to make magnetic observations at locations throughout the Southern Ocean world, from the Falkland Islands to the Kerguelen archipelago, and to establish permanent magnetic observatories in British colonies at Saint Helena, Cape Town and Hobart. Simultaneous observations were to be made at these stations, on board the expedition's ships, and at Northern Hemisphere observatories on predetermined 'term days', in the hope that, when combined with existing records, this data would lead to a decisive breakthrough in the science of terrestrial magnetism.[45] In addition to data collection, Ross was to investigate previously sighted stretches of land in the Antarctic, such as Enderby and Graham Land, and to search hitherto unexplored areas for new discoveries. The expedition's medical officers, Robert McCormick and Joseph Hooker, would also act as naturalists responsible for collecting geological, zoological and botanical specimens throughout the voyage.[46]

To complete this ambitious task, Ross was given the *Erebus* and *Terror*. The two bomb vessels were better suited to pushing through pack ice than any ships previously despatched to the Antarctic, including those belonging to the US and French expeditions. Ross was also able to call on the expertise of several Arctic veterans, notably his second-in-command Francis Crozier and the *Erebus*'s gunner Thomas Abernethy, who had been a member of Ross's north magnetic pole party. And Ross had one final advantage over his rivals: a logbook given to him by a man called Charles Enderby.

'Enderby' was a famous name in the late-eighteenth and early nineteenth centuries, a name associated with whaling, sealing and all kinds of entrepreneurialism in the farthest flung corners of the world. Only a few vestiges of the Enderby family's fame remain, mostly in the names of a handful of desolate landmarks on the map and a casual aside in *Moby Dick*, which refers to the family firm Enderby & Sons as 'a house which … comes not far behind the united royal houses of the Tudors and Bourbons, in point of real historical interest'.[47] The company's renown had been built on discovering and exploiting whaling grounds throughout the Atlantic and Pacific worlds. It had been the Enderbys, for instance, who pioneered whaling off the coast of Australia and New Zealand in the 1790s, accepting government premiums to take convicts to New South Wales to subsidise their whaling experiments. Charles, the third generation to helm the company, must have grown up on stories of his family's various achievements, such as the discovery in 1806 of the Auckland Islands by Enderby captain Abraham Bristow, a discovery which sparked a subantarctic sealing boom. This may explain Charles Enderby's passion for exploration.[48]

Charles and his brother George became directors of the company in 1830, a time of precipitous decline for the British whaling industry. The unsustainable slaughter of whales had made many older whaling grounds unprofitable, while whalers in North America and Australasia had a geographical advantage that helped them outcompete the old British companies, and the whales themselves had developed more effective tactics to evade hunters.[49] In the context of this malaise for British whaling, Enderby began commissioning company captains to undertake dedicated voyages of exploration in the Southern Ocean, hoping to both discover new whaling or sealing grounds and bring glory to the company. The first of these voyages, commanded by John Biscoe in 1830–33, became only the third (after Cook's and a Russian expedition in 1820) to circumnavigate Antarctica. Biscoe also discovered several islands and sighted two hitherto unknown stretches of coastline: Graham Land, on the Antarctic Peninsula south of Chile and Argentina, and Enderby Land, south-east of South Africa.[50] Enderby was a relentless self-promoter and presented a paper on Biscoe's discoveries to

London's Royal Geographical Society in 1833 that was subsequently published in the society's journal. Enderby's belief that 'the probability seems thus to be revived of the existence of a great Southern Land' therefore circulated widely and shaped the programs of the three national expeditions of 1839–41.[51]

Biscoe's voyage had been a financial failure for the company, but Charles Enderby remained bullish about the prospects of this kind of private exploration. A second voyage in 1833–34 had been aborted when a ship was crushed by pack ice on the edge of the Antarctic Circle, but Enderby & Sons nonetheless financed a third in 1838–39, led this time by veteran captain John Balleny. Balleny opted to take an unusual route, sailing first to subantarctic Campbell Island, around 600 kilometres south of New Zealand's Stewart Island / Rakiura. Taking his two small ships south along a more easterly route than previous Antarctic voyages, roughly following the 172nd meridian east, Balleny was surprised to find a relatively open sea. He reached 69°S before encountering the icepack, and while he had no hope of breaking through it in his small schooner, the ice had not seemed impenetrable here. Returning north from this point, Balleny had discovered a previously unknown chain of islands and a short stretch of land, which he named Sabrina Coast in tribute to his second ship, which had disappeared in a storm a few days earlier.[52] Balleny returned to London on 17 September 1839, just a week before the *Erebus* and *Terror* were due to depart. Charles Enderby had therefore raced to ensure that Balleny's journal made it into Ross's hands before his departure.[53] This action would prove significant. Armed with Balleny's journal, Ross knew something Wilkes and d'Urville did not: a more easterly route might offer a way through the icepack.

The *Terror* and *Erebus* reached Hobart on 15 and 16 August 1840 respectively, after a meandering voyage that had seen them stop to make magnetic observations at Madeira, Cape Verde, the Saint Peter and Saint Paul Rocks, Trinidad, Saint Helena, Cape Town, Possession Island and Kerguelen.[54] As had been the case with the French expedition eight months earlier, their arrival had been keenly anticipated.[55] Undoubtedly the most enthusiastic person in Van Diemen's Land about the expedition, though, was lieutenant-governor Franklin. As his biographers have shown, Franklin cut an isolated figure in the colony. Unprepared for the ruthlessness of Vandemonian politics and frustrated by public disinterest in the kinds of cultural and intellectual pursuits he favoured, he had proved ill-suited to a position in colonial administration.[56] The presence of his old Arctic companions Ross and Crozier, and a chance to assist in their new voyage of polar exploration, was a rare delight for Franklin, and he threw himself into supporting the expedition wholeheartedly.

Ross's priority on arrival in Hobart was to commence construction of a magnetic observatory. He was delighted, then, that the endlessly enthusiastic lieutenant-governor had already prepared the necessary materials and drawn up a shortlist of possible sites. Once Ross had chosen a site near the planned location for a new government house, Franklin assigned no fewer than 200 convicts to work on the project and began supervising construction himself. With such unequivocal government backing, 'Rossbank Observatory', as Franklin dubbed it, was completed and its instruments fully installed within nine days.[57] While work on the observatory was underway, the expedition was granted a private anchorage, renamed 'Ross Cove' by Franklin, upriver from the town's crowded main harbour. As the ships underwent repairs, the colony's commissary-general was assigned the daunting task of providing the expedition with the diverse range and 'unusually large' quantity of provisions required for an Antarctic voyage. These provisions from the public store were supplemented by daily deliveries of fruits and vegetables from Franklin's private garden.[58]

While few could rival Franklin for enthusiasm, there was certainly significant interaction between the expedition and Vandemonians. Even with the *Erebus* and *Terror* tucked out of the way at Ross Cove, locals were eager to visit and inspect the ships.[59] On 29 October, Hobart was 'disturbed from its uniform aspect of settled dullness' by a ball held at the town's customs house in honour of 'the distinguished sons of science now amongst them'. The *Courier* estimated that 300 people, roughly one in every forty-nine residents of Hobart, attended this party.[60] Ross was a guest of honour at various local ceremonies, such as those to lay foundation stones for the new government house and college buildings. Several expedition members struck up friendships with the soldiers from Hobart's local regiment, while the expedition's young botanist Joseph Hooker and the lieutenant-governor's secretary Ronald Campbell Gunn roamed the island together whenever they could, collecting specimens of plants, animals and minerals.[61] Other locals volunteered to assist with the painstaking task of recording magnetic data on term days, when observations were made at two-and-a-half-minute intervals for twenty-four hours by the expedition and at observatories around the world.[62]

It was during this time in Hobart that Ross became aware of the outcome of the southern voyages undertaken earlier that year by the US and French expeditions. He learnt of d'Urville's discoveries from the account published in the Hobart newspapers, but also found a letter from Wilkes waiting for him. Disregarding his orders to maintain secrecy, Wilkes had drawn up a rough chart of his discoveries after leaving Sydney and sent it to Ross, along with a set of practical suggestions about where Ross should focus his attention. Wilkes' motive for sending this letter this may have been earnest—the two men had met when Wilkes travelled to England to purchase charts and instruments and had been on good terms—but it was a source of enormous frustration for Ross. His plans to explore precisely the region visited by the US and French expeditions had been publicly known, leaving him astounded that both Wilkes and d'Urville had chosen to forestall him. As far as Ross was concerned, this left him with only one option. He felt it would be inconsistent with the expedition's objectives and the traditions of British polar exploration to 'follow in the footsteps of the expedition of any other nation'.[63] He therefore hastily drew up a new plan: the *Erebus* and *Terror* would take a far more easterly route, sailing south along the 170th meridian east to take advantage of the open sea reported by Balleny.

The expedition left Hobart on 12 November 1840. It paused for three weeks at the Auckland Islands, 465 kilometres south of New Zealand, to chart them and take magnetic observations for November's term day. While there, Ross took the opportunity to release sheep, pigs, poultry and rabbits on the islands, and to instruct Hooker to scatter gooseberry, currant, raspberry and strawberry seeds wherever he roamed while collecting specimens.[64] While this would have ramifications for the islands' environment, it was a common practice at the time. Introducing various plant and animal species offered a way to test the potential of uninhabited islands like the Aucklands, which Ross believed were the ideal candidate for Britain's next penal colony. It also had a humanitarian dimension, the idea being that plants and animals would provide a food source for future visitors or shipwreck survivors. These dual developmental and humanitarian ideas would become a recurring theme in discussions over the next century of how to approach the uninhabited islands scattered throughout the Southern Ocean.

After another brief stopover at Campbell Island, Ross took the *Erebus* and *Terror* south. They encountered a belt of pack ice around 66°S, but, as Balleny had suspected, it was simple enough for Ross to break through into the sea that bears his name today. Both ships made directly for the magnetic pole's approximate location, but their progress was halted by a spur of land that Ross named Cape Adare, beyond which lay imposing cliffs and a range of high mountains. This left Ross and Crozier with two options: they could go north around the cape and continue westwards towards the region explored by d'Urville and Wilkes, hoping to find a way to cut back south towards the magnetic pole, or they could follow the cape southwards. Reasoning that if they could not reach the magnetic pole they could at least obtain a high latitude, they headed south.

For the next two weeks, then, they sailed southwards, charting and naming the mountains and promontories they passed after various patrons, Admiralty figures, scientists, family and expedition members. Twice they stopped to land on islands, hastily collecting geological specimens and performing proclamation ceremonies to claim the nearby coast, which Ross called Victoria Land. Weddell's farthest south record was broken on 23 January with open sea still ahead. Not until the 27th were *Erebus* and *Terror* finally halted in their tracks. Glimpses of mountain peaks in the distance indicated that Victoria Land continued to the south, but the expedition was blocked by a towering active volcano, Mount Erebus, and by what appeared to be a solid wall of ice. Having reached 77°30'S, they were forced to turn east, hoping to find a way around this 'Great Ice Barrier' (known today as the Ross Ice Shelf). But after sailing along the barrier for 460 kilometres, they were forced to call an end to the southern voyage on 14 February 1841.[65] Returning north, Ross sailed north-west from Cape Adare, expecting to come across a stretch of mountainous coastline marked on the chart given to him by Wilkes, but instead finding only deep sea. This would later become the centre of another acrimonious polar dispute.

While Ross and Crozier were occupied with redrawing the map of the Antarctic, the infinitely less dramatic work of magnetic observation continued apace in Hobart. The *Terror*'s lieutenant Joseph Kay had been left in charge of a five-man party at Rossbank Observatory. In characteristic fashion, Franklin accommodated Kay's team of observers in Government House until dedicated quarters were ready for them next to the observatory. But while the five expedition members were able to keep up with most of the scheduled observations, they relied on the assistance of a group of local volunteers to get through the 'tedious and laborious work' required on the monthly term days. Franklin, of course, headed this group (his biographer Andrew Lambert refers to the observatory as the lieutenant-governor's 'garden shed'), and was joined by Ronald Campbell Gunn, Franklin's private secretary Francis Henslowe, Tasmanian Society secretary John Philip Gell, port officer William Moriarty, government printer James Barnard, the commander of the visiting Royal Navy ship *Britomart* Owen Stanley, and five free settlers.[66]

The expedition's return to Van Diemen's Land was eagerly anticipated in the colony. When the *Erebus* and *Terror* were sighted off the coast, Franklin immediately sailed his barge down the Derwent to meet the ships and escort them to their former moorings at Ross Cove. The expedition's second spell in Hobart generated even greater excitement than its first. The voyage was heralded as a 'complete success', having discovered islands and volcanoes, charted 900 kilometres of coastline, accurately calculated the position of the magnetic pole, and set a new farthest south record while tracing the edge of the astonishing Great Ice Barrier for 460 kilometres. While the US and French expeditions had been regarded well while they were in Australia, the press soon began comparing their achievements unfavourably with Ross's. Hobart's *Courier*, for instance, seized on Ross's mention of having sailed over mountains marked on Wilkes' chart to accuse the Americans of 'an extraordinary mistake'.[67] A casual press mention of how 'seals and sperm whales were seen in abundance' led to a flurry of excitement, with investors speculating about the possibility of lucrative industries, before hopes were scuppered by a clarification that Antarctic conditions made whaling impractical and that the seals seen were 'not of the valuable kind'.[68]

Perhaps the most intriguing response to Ross's return was a dramatisation of the expedition's Antarctic voyage in the form of a play. This 'much talked of and anxiously looked for spectacle', the sets of which offered the first visual depiction of the Antarctic in Australia, was written and staged within a month of the expedition's return.[69] While only fragments of the play's content are known, it offers a tantalising glimpse into how ordinary Vandemonians responded to the expedition. It is notable that the play's closing monologue looked forward to a future in which 'those cold seas, to all but him unknown / May furnish wealth, that might uphold a throne'.[70] Even with the press downplaying the prospect of Vandemonians exploiting the whales and seals Ross had seen, the idea that his Antarctic discoveries might one day have commercial value remained an alluring one.

Much of the officers' time in Hobart was again taken up by magnetic observations, or else by calibrating the instruments required to take them. But while Crozier stayed at Ross Cove to oversee the repair and restocking of the ships, Ross and his two surgeon-scientists, McCormick and Hooker, travelled around the colony with Franklin. These excursions included an overland journey to Launceston, a trip to a fossilised forest at Macquarie Plains, and a tour of the convict facilities at Port Arthur.[71] Several expedition members also became involved in the fledgling Tasmanian Society, attending meetings and presenting papers during their winter in Hobart. Kay presented two papers to the society on terrestrial magnetism and the instruments and techniques used at Rossbank. McCormick spoke on the results of his geological investigations of Kerguelen, the Aucklands, Campbell Island and Victoria Land. The *Terror*'s surgeon John Robertson gave an account of the southern voyage and the expedition's geographical discoveries. Ross, Crozier, Hooker, McCormick and Robertson were all elected members too, as d'Urville and Jacquinot had been.[72] And in amongst the work of the expedition, Ross and Crozier found time to organise their spectacular party aboard the *Erebus* and *Terror* on 'the memorable First of June'.

Ross's charisma, his ability to host a unique and memorable party, and his wholehearted participation in Hobart life, along with his openness in sharing the story of the southern voyage, endeared him to Vandemonians throughout the expedition's two spells in the colony. When the expedition finally left on 7 July 1841, bound initially for Sydney and then for two more dramatic Antarctic voyages in the summers of 1841–42 and 1842–43, the *Erebus* and *Terror* were farewelled by large crowds and escorted down the Derwent by Franklin's barge.[73] Fifty years later, South Australian politician Samuel Davenport recalled arriving in Hobart in 1842 and finding Vandemonians still 'all agog as to the expedition'.[74] Ross's every move was reported in the Vandemonian press long after his departure: the expedition's arrival at various ports; Ross, Crozier and Hooker's meeting with the king upon their return to Britain; the publication of the papers relating to the voyage, and later Ross's narrative of the expedition and Hooker's *Botany of the Antarctic Voyage*; Ross's involvement in the ultimately fruitless search for Franklin and Crozier, who famously disappeared while on an expedition in search of the North-West Passage in 1848; and, eventually, Ross's death in 1862.[75]

This fascination with Ross's career was not the passion of a single newspaper or editor; these stories were followed for more than twenty years by multiple publications in both Hobart and Launceston. Clearly, even two decades later, Tasmanian memories of Ross remained undimmed. This interest in Ross came to be shared with the other Australian colonies and continued even after his death. *The Sydney Morning Herald* coordinated an intercolonial campaign for Australians to donate to the construction of a memorial to Ross in England, while books and newspaper articles recounted his achievements throughout the 1860s and 1870s.[76] Sixty years after Ross's arrival in Hobart, Norwegian-Australian Antarctic explorer Carsten Borchgrevink was overwhelmed with joy when he was gifted a relic of the older era of Antarctic exploration: an Admiralty chart that had once belonged to Ross.[77]

The Antarctic voyages of Ross, Wilkes and d'Urville are often understood as a brief burst of interest that faded rapidly into obscurity.[78] There was simply little interest in Britain, France or the United States in following up on any of these projects. D'Urville's was the first of the three to return, but he never got the chance to articulate the significance of Adélie Land or to campaign for further investigations—the feted French explorer died, together with his family, in a horrific railway accident in May 1842.[79] The US Exploring Expedition became mired in various controversies: Wilkes behaviour as commander, the dispute over the 'land' Ross had sailed over, and allegations Wilkes had lied about the date his expedition first sighted land to falsely claim priority over d'Urville. Wilkes was acquitted on most of the charges against him at court martial, but his career stalled and the messiness of the expedition cast a long shadow over any possibility of further US exploration in the far south. Wilkes eventually became an even more controversial figure during the US Civil War. In an incident known as the '*Trent* Affair', Wilkes detained and boarded a British ship to remove two Confederate envoys travelling on it, violating Britain's neutrality and sparking an international incident.

Britain's Royal Navy, meanwhile, turned its focus back to the Arctic. When Ross returned in 1843, the *Erebus* and *Terror* were almost immediately refitted for a new expedition to search for the North-West Passage. Ross declined an invitation to lead this new voyage and overall command fell to Franklin, recently recalled from Van Diemen's Land, while Crozier retained command of the *Terror*. Franklin's 1845 expedition disappeared, sparking three decades of naval and private search efforts. Aside from a single, exceedingly small follow-up in 1845, when one of the *Terror*'s former officers was sent to collect magnetic data in a stretch of the southern Indian Ocean sector that Ross had missed, the focus of British polar exploration was directed north rather than south throughout the rest of the nineteenth century.

This standard narrative of a singular burst of interest in the Antarctic followed by an extended period of disinterest makes sense from a Northern Hemisphere perspective. It is unsatisfactory, though, in an Australian context. For one thing, the Antarctic expeditions of 1839–41 were not quite as novel to the people of the Australian colonies as they first appeared. By the time Wilkes and d'Urville arrived, there had been close connections between the colonies and the Southern Ocean and its islands for at least thirty-five years. The first staple export industries in New South Wales and Van Diemen's Land were whaling and sealing, and the latter especially drew mariners to the region south of Australia and New Zealand. As early as 1805, colonial investors, ships and workers were involved in a sealing boom that had broken out on the subantarctic Antipodes Islands. The unsustainable slaughter of seals on those islands meant the boom was all but over by 1807, so sealers shifted their focus to butchering fur seals on the newly discovered Auckland Islands further south. The unrestrained slaughter continued, and sealers searched for new populations to exploit. Sydney sealer Frederick Hasselborough discovered Campbell and Macquarie islands in 1810, and within two years the sealing frontier had shifted to these islands. To give a sense of the scale of this industry, a single merchant firm obtained at least 101,200 seal skins from Macquarie Island alone in the decade after its discovery.[80] By the 1820s, fur seal populations throughout this stretch of the Southern Ocean had been decimated, so sealers turned to hunting other species such as elephant seals, which had no value for the fur trade but had blubber that could be boiled to produce an alternative to whale oil. Others travelled further afield to work islands like the Kerguelen archipelago, or else revisited the already denuded subantarctic islands south of New Zealand to exploit any fur seal populations that had begun to recover from the earlier booms.

Sealing in the subantarctic was grim work. Groups of sealers would be deposited on islands for weeks or months at a time, tasked with slaughtering seals and preserving the skins or boiling down the blubber for oil. Yet this arduous and unpleasant work, often in cold, wet conditions, offered significant opportunities. For some maritime workers, former convicts, and First Nations people, the mobility and employment it offered was a more attractive alternative to conditions in the colonies.[81] For colonial merchants and investors, it was a way to earn quick profits with relatively little up-front investment. Many former convicts such as Simeon Lord, Henry Kable, James Underwood and Mary Reibey, as well as the first generation of free merchants such as Robert Campbell, took advantage of the various sealing booms to generate substantial wealth. This wealth could then be reinvested, either in more capital-intensive industries like whaling or in the physical and financial infrastructure of the colonies. Fur, blood and blubber extracted from the Southern Ocean world was transformed into ships and wharves, homes and warehouses, banks and insurance corporations.[82]

This entanglement of the Australian colonies and their Southern Ocean hinterland was no secret to people in Sydney and

Hobart. By 1839 there were still many people living and working in these towns with first-hand experience of Southern Ocean industries. The colonial press had also consistently reported on the discovery of new islands in the subantarctic and the success of sealing expeditions.[83] A decade before Wilkes and d'Urville arrived, the possibility of developing a colonial whaling industry in Antarctic waters had been discussed in the press.[84] There was even some degree of familiarity with the idea of exploring and undertaking scientific investigations in the Southern Ocean. A Russian naval expedition, commanded by Fabian von Bellingshausen, had visited Sydney twice in April and September 1820 while searching for an Antarctic continent.[85] Bellingshausen's reception in Sydney closely resembled that of Wilkes: there were inspections of the expedition's ships, a welcome ball, a farewell dinner, and even a party to celebrate the anniversary of the coronation of Russia's Emperor Alexander I that commenced in a villa at Point Piper and continued on the harbour in a chartered schooner.[86] The Philosophical Society of Australasia, the first attempt to establish a scientific society in New South Wales, chose the subantarctic for its first project, commissioning mariner Thomas Raine to report on Macquarie Island's geology, flora and fauna when he sailed there to deposit an elephant sealing gang in 1821.[87] This prior history of colonial engagement with the Southern Ocean added up to a store of residual vernacular knowledge about the region to Australia's south, knowledge that shaped interactions between the colonists and the visiting expeditions.

Clearly, then, 1839 did not mark the *beginning* of an Australian interest in the Antarctic. It did, however, mark a significant turning point in how people in Australia thought about the region that lay to the continent's south. Until this time, this region was overwhelmingly imagined in entirely extractive, bluntly commercial terms—as a maritime hinterland to be exploited to help fuel the colonies' development and expansion. This mentality did not disappear. It can be seen, for instance, in the play that celebrated Ross's return to Hobart by imagining a future of Vandemonian prosperity built on polar wealth. But where this had been the default way of thinking about the Antarctic, after 1841 it became one of several overlapping ways of thinking and talking about this part of the world.

The Philosophical Society's singular effort to promote the basic scientific observation of Australia's southern hinterland aside, science and geographical exploration scarcely figured in discussions of the Southern Ocean in the Australian colonies before 1839. The presence of the three national expeditions of 1839–41 energised those with an interest in these topics, however, and the willingness of expedition members to become involved with the colonies' fledgling scientific societies gave these institutions a significant boost. Antarctic science did not suddenly become a topic of mass interest, but the idea that exploration and research in the Southern Ocean was fundamentally valuable would become increasingly evident in the decades after 1841. The three national expeditions also excited patriotic sentiments in the colonies, establishing that Antarctic exploration was a project of national significance. This was a broad kind of patriotism, one that could proclaim the US explorers as 'blood relatives' as easily as it could hail 'the gallant tars of England'.[88] Yet the expression of such sentiments served to clearly link Southern Ocean exploration and national achievement and glory in colonial discussions of the Antarctic.

The three expeditions of 1839–41 are essential to understanding how Australians have thought about the world to their south. Ross, Wilkes and d'Urville's voyages have conventionally been framed as a brief surge of interest in the Antarctic that emerged out of the Magnetic Crusade and soon faded. Yet this narrative underestimates the legacy these expeditions left in the Australian colonies, where they gave momentum and legitimacy to local scientific institutions, stimulated patriotic sentiments, and gave hope to local expectations of profiting from new discoveries in the icebound seas to the south. These local impacts ensured that, while Britain, France and the United States had little interest in following up their grand expeditions, an idea began to emerge that the further investigation of this part of the Antarctic was not only desirable but was the duty of those living in the Australian colonies. This idea would develop slowly over the next three decades before exploding into life in the 1870s.

2

'THE RADIUS OF THEIR DUTY'

Debating the Value of the Southern Frontier

In May 1873, a surprising schism appeared in Victorian society and politics. Its origins lay in a seemingly straightforward question asked in the colony's Legislative Assembly by the Liberal member for Avoca. Was the government prepared, asked James Macpherson Grant, 'to take any steps, either separately or conjointly with the other colonies, to fit out an expedition to Possession Island'?[1] Grant was the parliamentary mouthpiece of a growing movement that saw despatching an expedition to Possession Island—the small island off the coast of Victoria Land that James Clark Ross had landed on in January 1841—as a task of vital and urgent importance. Significantly, Grant and his allies believed that it was the responsibility of the Australian colonies generally and Victoria especially to shoulder this burden.

The Argus, one of Melbourne's most influential dailies, resoundingly endorsed Grant's proposal. In an unflinching editorial, the paper proclaimed that it would be 'a lasting disgrace to the whole of the Australian colonies, and to Victoria in particular', if the expedition did not go ahead.[2] Conservative premier James Francis, however, was not swayed, announcing that his government 'did not feel called upon to undertake an obligation which did not come within the radius of their duty'.[3] Francis's decision was decried in newspapers across the colony.[4] So outraged were the editors of *The Argus* that they continued a campaign for urgent colonial action even after Francis had categorically ruled it out.[5] The decision even attracted staunch criticism in South Australia, where it was erroneously reported that New South Wales had committed £1,000 to an intercolonial Australian Antarctic expedition, so that if South Australians 'may be induced to do our part' then the expedition could yet be despatched in time.[6] Evidently, many people in Australia felt that Antarctic exploration *did* fall within the radius of the colonial governments' duty.

The impetus for the wave of Antarctic expeditions in 1839–41 had been the Magnetic Crusade, the campaign to accumulate data from around the world to better understand the forces that govern the planet's magnetic field. The Victorian proposal for a new expedition in 1873 likewise had its origins in a desire to better understand a fundamental scientific problem. The transit of Venus, when Venus passes directly between the earth and the sun, offers the best opportunity to measure the distance between these two celestial objects. The transit is a rare but predictable astronomical phenomenon: two transits take place eight years apart, then after 121 years another pair of transits takes place eight years apart, then after another 105 years the pattern repeats. By observing the transit simultaneously from multiple locations around the world, the distance between the earth and the sun could be calculated using trigonometry. Observations had been made during the twin transits of 1761 and 1769, mainly in the Northern Hemisphere, from which a figure of roughly 153 million kilometres had been calculated. To improve the accuracy of this calculation (eventually found to be approximately 3.4 million kilometres off), observations needed to be made as close to the poles as possible, and the twin transits of 1874 and 1882 offered the last chance to do so until 2004. When it became apparent that no other state had committed to an expedition to observe the transit from the Antarctic, the campaign for a last-minute Australian expedition kicked into gear.

This campaign ultimately proved unrealistic. While there was no shortage of enthusiasm, there was simply too little time and insufficient political will to get an expedition off the ground. Yet the very existence of this debate draws attention to a significant change in how people in Australia thought about the Antarctic at the time. This chapter traces the steady emergence of the idea that the Australian colonies had a special interest in the Antarctic, one that brought with it both a responsibility to take a leading role in the further exploration of the colonies' southern frontier and an opportunity to reap the benefits of this work. Existing accounts of this era of Antarctic history have tended to treat the period from the 1840s to the 1880s as one of relative disinterest in Antarctic science and exploration. I argue that this overlooks a sustained engagement with the world to their south that is evident in the Australian colonies throughout this period and which shaped the emergence of fundamental ideas about Australia's southern frontier.

Well after the British, French and US expeditions had returned to their ports of origin, the Antarctic remained a topic of interest and discussion in the Australian towns they had visited. The Tasmanian Society, dedicated to fostering science in the colony, did much to promote the work of the expeditions, publishing a series of articles on the Antarctic between 1842 and 1847 in its journal. Most of these were papers that had been presented by members of the British expedition, though they also included accounts of the French expedition, reviews of Joseph Hooker's book *The Botany of the Antarctic Expedition*, and re-publications of papers presented to European societies.[7]

While the Tasmanian Society itself was a small group with strict membership requirements, each issue of the journal was promoted widely in the Vandemonian press, with the Antarctic articles often prominent in the descriptions.[8] *The Courier*, for instance, republished Robert McCormick's paper on the geology and ornithology of the Antarctic regions to promote the journal.[9] Antarctic science was hardly a subject of mass interest in Van Diemen's Land, but nor was it something restricted to the dozen or so enthusiasts who had volunteered to help record magnetic data at Rossbank. In 1850, a lecture at the Hobart Mechanics' Institute by public servant Adam Turnbull, in which Turnbull argued that the origins of the world's tides were to be found in the Antarctic and southern Indian oceans, attracted an audience of around 400 people.[10] In the same year, the Mutual Improvement Class at Hobart School of Arts debated whether there was land at the South Pole.[11]

Discussions like this were how knowledge about the Antarctic, and its role in addressing the major scientific questions of the day, circulated in Australia in the middle part of the nineteenth century. This knowledge was not always accurate, of course, and its circulation was often limited by geography, or else to readers of certain publications or members of certain organisations. But it circulated nonetheless, and as it did so it built a degree of familiarity with the idea of Antarctic science and exploration. An 1857 article on magnetism published in the *Illustrated Journal of Australasia* is indicative of this kind of discussion. The value of more abstract branches of science, such as magnetism and astronomy, was a heated topic in Victoria at this time. The colony's recently established Philosophical Institute—known from 1859 as the Royal Society of Victoria—had begun a campaign for the construction of a government astronomical observatory in 1856. A year later, the young German scientist Georg Neumayer had applied for government funding to construct a separate magnetic and meteorological observatory in Melbourne.

The anonymous author of the *Illustrated Journal* article was therefore engaging with a topic of considerable public interest when they asked what a branch of science like terrestrial magnetism can 'do for us'. In the author's opinion, the Australian colonies would be better served focusing on applied projects like mapping the Victorian goldfields than trying to accumulate magnetic data from sites in Australia, since they could never compete with the 'old nations of the northern hemisphere in branches of science peculiarly their own'. If colonists *did* want to 'advance the cause of pure theoretical science', then they should do so in a field suited to them. If they wanted to make a real contribution, they should abandon the idea of an observatory and instead 'fit out an expedition to the south pole and really obtain something for our money'.[12] In this public debate over the merits of various scientific projects can be seen the germ of an idea that the Antarctic was a sphere of investigation peculiarly suited to the peoples of the Australian colonies.

The proposal for the construction of two observatories in Melbourne, both of which were eventually taken up, was symptomatic of the growing enthusiasm for science in Australia in the mid-nineteenth century. Science, in its broadest sense as a way of understanding the natural and physical world, was embedded in Australian colonial life. The farming, mining and maritime trade that underpinned processes of dispossession and settler colonial expansion in Australia required constant improvements in understanding weather patterns, soil characteristics, human and animal health, the distribution of minerals, hydrology and magnetism. This kind of environmental knowledge was built on the observation of phenomena like weather and magnetic variation, the collection of specimens and data, and engagement with theories, observations and practices from around the world.[13]

A variety of institutions and media developed to promote this work of observation, collection and research. Early attempts at establishing dedicated associations were often abortive, undermined by political differences, onerous membership requirements and wider economic conditions. The Philosophical Society of Australasia, the short-lived, Sydney-based association that had commissioned a report on Macquarie Island, enjoyed a burst of activity in 1821 and 1822 before collapsing. In Hobart, a Van Diemen's Land Scientific Society had a similarly tumultuous trajectory from ambitious beginnings in 1829 to total collapse in 1831. In Sydney, several members of the Philosophical Society jumped ship to the new Agricultural Society in 1822, before it too lapsed in 1834. Later attempts were more stable and successful, however, and by 1855, Tasmania, New

South Wales, South Australia and Victoria each had their own generalist scientific association that would come to be designated a 'Royal Society'. By this time, the colonies also had dedicated museums and botanic gardens, hundreds of mechanics' institutes and schools of arts committed to adult education, universities in Sydney and Melbourne, and the first public library in Melbourne.

Over the course of the 1860s and 1870s, a variety of other, more specialised scientific associations were formed throughout Australia, including agricultural, acclimatisation, zoological, entomological and Linnaean societies. Similar associations were established in New Zealand, both at the provincial level and in the form of colony-wide groups like the generalist New Zealand Institute. In the 1880s, geographical societies, field naturalists' clubs, the Royal Society of Queensland, and the intercolonial Australasian Association for the Advancement of Science were all added to this burgeoning coterie of scientific associations. These associations both promoted and supported new research, be it lobbying for government funding for projects or organising expeditions themselves, and provided a space for the presentation, discussion and publication of scientific work. Such discussions frequently reached wider audiences. Public lectures, such as those organised by the flourishing mechanics' institute movement, were common, as were public events like the Royal Society of Victoria's annual 'conversazione' and exhibitions devoted to science, technology and industry. Scientific topics would be summarised and commented on in the press, including in dedicated columns such as the weekly 'Scientific Gossip' section of Melbourne's *Leader*. Public science was, in short, an integral and highly visible dimension of colonial culture in Australia.[14]

Australia's southern frontier fit neatly into this world of colonial science. In the 1860s and 1870s, the colonial press played host to a range of letters and articles on Antarctic topics, such as whether the cause of droughts in Victoria might be found in the Antarctic, whether an Antarctic continent existed, and whether the Antarctic was 'the nursery of the terrible earthquakes and volcanic thunders of South America and the Pacific'.[15] These kinds of articles were commonly syndicated in regional papers and those in other colonies, while original discussions also emerged in the regional press. The *Ballarat Star*, for instance, was the outlet of choice for a resident of the country town of Skipton to share their theory that cold northerly winds in that region were caused by winds blowing from Antarctica and then being deflected back south by an as-yet-undiscovered mountain range in central Australia.[16] The Mount Gambier–based *Border Watch* similarly hosted a discussion between farmers in 1868 of a theory that unseasonably cool temperatures in South Australia were caused by the northerly drift of Antarctic icebergs.[17] The most prominent and sustained example of this public discussion of Antarctic science came from James Harrison, a pioneer of artificial ice and refrigeration technologies who moonlighted as the *Leader*'s 'Scientific Gossip' columnist under the nom de plume 'Oedipus'. Harrison's column regularly drew readers' attention to topics and debates in Antarctic science, such as the recurring debate about the existence of an Antarctic continent. Despite Wilkes and d'Urville both believing they had found evidence of a continent in 1840, this debate remained unresolved until the twentieth century.

The work of Ferdinand von Mueller, director of Melbourne's Royal Botanic Gardens from 1853, provides another example of how Antarctic knowledge circulated. Mueller was one of the dominant figures of nineteenth-century Australian science and would eventually become a prime mover in the campaign for an Australian expedition to explore the Antarctic in the 1880s. His interest in the Southern Ocean began much earlier, though. Mueller was vice-president of the Acclimatisation Society of Victoria when, in 1865, the society arranged for pigs, goats, rabbits and chickens to be released on the Auckland and Campbell islands. Following in Ross's footsteps, the society hoped that the animals would proliferate and 'prove of value to persons who may be shipwrecked upon the islands'.[18] This acclimatisation project also sparked Mueller's interest in the unique flora of the subantarctic, conducting studies of *Azorella polaris* in the 1860s and *Pringlea antiscorbutica* in the 1870s, more commonly known as 'Macquarie Island cabbage' and 'Kerguelen cabbage' respectively.[19] Reflecting a contemporary focus on applied science, Mueller advocated cultivating the latter plant in Australia, but despite a concerted campaign to introduce it to New South Wales, Kerguelen cabbage never did become the 'first-class fodder plant' boosters like Mueller predicted.[20] The dream of acclimatising and commercialising subantarctic flora did prove surprisingly durable, though; as recently as 1998, an Australian research project investigated the possibility of cultivating Kerguelen cabbage.[21]

In this way, people in the Australian colonies were regularly exposed to discussions about the importance of the Antarctic for addressing scientific questions. These questions ranged from ones of clear and immediate local significance, such as the role of the Antarctic and the Southern Ocean in Australian weather, through to more abstract questions, such as the existence or otherwise of an Antarctic continent, but there was a broad awareness that whatever lay south of Australia was of clear scientific value and interest. As this awareness spread through the increasingly established institutions and media of Australian public science in the mid-nineteenth century, it overlapped and interacted with the older way of thinking about the colonies' southern frontier as a site of economic and commercial interest.

‹ ›

The early 1840s marked the Australian colonies' first major economic depression. The effects of this downturn were felt across Australia, but where most of the colonies rebounded quickly and boomed following the onset of the gold rushes in the 1850s, the freshly renamed colony of Tasmania languished.[22] In this context, a belief began to circulate that the Antarctic might offer a panacea for Tasmania's woes. Alexander Smith, a lieutenant on *Erebus* who had remained in Hobart to work at Rossbank Observatory, wrote a letter to the Hobart *Courier* in November 1848 to lay out his thoughts on the promise of Antarctic whaling. Drawing on his authority as one of the few Tasmanians to have sailed beyond the Antarctic Circle,

Smith argued that 'a field is open to the southward of 60°, which I am convinced would richly repay the enterprising master there'. He outlined a plan for a whaling voyage in this region, recommending that a ship leave Hobart in mid-December, follow Balleny and Ross's easterly route south along 166°E, and travel eastwards while hunting whales in the seas between 63° and the main icepack at around 66°. Smith was confident that whaling would be highly profitable in this area and hoped that Tasmania would 'take the first share in so vast a field'.[23]

Smith's optimism echoed Ross's. In his published account of the Antarctic voyage, Ross had discussed encountering vast numbers of whales amidst the ice, where they 'enjoyed a life of tranquillity and security' free from predation by humans. Reflecting on this discovery, Ross declared that 'a fresh source of national and individual wealth is thus opened to commercial enterprise' that would undoubtfully prove 'abundantly productive'.[24] *The Courier* was sufficiently impressed by Smith's detailed suggestions that it drew attention to them in a separate article for its Saturday edition, declaring that the colony's interests 'are closely interwoven and mainly dependent upon the prosperity of the whale fishery', and supporting the idea of extending Tasmania's whaling grounds southwards.[25] A fortnight later, an editorial in the *Colonial Times* endorsed the call for Tasmanians to take advantage of the 'mine of inexhaustible wealth ... at our very doors'. The *Colonial Times* felt that, in addition to the direct profits from the oil trade, Antarctic whaling would lift the colony out of its economic malaise by stimulating demand for agricultural products; a larger fleet of whalers calling at Hobart to resupply would boost the entire economy.[26]

This brief period of optimism about the potential for Antarctic whaling to revitalise the Tasmanian economy came to an end in 1850. When the captain of the American whaling ship *Franklin* met Smith in Hobart, he was persuaded by stories of icy seas teeming with whales to test Smith's theory. The *Franklin* spent twenty days 'among the tumbling mountains of ice', sailing as far south as 66° along Smith's recommended 165th parallel. But despite seeing plenty of whales, the crew of the *Franklin* did not slay a single one. The species they encountered—mainly humpback, fin and blue whales—were not suited to the technologies and techniques of mid-nineteenth-century open boat whaling. The favoured targets of whalers like those aboard the *Franklin* were right whales, a species characterised by their gentle natures, tendency to swim and feed close to the surface, and the fact that they float when killed. Southern right whales do feed in Antarctic waters, but their numbers had already been badly affected by coastal whaling in places like Australia and New Zealand. This early attempt at whaling on the fringes of the Antarctic icepack was therefore a failure, and after its three-week stint in Antarctic waters the *Franklin* sailed for the Arctic, where 3,000 barrels of oil were harvested in short order. News of this reached Hobart in 1850, puncturing the belief that the Southern Ocean held the solution to the colony's economic woes.[27]

If further evidence was required that the Southern Ocean was not quite the 'mine of inexhaustible wealth' predicted by the *Colonial Times*, it came in the form of one of the smallest, most remote and least successful settler colonies in the history of the British Empire. Charles Enderby, third-generation director of the Enderby & Sons whaling company and self-appointed patron of Antarctic exploration, became convinced that the Auckland Islands held the key to revitalising the fortunes of his family firm. The 1830s and 1840s was a period of precipitous decline for the entire English whaling industry, with the withdrawal of various government subsidies, competition from the United States and Australasia, and declining catch rates combining to make whaling from a base in London unprofitable. For Enderby & Sons, this crisis was exacerbated by the three loss-making voyages of Antarctic exploration in the 1830s and a fire that destroyed the company's only alternate revenue stream, a rope-making factory in East Greenwich, in 1845. Charles Enderby's solution was to call on the English whaling industry's remaining firms and investors to form a single corporation, the 'Southern Whale Fishery Company', and invest in a grand new whaling station on the Auckland Islands.

Enderby's plan was startling in its ambition. Instead of a single small whaling station on the islands, such as those that dotted the coasts of Australia and New Zealand, he envisaged full-scale colonisation. The islands' dense and windswept southern rātā forests would be cleared to build a flourishing port town. Port Ross, as it would be known, would host a fleet of 600 whaling ships and become a stopover for ships traversing the Southern Ocean on voyages between Europe, South Africa, Australasia and the Americas. The whaling fleet, meanwhile, would employ a radical new model. Instead of the traditional multi-year voyages, with crew members signing on for a single voyage, the Southern Whale Fishery Company would despatch its ships from Port Ross to hunt whales for a few weeks or months. The ships would then return with a full cargo of blubber, which would be refined into oil at Port Ross and shipped to London for sale while the whalers returned to sea to continue the hunt. The whaling crews would be permanent employees of the company on fixed wages and would be given opportunities to purchase land from the company to become settler farmers.[28]

Charles Enderby spent five years promoting his plan. He secured if not the wholehearted support then at least the lukewarm acquiescence of the British Government. Aided by endorsements from the likes of Ross and a horrifically exaggerated account of the islands' climate and suitability for settlement by American sealer (and infamous fantasist) Benjamin Morrell, Enderby raised nearly £100,000 from investors.[29] This was well short of his target of £300,000, and the largest investors were members of the Enderby family, but he ploughed on regardless. After receiving a dual appointment as both the company's resident commissioner and the new colony's inaugural lieutenant-governor, 52-year-old Charles Enderby took charge of the first fleet of three ships and approximately seventy-five settlers when it departed London in July 1849.[30]

Given the Australian colonies' long history of subantarctic whaling and sealing, and the very recent interest in despatching a Tasmanian whaling fleet beyond the Antarctic Circle, there was naturally intense interest in the fortunes of this southernmost outpost of the Australasian colonial world. There was a healthy scepticism towards the company's plans, and there was also a degree of consternation that so much British capital was being devoted to establishing a new colony when existing ones were eager for metropolitan investment.[31] Yet early reports on the colony's development were broadly positive. It was noted that fresh supplies were needed from Sydney and that Enderby's dual position as both lawmaker and magistrate was proving problematic, but it seemed like the colony would grow to become a valuable trading partner for Sydney, Hobart and Dunedin.[32] Further positive reports came when Enderby visited New Zealand and Sydney, and when NZ governor George Grey visited Port Ross.[33] The Auckland Islands were even added to the guidebooks sold to prospective migrants in Britain to help them decide which colony to emigrate to and what to expect on arrival.[34]

On the island, however, circumstances were far more dismal than the cautiously optimistic picture painted in the Australian press suggested. While the tiny town of Port Ross was taking shape, peaking at a population of roughly 300, the island's environment was more hostile than anticipated. Enderby had promised 'fine harbours, ready formed, and land ready for the ploughshare'; what the colonists found was a densely forested coast, swampy interior, constant rain, and brutal winds that ripped the roofs off buildings.[35] The settlers were miserable, and had scarcely 2 hectares of farmland to show for two years of arduous labour. The harvest from these farms was meagre, leaving the tiny community reliant on an irregular supply of rations imported from Australia or New Zealand. To make matters worse, the company's whaling operations proved an utter disaster. By July 1851, the whalers had harvested 919 barrels of oil worth £5,200, against expenses of £98,332 for the same period.[36]

Enderby's ambitious experiment was a failure. The company's directors despatched two special commissioners to investigate the situation at Port Ross and, if necessary, to oversee its relocation to Australia or New Zealand. Enderby and the commissioners clashed immediately, resulting in a farcical situation whereby Enderby resigned from the company but retained his commission as lieutenant-governor. With everything on the island being company property and every colonist a company employee, the situation was untenable. Enderby was eventually persuaded to leave the islands—though he launched legal action against the commissioners as soon as he arrived in New Zealand—and the scheme was abandoned.[37] Giving up on the idea of relocating the whaling station, the commissioners sold every bit of company property they could in Sydney, Hobart and Dunedin.[38] Even with this measure, the company's investors suffered huge losses, receiving only 15 shillings for every £50 they had invested when the company was liquidated.[39] Naturally, all of these developments were widely discussed in the Australian press, which was generally critical of the special commissioners' treatment of Enderby, but agreed that the Aucklands had always been a poor choice for a whaling colony.[40]

The voyage of the *Franklin* and the spectacular failure of the Southern Whale Fishery Company had proved that, however rich in resources Australia's southern frontier might be, it was not the El Dorado the most vociferous colonial boosters had imagined. Yet the dream of deriving value from the Southern Ocean continued to sporadically rear its head, animating a steady stream of proposals and experiments to find new ways to extract wealth from this region. Small-scale, ad-hoc sealing ventures returned to the islands south of New Zealand to pick over the sites of former booms, slaughtering recovering fur and elephant seal populations. This regular gleaning of the subantarctic islands prompted New Zealand's colonial government to introduce the first limitations on sealing in this region, passing legislation in 1872 and 1878 that significantly restricted the killing of seals on the Aucklands, Antipodes, Bounty and Campbell islands.[41] Poaching remained a problem, however, and sealing was unrestricted on Macquarie Island, which fell under Tasmanian rather than New Zealand jurisdiction.

More substantial sealing operations continued far to the southwest of Australia in this period. The Kerguelen archipelago had attracted fur sealers, elephant sealers, and whalers from around the world since the turn of the nineteenth century, though Australian ships, labourers and investors were only ever minor players at best in the exploitation of these exceptionally remote islands. It was a similar story at the Heard and McDonald islands, 400 kilometres south-east of Kerguelen. US sealers led the way in exploiting these islands, which had been discovered in the mid-1850s. News of the value of whaling and sealing in this stretch of the Southern Ocean did reach Australia, however, most notably when an American vessel arrived in Melbourne from Heard Island with a rich cargo of elephant oil in 1858.[42] This captured the attention of Tasmanian whaling captain James Robinson and businessman William Crowther, who almost immediately despatched a whaling and sealing expedition of their own.[43] Crowther and Robinson's well-equipped Tasmanian venture was another financial failure, however, with one ship forced to retreat to Mauritius for repairs after sustaining damage off Heard Island, and the other returning to Hobart with only 1,000 barrels of oil to show for eighteen months of difficult labour.[44]

Crowther made a significant loss on his attempt to force his way into the Heard and Kerguelen oil trade. This was hardly surprising. As Briton Cooper Busch notes in his sprawling history of North American sealing, this branch of the trade required an intimate knowledge of local coasts and conditions that created a high bar to entry.[45] Yet even as Crowther's expedition made it clear that investing significant sums in Southern Ocean industries was a high-risk proposition, it drew attention to the possibility that these islands could be rendered profitable in other ways. Robinson returned with several mineral specimens that were handed over to Tasmania's geological surveyor, Charles Gould. Gould announced that the minerals found in Robinson's samples usually occurred 'in association with minerals of a more valuable character', drawing attention for the first time to the possibility of subantarctic mining.[46] The Kerguelen archipelago's remoteness meant that the idea of mining the islands was little more than a curiosity in 1861, but it would eventually be taken much more seriously as a possibility in the 1890s and 1900s, when the hitherto obscure question of Kerguelen's legal status briefly exploded into wider prominence.

Other forms of commercial activity in the Southern Ocean also had their champions. An 1864 letter to *The Australasian* called for investigations into guano mining, for instance, citing Ross's observation that guano-rich Possession Island might prove 'valuable to the agriculturists of our Australasian colonies'.[47] Another possible solution to the financial risk associated with attempting to exploit the southern frontier was to share that risk. This was the model proposed in 1866 by supporters of an Australian joint stock company that would be dedicated to developing Antarctic whaling.[48] This idea gained plenty of interest but little traction, leading to concerns eight year later that New Zealand was on track to forestall the Australian colonies in developing the Antarctic whaling grounds.[49] None of these ideas came to fruition. Boosters continued to seize on old quotes and comparable enterprises to promote the tantalisingly inchoate wealth of the Southern Ocean, but there was no shortage of investment opportunities closer to home. The idea of profiting from the southern frontier therefore endured, fuelled by memories of its past role in driving colonial prosperity and by explorers' tantalising accounts, but practical factors ensured it remained a colonial fantasy.

‹ ›

There was, then, a booming interest in the possible scientific and commercial value of the Antarctic in Australia in the mid-nineteenth century. This, along with memories of the three expeditions of 1839–41, made the possibility of further voyages of Antarctic exploration a topic of considerable public interest in the colonies. The fact that there were no attempts to follow up on the voyages of Ross, Wilkes and d'Urville meant there was little to actually report on in the 1840s and 1850s, but rumours and scraps of news were seized on nonetheless.[50] Things changed in 1860, when US hydrographer Matthew Fontaine Maury began outlining his idiosyncratic vision for a renewal of Antarctic exploration.

Maury was an influential figure. His active naval career had been ended by an injury in 1839, but he had taken to a desk job at the Depot of Charts and Instruments with gusto, focusing his efforts on improving maritime navigation by accumulating and systematising data on winds, weather and ocean currents. This research had allowed Maury to devise new sailing routes that dramatically shortened long-distance voyages. His recommended route from London to Melbourne, for instance, shaved thirty to forty days off the voyage by sailing at least six degrees further south than the conventional route.[51] Having pioneered the science of oceanography and transformed the movement of goods and people around the world, Maury's voice carried weight.

Maury's analysis of the vast quantities of data he accumulated was not always correct, though. He subscribed to a theory known as the 'open polar sea', which stated that the Arctic pack ice that had long stymied explorers in the far north was only a relatively narrow ring—if explorers could break through the ice, they would find a temperate, ice-free polar sea beyond it. Maury's analysis of meteorological data from ships traversing the Southern Ocean led him to believe there was a similar phenomenon at work in the Antarctic, so that if explorers could break through the ice they might find the Antarctic 'to grow milder instead of colder' as they approached the South Pole.[52] To confirm his theory that the Antarctic experienced mild winters, Maury needed more data. He therefore began advocating for a new Antarctic expedition, initially calling on Britain or the United States to take the lead and later suggesting multinational cooperation.[53]

This proposal excited particular interest in Australia because Maury recommended Melbourne as the expedition's base. The plan was heartily endorsed by *The Age*, which felt that Britain—and its Australasian colonies—should take the lead in exploring a continent 'immediately opposite our own shores'.[54] Both Maury's proposal and *The Age*'s endorsement were widely reported on and syndicated throughout the colonies. The proposal was ridiculed by the Launceston-based *Cornwall Chronicle*, which mocked the notion of a warm, habitable Antarctic continent, but otherwise generated enthusiasm.[55] Not that Australian enthusiasm counted for much. Maury's proposal was vague, uncosted, and lacked the support of any nation. When he resigned to take up a position in the Confederate Navy at the outbreak of the Civil War in 1861, he no longer had even a government role to lend gravitas to his proposal, and what little momentum it had faded away. In the history of polar exploration, Maury's proposal is little more than an eccentric curiosity. For Australia, however, this loose scheme represented a significant moment. It was in response to Maury's suggestion that Melbourne was the natural forward base for exploring the Antarctic that the idea that the Australian colonies should take a leading role in the renewal of Antarctic exploration was first articulated. This idea was tentative, envisaging little more than colonial cooperation with a wider imperial project, but it marked the beginning of a distinctly Australian way of thinking and talking about exploring the Antarctic.

Just a few years later, in 1866, *The Australasian* made a case for the Australian colonies to step up to address the yawning gaps that existed in the world's knowledge of the Antarctic. With Britain focused on exploration in Africa and the Arctic, if Australians wanted to flesh out the map of the Antarctic, they would have to 'do it for ourselves'.[56] The best way of achieving this, the newspaper suggested, was via a whaling and sealing company based in Tasmania. The hypothetical company's whalers and sealers would, in the course of their work, systematically explore the region south of Australia, so that 'scraps of intelligence, voyage after voyage, would fill up the measure of information'. This was far less ambitious than either Maury's proposal or the elaborately equipped multi-vessel expeditions of 1839–41, but the idea that Australians should, in their own fashion, take responsibility for investigating the largest blank space left on the world's maps was a radical assertion of colonial confidence and competence.

This idea was endorsed by other papers, although the *Tasmanian Morning Herald* rather missed the spirit of the proposal by recommending it drop the exploring component to focus on whaling.[57] The *South Australian Register* was especially enthusiastic, piggybacking on the original idea to outline its vision for an intercolonial company based in Williamstown, Victoria. While it estimated that an initial investment of £50,000 would be required, an Australian whaling company would, it argued, be 'as safe a source of profit as a Bank or an Insurance Company, and a far safer and ... more profitable investment than four fifths of mines in Victoria'.[58]

An article in Melbourne's *Leader* offered another way of tackling the exploration of the Antarctic in a manner suited to Australian circumstances. The *Leader* offered three reasons in favour of an expedition: the prospect of scientific discoveries, the 'healthy spirit of mere adventure', and the possibility of great commercial rewards from whaling, guano and more-novel enterprises such as harvesting natural ice from icebergs. To raise funds for an expedition, the *Leader* suggested a number of Melbourne elites 'club together' to hire a steamer to escape the hot summer with a 'pleasure trip' to the cooler subantarctic regions, all funds raised going to a scientific expedition.[59] In a follow-up article three weeks later, the *Leader* noted that its earlier suggestions had 'excited more attention that we had hoped for; though certainly not more than the subject deserves', and reiterated that great discoveries were there to be made in Antarctica, including the possibility of encounters with unknown animals and perhaps even an undiscovered race of men.[60] Nothing ever came of this creative suggestion for financing a colonial Antarctic expedition, but the *Leader* continued to promote the idea of Australian Antarctic exploration over the next few years.[61] This meant that when a more concrete proposal for an expedition to observe the transit of Venus from Possession Island came in 1873, the general idea had already been percolating for some time and there was already a community of enthusiasts and supporters to lobby for it.

Science, commerce and adventure were, as the *Leader*'s tripartite rationale indicated, the driving motivations behind the emerging idea that Australians could and should explore the Antarctic. But while it was less prominent among colonial boosters, safety also played a key role in popularising this idea. While Maury's proposal for an international Antarctic expedition had quickly lapsed into obscurity, his recommended sailing routes became a staple of the experience of travelling to or from Australia. Following Maury's recommended route meant dropping down to at least 45°S, with every extra degree of latitude beyond this shaving additional time and distance off the voyage. Shipping companies servicing the Anglo-Australasian route competed to offer the fastest passage, with their captains dropping as far south as they dared. Routes along the 55th parallel were not unheard of.[62] Sailing in these latitudes was a boon to the colonies' development and their connectedness with other parts of the world, but it came at a cost. Hitherto the scourge only of explorers, whalers and sealers, icebergs became a standard threat to Australian seafaring.

In the 1850s and 1860s, ships on the Anglo-Australasian route experienced a series of collisions, disappearances and near misses in high latitudes. The *Ralph Waller*, for instance, struck an iceberg head-on in 1855 but was kept afloat by jury-rigged repairs and continuous pumping by the passengers and crew.[63] That same year, six other ships were fortunate to escape from icefields unharmed, while the *Guiding Star* disappeared somewhere in the Southern Ocean with 543 people on board.[64] Dramatic stories, such as the collisions with icebergs suffered by the *Marco Polo* and *Royal Standard* in 1861 and 1864 respectively, or the four anxious days the *George Thompson* spent trapped in an icefield in 1868, created a media frenzy around the problem of Antarctic ice in Australian sea lanes.[65] Other close encounters were captured in the letters and diaries of passengers, such as the *Norfolk*'s encounter with a 2.4-kilometre-long iceberg at 55°S in 1868.[66] Public interest was further fuelled by reports of a 96-kilometre-long iceberg seen by Australian-bound ships, and by the captivating story of the *Grafton*.[67] A Sydney-based consortium chartered the *Grafton* in 1863 to hunt seals and investigate rumours that silver and tin could be mined on the Auckland and Campbell islands. The ship was wrecked at the Aucklands, forcing its five-man crew to subsist for a year-and-a-half on salvaged supplies, birds and seals. When no ship came to search for them, three of them sailed a salvaged and repaired dinghy to New Zealand to seek help before returning to rescue the others.[68]

The wreck of the *Grafton* had nothing to do with ice conditions, but it fitted easily into contemporary concerns about the safety of Southern Ocean shipping. The wrecks of the *Grafton* and two other ships on the same island within two years drew attention to another problem: poor and inaccurate charts of the Southern Ocean and its islands, reefs and harbours.[69] These mounting concerns culminated in calls for a grand oceanographic survey to improve the safety of navigation at high southern latitudes by correcting errors and inconsistencies.[70] Separately, an effort was made to compile information about Southern Ocean iceberg sightings to aid navigators.[71] While this campaign called for a British-organised expedition with practical rather than financial support from Australia, it was another significant precursor to later campaigns. It stopped short of suggesting that Australians should fund and organise this work themselves but recognised that the colonies had a significant shared interest in the investigation of the Southern Ocean world.

‹ ›

It was in this context that debate erupted over whether the Australian colonies could and should despatch an expedition to observe the transit of Venus. As early as 1864, Australian newspapers were reporting that the twin transits of December 1874 and 1882 represented the last opportunity to measure the distance between the earth and the sun until 2004, and that a global network of observatories would be needed to observe the transits. A series of preliminary Antarctic expeditions to investigate the region and lay the groundwork for a south polar observatory by 1873 were envisioned. And despite a lack of any real developments, this suggestion was reported on and discussed in the Australian press for the better part of eight years.

Until 1873, the assumption was that *something* would be organised. In April that year, though, a report from British magazine *The Spectator* began to circulate in the colonies suggesting that a series of failures meant there was now no chance an expedition could be organised in time. The only lingering hope for the enterprise, the report claimed, was if the Australasian colonies could outfit an Antarctic expedition themselves.[72] The suggestion of an intercolonial Australian expedition to fill the void was enthusiastically taken up by the local press. Melbourne's *Age*, for instance, declared that a failure to establish an Antarctic observatory would leave 'the scientific honour of our country at stake', and concluded that 'an Australian (Victorian if possible) Antarctic expedition should be organised without delay'. James Harrison used his 'Scientific Gossip' column to lambast Britain for failing to mount an expedition, but also suggested that 'we Victorians should seriously ask ourselves whether these words do not apply to us as to the mother-country'.[73] These criticisms were not particularly fair—governments and scientific bodies in Britain, Germany and the United States had all organised for parties to travel to Kerguelen to observe the transit, while a French expedition had been despatched to Campbell Island and a German expedition to the Aucklands—but they were effective in creating a sense of urgency.

Victorian premier James Francis quickly distanced his government from the proposal. Francis acknowledged that the idea of an expedition to Possession Island was a worthy cause but noted that the Victorian Government had contributed £30,000 to construct a first-class observatory only ten years ago, was providing upwards of £3,000 a year to maintain it, and had recently obtained £800 worth of instruments to observe the transit from Melbourne. This decision to focus government funds on observing the transit from Victoria rather than outfitting an ambitious expedition to the Antarctic had been endorsed by the government astronomer, Robert Ellery, lending scientific credibility to Francis's refusal.[74] While there was plenty of criticism of this decision, the Royal Society of Victoria endorsed the position adopted by Francis and its own president, Ellery.[75] One Melbourne paper, *The Australasian*, broke ranks to support the decision, arguing that any meaningful expedition would require instruments to be sent from London, eroding any time savings to be gained from outfitting the expedition in Melbourne.[76]

The 1873 expedition was never likely to succeed. There was too little time—around eight months—for an expedition to be organised, and despite the enthusiasm evident in the colonial press and among the Liberal opposition, there was no individual or body capable of organising one. The only comparable Victorian exploring expedition—the disastrous Burke and Wills expedition of 1860—had been organised by the Royal Society of Victoria in an attempt to cross the Australian continent from south to north. This had taken more than three years to finance, cost £57,840, and resulted in the deaths of seven expedition members in largely preventable circumstances.[77] An Antarctic expedition, particularly one that aimed to break through the icepack into the Ross Sea to reach Possession Island, would have been an altogether more complex and costlier undertaking.

While the debate about rushing to organise an expedition in 1873 was settled by Francis's swift refusal to pledge government funds, the broader idea of the Australian colonies taking steps to explore the Antarctic continued to circulate. In 1880, CW Purnell of Ashburton, New Zealand, published an article in the *Melbourne Review* that lambasted 'the want of curiosity, of geographical enthusiasm, and of exploratory enterprise, exhibited by the people of these colonies with respect to the vast antarctic region', and called for the colonial governments to collectively equip an expedition.[78] Purnell's argument won support in the Sydney and Melbourne press, although *The Argus*—still stung by its unsuccessful 1873 campaign—commented acerbically that 'Mr. Purnell must be a very sanguine gentleman if he imagines that professional politicians here or elsewhere care two straws about geographical or any other science'.[79] The *Leader* revived the idea of exploration through whaling in 1881.[80] The same magazine then commented on reports in 1885 that Swedish explorer Adolf Nordenskiöld was attempting to win Russian backing for an Antarctic expedition. While welcoming Nordenskiöld's plan and predicting that an appeal for funding in Australia to support it would likely 'be liberally responded to', the *Leader*'s contributor demanded more than this. 'Australians', they argued, 'must bestir themselves. It is part of their destiny to explore these southern solitudes.'[81]

The *Leader*'s mobilisation of the concept of destiny in 1885 was something of an outlier. This idea that Australians were especially obliged to unlock the mysteries of the south would be invoked more frequently in later decades, but it remained more common to see *any* attempt to explore the Antarctic as a good thing for Australia. This attitude was evident in the way the Australian press latched onto rumour or report of possible projects to explore the Antarctic. Only one of these—the five-year world-ranging oceanographic survey known as the *Challenger* expedition—actually eventuated, and even this only went as far south as the icepack rather than trying to make new discoveries in the Antarctic. But there was no shortage of rumours to occupy column inches. There were reports in 1870 of an expedition organised by Georg Neumayer and financed by the Austrian Government, and of a new British expedition in 1878 under *Challenger*'s commander George Nares.[82] A fresh round of rumours in 1880 and 1881 suggested that Sir Allen Young, a veteran of the searches for Franklin's lost expedition, would soon be heading south.[83] Another burst of interest focused on a mooted Italian expedition in 1880 and 1881.[84] The project swiftly fell apart due to funding difficulties, leading to a suggestion that there should be 'some co-operation on the part of the Australian colonies' to ensure that the expedition went ahead.[85]

‹ ›

The time from the early 1840s, when the British, French and US expeditions concluded, to the 1880s, when there was a resurgence of international interest in Antarctic exploration, has tended to be treated by historians as something of a fallow period. In his account *Australia in the Antarctic*, RA Swan describes this as a 'period of averted interest' spanning forty odd years.[86] Joy McCann's *Ice Bound: The Australian Story of Antarctica* jumps from the 1840s to the 1880s, as do accounts by Marie Kawaja and Tom Griffiths.[87] David Day, in an otherwise comprehensive synthesis, devotes roughly a page to the years 1845–86.[88] Even Andrew McConville's dedicated account of Australia and Antarctic exploration in the nineteenth century rushes through this four-decade interregnum, while RW Home explicitly states that 'in the 1870s … expeditions to the Antarctic, scientific or otherwise, were on scarcely anybody's agenda'.[89]

Yet Australian interest in the Antarctic did not simply fade away after 1841. Far from a fallow period, this was the era in which fundamental ideas about the colonies' relationship with the world to their south were forged. There was an awareness in the colonies that the Antarctic was a site of scientific value and interest, both for questions of practical concern (what is the role of the Southern Ocean in Australian weather conditions?) and more abstract issues (what is the distance between the earth and the sun?). As the colonies developed cultures of public science underpinned by a proliferation of associations and media that facilitated discussion, there was growing interest in how Australia could both benefit from and contribute to this kind of scientific investigation of the Antarctic. At the same time, the Antarctic was increasingly imagined as a source of vast, untapped wealth in the form of whales, seals, guano and minerals. Optimism about the region's commercial potential was fuelled by both promising reports from explorers like Ross and memories of how the colonies had profited in the past from whaling and sealing in lower latitudes in the Southern Ocean. And from the 1850s, new sailing routes took ships bound to and from Australia into higher latitudes than ever before. As these routes became busier, the threat posed by poor charts and drifting icebergs gave further impetus to the idea that a better understanding of the Southern Ocean world was a necessity.

There may not have been the genuine mass interest seen when Ross arrived in Hobart, which would be seen again in the early twentieth century, but people in Australia were clearly interested in and engaged with the world to their south. This was an era not of 'averted interest' but of *sustained* interest, an era in which memories of the past and optimism—however misplaced—about the future generated a set of increasingly coherent ideas about the colonies' relationship with their southern frontier. By the turn of the 1880s, the idea that the Antarctic was a place of enormous potential for science and industry, ripe for exploration and development, had become the dominant way of imagining this region in the Australian colonies. It had become almost a truism, whenever the Antarctic was discussed, to say that any exploration of this region would be a good thing generally and an especially good thing for Australians. And it had become commonplace to assert that the Australian colonies, by virtue of their proximity to the Antarctic and the benefits they stood to derive from its further exploration, should take a role, perhaps even a leading one, in unravelling the mysteries of the frozen south.

3

'DESTINY'

Antarctica and Visions of Australia's Future in the 1880s

On a warm Wednesday evening in late January 1886, George Samuel Griffiths took to the stage of Melbourne's Town Hall. A Collins Street stockbroker by trade, Griffiths was one of the city's growing cohort of Antarctic enthusiasts. These were men—and they were overwhelmingly men, middle-class and middle-aged—who shared a keen amateur interest in Antarctic science and an appetite for publicly championing the idea of exploring the frozen south. In the audience was another enthusiast, Irish-born politician John Gavan Duffy. Only a month earlier, Duffy had tabled an ambitiously worded motion on the final sitting day of the state parliament for 1885, declaring that

> the time has arrived when … Victoria, in consideration of its important position in the Southern hemisphere, in the interest of science and for the advancement of commerce, should undertake the task of exploration and discovery in the Antarctic regions.[1]

Duffy's colleagues laughed off his suggestion, but he could at least take comfort in the knowledge he had allies beyond parliament.[2]

Chief among these allies was botanist Ferdinand von Mueller. In April 1884, Mueller had used his inaugural address as president of the inelegantly named Geographical Society of Australasia (Victorian branch) to argue that 'some of the grandest results of geographic science' for Australians were to be found in the Antarctic and the South Pacific. 'To no other people,' Mueller insisted, 'can research connected with the antarctic regions be of that value which it must ever have for the Australian Colonies.' To him, a vast sector of the Antarctic was 'more readily within our reach than that of any other nation', and offered remarkable commercial opportunities should exploration lead to the discovery of coal or new whaling grounds.[3]

These were Mueller's words, but they were read that evening by another enthusiast, Alexander Cameron Macdonald. Macdonald was an accountant and land speculator who would later recollect that he became deeply interested in Antarctic exploration in the early 1880s, inspired by a chance conversation with a woman who had toured the *Erebus* and *Terror* as a young girl in Hobart in 1841.[4] While his first public pronouncements about the Antarctic were simply ventriloquising Mueller, Macdonald would soon become one of Victoria's most vocal proponents of Antarctic exploration. Newspaper proprietors James and Daniel Harrison were another pair of early advocates. The brothers had been commenting on Antarctic research and calling on Australians to take action to explore their southern frontier throughout the 1870s, most notably in the pages of the *Leader*.

Griffiths, though, was the most enthusiastic of the enthusiasts. He compiled every scrap of information about the Antarctic he could, and this fed into the paper he presented to the Geographical Society in January 1886. Titled 'South Polar Problems, or the Objects and Value of Antarctic Research', Griffiths' paper gave an overview of the current state of knowledge of the Antarctic. This was, he argued, meagre. It was still unknown, for instance, whether Biscoe's Graham and Enderby lands, Ross's Victoria Land, d'Urville's Adélie Land and Wilkes's patchwork of sightings were all part of an enormous continent, or whether these were islands and coastlines of a fragmented Antarctic archipelago. There were therefore many questions that could only be addressed by further exploration. Was there geological evidence for a 'common fatherland' for Australia, New Zealand, South Africa and South America in the Antarctic? Was there evidence that the Antarctic had once been, in the deep past, a temperate region filled with plant and animal life? What weather conditions prevailed in the Antarctic in winter? How did the Antarctic affect Australia's weather? Was there any relationship between the aurora australis and the weather?[5]

Many of Griffiths' fellow Antarctic enthusiasts were in attendance, and the paper provoked fervent discussion. Daniel Harrison argued that an expedition could not only address the questions raised by Griffiths but make a substantial profit in the process by hunting whales and collecting guano en route to conducting scientific investigations. Macdonald was less optimistic about the profitability of a scientific expedition but felt its value should not be judged against 'a merely commercial standard'. He reported that the British Association for the Advancement of Science and the Berlin Geographical Society had recently broached the possibility of an expedition to the Antarctic, and he felt that 'Australia could not afford to be left out of such an enterprise'. Duffy vowed to again raise in parliament the possibility of mounting an expedition.[6] Griffiths' arguments about the importance of Antarctic research were also picked up by the Melbourne press.[7]

Griffiths followed up his paper to the Geographical Society of Australasia with another to the Royal Society of Victoria in May, this time on the Kerguelen archipelago. Again, his overview captured the audience's imagination. After prolonged discussion of the value of Antarctic exploration, both scientific and 'practical', attention turned to what could be done. Since there was seemingly interest among scientific societies in Europe in despatching an expedition, and this was matched by clear interest among the members of both the royal and geographical societies in Melbourne, it was suggested that a joint committee of the two societies be formed to investigate 'the antarctic question'.[8] Thus was the Australian Antarctic Exploration Committee born.

This chapter tells the story of how a group of largely self-taught enthusiasts in Melbourne—accountants, an auditor, a stockbroker, an engineering professor, a botanist, an astronomer, an ex–naval officer and a politician—set themselves the task of mobilising the Australian colonies to 'open up' the Antarctic for scientific exploration and commercial exploitation. The Antarctic Exploration Committee's quest to lead the world in exploring the Antarctic would ultimately prove quixotic. Despite years of effort and many promising leads, no ship ever sailed south under the committee's auspices. Yet it was nonetheless significant in how Australians thought about the southern frontier. The committee's promotion of Antarctic exploration as the 'destiny of the federated colonies of Australia' was closely aligned with the popular idea that the colonies were destined not only to federate but to exercise control over a swathe of territories in the Pacific and the Southern Ocean.[9] While the committee members never achieved their dream of putting boots on the ground, they played a key role in positioning the Antarctic as part of Australia's natural sphere of influence.

‹ ›

Geographical societies were relative latecomers to the world of colonial scientific associations. Geography was usually understood in the nineteenth century to be an applied science, one involving the exploration, surveying and mapping of territory, and the study of its current and future uses and resources. It has been described as 'the science of imperialism *par excellence*', a discipline intimately bound up with the acquisition and exploitation of land by expansionist imperial states.[10] Geographical societies were key nodes in this enterprise, supporting and promoting the exploration and investigation of targeted areas and seeking to disseminate geographical information through lectures, publications, and school and university courses. In Australia, geography technically fell within the scope of the earlier generation of generalist scientific societies but was, in practice, an afterthought. The Royal Society of New South Wales, for instance, had a dedicated geographical section between 1876 and 1879, but this forum was abandoned when, after four years of sporadic and sparsely attended meetings, its membership dwindled to two.[11]

When news of a possible Italian Antarctic expedition swept through the colonies in 1881, one of the Royal Society of New South Wales's erstwhile geographical duo, Sydney draftsman Eccleston du Faur, lamented that the colony had no dedicated association to promote and support such enterprises.[12] The lack of such an institution continued to chafe, and in April 1883 a dozen or so supporters of the idea met in Sydney to establish a new, intercolonial 'Federal Geographical Society of Australasia'. This would be a body to promote, support and systematise the exploration not only of the Australian continent but of the Pacific and the Antarctic too, as well as promoting the study of commercial geography to fuel Australia's development, and disseminating geographical information about the region.[13]

The institution that emerged from those early meetings had three important features. While 'federal' was swiftly dropped from the society's name to avoid any whiff of republicanism that might alienate potential members, it remained avowedly federalist in character. Rather than inviting supporters throughout Australia to join a body based in Sydney, the founders opted to encourage acquaintances in other colonies to set up autonomous local branches. A Victorian branch, headed up by Mueller and Macdonald, was established in 1884, followed by branches in Queensland and South Australia the following year. To coordinate their activities, it was intended to hold regular intercolonial conferences.

The Geographical Society also differed from many of its contemporaries in its relatively egalitarian approach to membership. Rejecting the stricter nomination-based qualification process of the royal societies, the founders resolved instead to open membership to anyone with the 'patriotic desire of seeing the natural resources of this great country brought to light and developed', including women.[14] Many of the society's members were serial joiners of scientific associations, but a focus on applying geographical knowledge to fuel the colonies' development did attract a wider membership. The New South Wales branch, for instance, boasted 178 founding members.

Finally, the society's understanding of its own area of operation was both expansive and expansionist. The association was intended from its outset to be active in exploring and developing the colonies' Antarctic and South Pacific hinterlands, with a view to supporting the future annexation of valuable territories by the Australian colonies. The society's first major project was to work with the governments of the eastern colonies to organise an expedition to New Guinea, which aimed explicitly to gather geographical information 'as to the aspect and capabilities of New Guinea' so that 'efforts to colonize the country might be in the future guided by the results obtained'.[15] When this expedition returned to Sydney in 1885, the society continued to advocate both for further exploration and a permanent Australian settlement in central New Guinea to develop its resources.[16] In common with its counterparts around the world, then, the Geographical Society of Australasia was entangled in processes of imperial expansion and administration.

While the NSW branch of the Geographical Society looked north, it was the Antarctic that most occupied the minds of Victorian members. The Geographical Society was an ideal forum for Melbourne's band of Antarctic enthusiasts. It viewed geographical exploration, scientific research and the development of commercial opportunities as interlinked. This aligned with the way the Southern Ocean had, for the better part of four decades, been discussed as simultaneously a space of scientific importance, future commercial value and national prestige. The society's relatively open membership made it more accessible to enthusiasts, while its federal structure offered hope for coordinated intercolonial action.

News that the royal and geographical societies had partnered to investigate the possibility of exploring the Antarctic generated interest throughout the colonies. Writers speculated about what the resultant committee might work towards, ranging from depositing self-recording meteorological instruments on subantarctic islands to inviting scientific societies in Britain, France and Germany to cooperate with Australia on a full-scale Australian or even Victorian expedition.[17] Yet even from the outset there were signs of the tensions between scientific and commercial objectives that would perpetually plague the committee. *The Age* was enthusiastic about the project, highlighting the wealth of possible commercial opportunities it might instigate, including trades in whale oil, whalebone, seal skins, guano, coal, and walrus oil and ivory (reflecting the limited state of Antarctic knowledge, it was not yet known that walruses do not exist in the Antarctic). It warned, though, that separate commercial and scientific expeditions should be organised, to avoid the interests of one compromising the other.[18] One of the Royal Society of Victoria's representatives on the committee, engineering professor William Kernot, pushed back against *The Age*'s commercial boosterism, telling a rival paper that the results of a Victorian expedition would be 'of purely scientific value'. He also downplayed the scale of the task, suggesting that since the Antarctic was only twice as far from Melbourne as New Zealand, he might join the trip himself and 'stop for a few weeks in these unknown regions'.[19]

In response to these discussions, the Swiss-born, Melbourne-based artist John Wild, who had spent four years with the *Challenger* oceanographic expedition, wrote to *The Age* to outline his own vision for an Antarctic expedition.[20] Wild suggested a more modest preliminary expedition, with a few 'enterprising Victorian explorers' deposited on the largest of the islands in the Kerguelen archipelago to survey its unmapped west coast, while the expedition's ship sailed as far south towards the pole as possible. Within three weeks of this letter appearing in the press, Wild was invited to join the committee as an additional expert member, alongside the considerably less expert Duffy.[21] Wild's involvement, along with that of Kernot, Mueller, naval veteran Crawford Pasco and government astronomer Robert Ellery, was a boon to the committee, lending it a greater degree of authority.

The committee's early meetings were preoccupied with preparing a fourteen-point 'Memorandum of the Objects to Be Served by Antarctic Research'. The memorandum, which was distributed to governments, scientific societies and the press, outlined the expected contributions of an Antarctic expedition to scientific knowledge and the likelihood of discovering whales, fur seals and 'shores elastic with guano'. The memorandum also mentioned more novel ways to capitalise on the Antarctic, including suggesting that islands in the Southern Ocean be 'stocked' with useful plants and animals or settled permanently to provide bases for Antarctic industries. The committee's first official public statement closed with a request for copies of logbooks or any other information relevant to Antarctic exploration.[22]

The committee's initial aim was simply to generate public interest in the idea of exploring the Antarctic, and in this it was successful. The memorandum was reproduced throughout the colonies, and discussions of it were generally positive.[23] An editorial in Sydney's *Daily Telegraph* is indicative. While doubting whether sufficient funds could be raised in Australia alone, it welcomed the idea that 'Australia secure the glory and trade' that would stem from an expedition.[24] The committee members therefore began turning their attention to just how they might raise the funds for a small, preliminary polar expedition. Perhaps the most interesting suggestion came from Kernot, who envisioned using tourism to fund exploration. He believed that it would be simple to find 'a couple of hundred people to go on an excursion to the South Polar Seas', and suggested negotiating with a steamship company to organise a summer cruise.[25] Kernot's idea attracted enthusiasm and scepticism in equal measure.[26] While *The Argus* believed an Antarctic tourist trip would be 'very enticing in the middle of summer', it feared that the risk of polar bear attacks (again reflecting the limited state of Antarctic knowledge) or of the ship being trapped in the ice might count against it.[27] Other outlets were more critical of the tourist idea itself, decrying the idea of exploration 'conducted on the Cook excursion lines'.[28]

With momentum for exploration increasing, the Antarctic Exploration Committee held a public meeting at Melbourne Town Hall in July 1886. Two invited guests, a Russian naval captain and a fellow of the Scottish Geographical Society, gave papers, and for the first time the committee discussed in detail what an Australian expedition might look like. It was eventually concluded that a full-scale expedition would require two ships, a naval crew, a large professional scientific staff, and a plan of action drawn up by experienced polar explorers—all of which was well beyond the funding or expertise available locally. Instead, they agreed to approach the British Association for the Advancement of Science (BAAS) with an offer to cooperate on the larger expedition it was rumoured to be organising, while still endeavouring to organise a smaller colonial voyage as a precursor. This precursor would be an experimental whaling voyage. The committee would pay a subsidy to an Arctic whaling company to insure it against the risk of an unsuccessful voyage, and would purchase passage for two scientists to join the expedition. A convoluted system of bonuses would incentivise geographical discovery, mapping, and the collection of scientific data and specimens, making for a useful yet affordable expedition.[29]

Having decided on a plan, the committee sent a ten-man deputation to meet with Victorian premier Duncan Gillies. Pasco and Kernot summarised the memorandum's overview of the value of the 'neglected' Antarctic region. Duffy added a geopolitical imperative to the more familiar rationales, warning that if Australia did not explore the Antarctic, 'another Power would do it, and we should realize their importance when too late'. Mueller suggested that the subantarctic islands, such as Campbell Island, 'might become valuable for colonising'. With the others having made a case for 'why', Griffiths outlined the committee's proposal for 'how' an expedition could be mounted.[30]

Early in the committee's planning, some supporters had been interested in the idea of a purely Victorian expedition. Kernot, for instance, had played into the New South Wales–Victorian rivalry, saying that 'if New South Wales could send troops to assist in the

Soudan, perhaps Victoria could send people of a more peaceful disposition to aid the old country in the Antarctic circle'.[31] But for the majority of Antarctic enthusiasts, exploration was imagined as a collective Australian responsibility that necessitated an intercolonial project. This was certainly how Gillies imagined it. He fully endorsed the committee's proposal but felt no colony could fund it alone. He offered the services of Victoria's agent-general in London, Graham Berry, to act as the committee's agent in negotiations with Scottish whaling firms. He also agreed to write to the other premiers on the committee's behalf but made it clear that a grant would only be forthcoming if it were matched by the other colonies.[32]

The committee's deputation to the premier, its letter to the BAAS, and Gillies' letters to Berry and the colonial premiers ensured the idea of an Antarctic expedition remained in public view, with the press enthusiastically covering every development.[33] The reportage was generally supportive, though it became clear that there was division over how any expedition should be organised and funded. An otherwise enthusiastic *Argus* editorial added to the earlier call for the whaling and scientific voyages to be kept separate.[34] The *Leader*, meanwhile, focused on the prestige that would come from the colonies taking action, arguing that if the committee's proposals came to fruition, 'the country would gain a degree of consideration in Europe which it has never yet enjoyed'. It added, however, that it would be 'more creditable' if the funds were raised privately rather than by government grant.[35]

While Gillies took up the question of intercolonial backing with his counterparts, the committee set about mustering support from the colonies' myriad scientific societies. Unsurprisingly, the NSW branch of the Geographical Society was the first to throw its weight behind the 'Federal Antarctic Expedition' and its 'glorious task'.[36] Over the next few months, other organisations—the royal and Linnaean societies of New South Wales, the South Australian and Queensland branches of the Geographical Society, and New Zealand's Otago Institute—gradually committed to supporting the committee's project, though they specified that their assistance would be practical, not financial.[37] An offer of non-pecuniary aid also came from the Scottish Geographical Society, which offered to facilitate cooperation between the committee and supporters in Britain.[38]

In Tasmania, premier James Agnew invited his colony's Royal Society to advise whether his government should support the project.[39] The society arranged a meeting for 13 September 1886, with deputy surveyor-general Charles Sprent tasked with presenting a paper on the subject to an audience of sixty-two fellows under the gaze of James Clark Ross's portrait on a wall. Sprent spoke as a representative of the Geographical Society, which had half a dozen or so Tasmanian members but no branch in the colony. He began with an overview of the history of Antarctic exploration, summarising the voyages of Cook, Bellingshausen, Weddell, Biscoe, Balleny, Wilkes, d'Urville and Ross. This detached account soon gave way to an impassioned call to arms, however, as Sprent turned his attention to what he saw as the two most common objections raised whenever the possibility of Antarctic exploration came to prominence. First, he rebuked those who felt such an expedition had little value, highlighting both the expected commercial opportunities and the fact that the future applications of abstract scientific knowledge were impossible to predict. And second, he rejected the idea that Australians could simply sit back and allow other nations to take the lead. Australians, he argued, 'aspire to be the leading power in these Southern Seas'. They were striving to enact 'a Monroe doctrine of our own' and sought to prevent the encroachment of foreign powers into what were considered 'our preserves'. Sprent therefore offered a warning: 'if we expect to be the ruling power in these seas, the sooner we show ourselves upon them the sooner we shall see our claims recognised'.[40]

To Sprent, exploring the Antarctic was a national imperative. Not only would it yield important scientific results and scope out potentially lucrative commercial opportunities for the colonies, but it would prove that Australians were serious about controlling their neighbouring islands and seas, and provide a training ground for the seamen of a future Australian navy. He urged his compatriots to show 'that although during our infancy we were content to share the benefits of scientific work, in our manhood we are ready to share the toil', before concluding his paper with another warning: it would be 'a standing disgrace to Australia if she took no part in the exploration of the seas that wash her own coasts'.[41]

These words certainly had the desired effect. One of the fellows in attendance, Hobart lawyer James Backhouse Walker, agreed that if Australia 'intended to hold the empire of the Southern Seas', it needed to 'take up the responsibilities that were attached to that position'. He moved a resolution affirming the society's support and calling on the Tasmanian Government to contribute to the cost of an intercolonial Antarctic expedition.[42] Alexander Morton, curator of the Tasmanian Museum, suggested that the expedition would be an apt celebration of the centenary of colonisation in 1888 and went so far as to volunteer to join the expedition as Tasmania's representative. Congregationalist minister George Clarke declared that it would be to Tasmania's 'unspeakable and everlasting disgrace' if the colony failed to support the proposed expedition. James Barnard, who could boast of hearing Ross's account of his Antarctic voyage from the man himself, added his own endorsement, and the resolution was adopted unanimously.

‹ ›

The September 1886 meeting of the Royal Society of Tasmania provides an unusually clear window through which to glimpse how Australia's future was imagined in the 1880s. Sprent's paper, and his eye-catching allusion to the idea of a 'Monroe doctrine of our own' (referencing the policy position articulated in 1823 by US president James Monroe that declared the entire Western Hemisphere fell within America's natural sphere of influence), has been discussed by historians and legal scholars before.[43] Yet its significance has tended to be downplayed. Marie Kawaja, for instance, says that talk of an Australian Monroe Doctrine in the 1880s 'was just that, and a doctrine that laid down how Australia would protect its northern and southern approaches was not introduced'.[44] This may be true in a literal sense, but it underestimates the significance of an Australian Monroe Doctrine as an *idea*, one that was both surprisingly durable and remarkably influential.

Federalism and imperialism were entangled concepts in nineteenth-century Australian political thought. Federalism emerged as a political force in the 1880s, fuelled by Australian anxieties about French and German colonial ambitions in the Pacific. These anxieties stemmed in large part from the fact that many Australian colonists considered the south-western Pacific to be, as Sprent would put it, 'our preserves'.[45] The colonies had been sustained and enriched by trading connections with various parts of the Pacific since the very start of the nineteenth century.[46] From the middle of that century, colonists had profited from both the forced labour of indentured workers brought to Australia from the south-western Pacific, and the appropriation of land for the development of plantations in the Pacific, particularly in Fiji.[47] By the 1880s, the continued exploitation of this Pacific frontier was widely imagined as integral to the Australian colonies' future. Were islands such as New Guinea, the New Hebrides (Vanuatu) or Samoa to fall under French or German control, Australia's development would be curtailed and the colonies exposed to new threats, such as the closure of vital shipping lanes in the event of a future European war. These fears existed alongside a wider suite of concerns about non-British imperial expansion in the South Pacific, such as persistent anxieties about the potential corruptive influence of French convicts travelling to Australia from France's penal colony in New Caledonia.[48] Seeing such a future as unpalatable, some colonists began to advocate pre-emptive acts of expansion to better align the colonies' political boundaries with their perceived sphere of interest.

John Dunmore Lang, Australia's most radical nineteenth-century republican, was an early advocate of this idea. Lang predicted in 1870 that the colonies would federate to form an independent 'Australian Empire', then acquire protectorates over Fiji, the New Hebrides and the Solomon Islands; annex New Guinea; and purchase New Caledonia and Tahiti from France.[49] In the same year, the conservative Melbourne newspaper *The Australasian* lambasted the British Government for its failure to annex Fiji and called on Victoria to 'take the initiative and boldly annex that group of islands'.[50] More than a decade later, in April 1883, Queensland premier Thomas McIlwraith sparked a political crisis by taking exactly the kind of unilateral action *The Australasian* had called for. Amidst rumours of German interest in the eastern half of New Guinea, McIlwraith ordered a police magistrate to make the short journey from Thursday Island to Port Moresby and claim possession of eastern New Guinea for Queensland. This was politically popular throughout the Australian colonies but swiftly disavowed by the British colonial secretary.

Britain's refusal to recognise and legitimise Queensland's annexation of New Guinea sparked a chorus of outrage in the colonies. To address the issue, an intercolonial 'Australasian Convention' was held in Sydney in November and December 1883. While there were clear tensions between the colonies' positions, the convention produced the first tentative experiment with federation via the Federal Council of Australasia.[51] The delegates also issued a remarkably bold resolution in response to the New Guinea issue, asserting that 'further acquisition of dominion in the Western Pacific, south of the Equator, by any Foreign Power would be highly detrimental to the safety and wellbeing of the British possessions in Australasia, and injurious to the interests of the Empire'.[52] This resolution drew on an emerging belief that the colonies had a sphere of influence encompassing most of the south-western Pacific that was effectively off limits to any state other than Britain, an idea commonly known by the short-hand term 'Australian' or 'Australasian Monroe Doctrine'. This was a reference to the US policy position that deemed the entire Western Hemisphere to be an American sphere of influence, and asserted that the United States would consider any attempt by European imperial powers 'to extend their system to any portion of this hemisphere as dangerous to our peace and safety'.[53] The influence of the US doctrine on the idea articulated at the Australasian Convention sixty years later is clear.

This belief in an Australian Monroe Doctrine remained a staple of public discourse in the late nineteenth century. The annexationists' worst fears were seemingly confirmed when, in November 1884, Germany claimed possession of north-eastern New Guinea, at the same time as the Colonial Office was slowly taking steps to declare the south-eastern portion of the island a British protectorate. Outrage at this incursion and Britain's failure to prevent it added further momentum both to the federal movement and to the popular conception of an Australian Monroe Doctrine.[54] Other practical and sentimental reasons would come to play a pivotal role in the federal movement, but these factors complemented rather than displaced the dream of an Australian empire. Federation and territorial expansion remained intertwined strands of the most widely held vision of Australia's future in the 1880s and 1890s. An article published by *The Age* in September 1900, when the final form of federation had become clear, is indicative. Assessing the future of the islands of the Pacific, the article's pseudonymous author declared that 'the time is fully ripe for the clear enunciation by Australia of a "Monroe doctrine" of her own, so far as the islands within 3000 miles of her shores are concerned'.[55] Prominent federal leaders, including early prime ministers Edmund Barton and Alfred Deakin, were committed to the idea that the new Commonwealth of Australia had an extracontinental sphere of influence, while the outbreak of World War I was seen in some quarters as a chance to rectify past wrongs and seize German territories in the region.[56] The same idea informed prime minister WM Hughes's postwar vision for Australia—Hughes proclaimed in 1918 that 'we stand committed to a policy of an Australian Monroe doctrine in the South Pacific'.[57] An Australian Monroe Doctrine might not have been enshrined in legislation, but it was one of the fundamental ideas of late-nineteenth and early twentieth-century Australian politics.

Some of the language in Charles Sprent's passionate defence of the need for Antarctic exploration appears peculiar or opaque to readers today. To his audience in 1886, however, it was loaded with meaning and symbolism. Sprent's references to familiar ideas and debates served to rhetorically connect Australia's Pacific and Southern Ocean frontiers. By invoking the concept of an Australian Monroe Doctrine, he was asserting that Australia's sphere of influence extended south as well as north, bestowing on Australians both a responsibility to explore the Antarctic and a right to reap the benefits of this work. Sprent's formulation of this idea was particularly emphatic, but he was certainly not alone in thinking this. Daniel Harrison asserted, in a similar vein to many advocates of Australian territorial expansion in the Pacific, that Australians had a 'destiny to explore these southern solitudes'.[58] Another article cast Antarctic exploration as being 'a duty laid upon us by our geographical position'.[59] Committee member HK Rusden made a comparable point, deeming it extraordinary that Australians had not yet taken up the project considering 'the contiguity of the land they proposed to explore to their own country'.[60] GS Griffiths similarly believed that 'the work, its profits and its glory ought to be the destiny of the federated colonies of Australia'.[61] The committee's own memorandum on the value of Antarctic exploration stressed that 'the Antarctic is situated so near to us, and it forms so considerable a region that, if its exploration will serve any valuable purpose, the interest Australasia has in its accomplishment ought to be greater than that of any other community'.[62]

Amidst this focus on destiny and distance, others emphasised the risk that foreign rivals would forestall Australia in exploring and developing its southern frontier. The spectre of the New Guinea annexation crisis loomed large in these discussions. A wry warning issued by Melbourne's *Herald* is indicative, with the paper arguing that the committee's scheme deserved the colonies' full support, but only on the condition that 'any territory discovered is not to be handed over to the Colonial Office, to be given to the first Foreign Power that may be inclined to ask for it'.[63] Channelling similar anxieties, SA newspaper *The Bunyip* warned that 'we have the Germans and French in our neighbourhood, and stimulated with a thirst for discovery, and a desire to increase their resources, so while we are dreaming they may be exploring'.[64] *The Australasian* warned that Germany was set to launch an Antarctic expedition of its own 'to occupy the position that ought to belong to Australia', arguing that while Australians were happy to talk about 'our manifest destiny', decisive action was required to ensure that Germany did not 'forestall us in exploration in our own seas'.[65]

These statements, and many others like them, capture a shift in how Australians talked about their southern frontier. Older ideas about the Antarctic—as a site of future scientific and commercial value and a region of particular interest for Australians by virtue of geographical proximity—were integrated into a far more extensive, multidirectional conception of Australia's natural sphere of influence. Anxieties about perceived security threats, lost commercial opportunities, and Australian interests being sidelined as part of a wider imperial strategy reached fever pitch in the 1880s as Australian colonists observed events in the Pacific. These anxieties informed discussions of the Antarctic. Enthusiasts, optimists and boosters had long argued that the colonies had *interests* in the Southern Ocean, from maritime safety to commercial opportunities; now, for the first time, they talked of the colonies having *rights*.

Perhaps the starkest example of this conception of Australia possessing natural rights in the Southern Ocean came when, in 1892, they were perceived to have been violated. The names of the Kerguelen and Crozet islands, subantarctic island groups in the southernmost stretches of the Indian Ocean between South Africa and Australia, mean little to most Australians today. In the nineteenth century, though, these islands loomed large in the Australian imagination. These were notorious landmarks on the Anglo-Australasian shipping route, remarked on in emigrants' guidebooks and infamous as the sites of shipwreck horror stories and near misses.[66] The wreck of the *Strathmore* is indicative of the stories that fuelled these islands' grim reputation. The *Strathmore* struck the rocky coast of one of the Crozets in heavy fog in 1875, killing half of its eighty-eight passengers and crew and leaving the survivors to subsist on the islands for seven months until they were rescued by an American whaler.[67] A similarly sensational story arose in 1887 when an albatross was found dead on a beach in Fremantle with a message stabbed into a tin band around its neck, saying in French that thirteen sailors were stranded on the Crozets. An urgent rescue effort was organised, but the crew of the *Tamaris* perished before help arrived, disappearing during an attempt to cross from one island to another when their food supplies ran out.[68]

The same thing that made these islands a threat to the safety of Australian shipping—their location in the middle of the optimum Anglo-Australasian sailing route—also marked them out as being of potential strategic value. As early as 1855, a letter to the *South Australian Register* highlighted Kerguelen's potential as a coaling station for steamships and called for Australians to 'occupy Kerguelen's Land in time, before any other nation should do so'.[69] Appalled by the *Strathmore* disaster, David Berry sparked a public debate in 1876 by calling for the colonies to cooperate in occupying and developing all of the Southern Ocean islands as lighthouses and coaling depots.[70] In the aftermath of the New Guinea annexation crisis, a letter to *The Age* warned that ownership of Kerguelen needed to be clarified at a time 'when every available island as yet uninhabited or unclaimed by any European power is being snapped up'.[71] While acknowledging its remoteness, the letter writer believed that the island's fine harbours would ensure it would become 'a coaling station for some power in the future, and could be made the base of operations against either these colonies or those at the Cape of Good Hope'.

There were dozens of individual calls for the colonies to do something about the islands that dotted its Southern Ocean shipping route, but the colonial governments did not take such concerns particularly seriously.[72] The islands were presumed to be British territories, even appearing in British pink on many maps and atlases, and attempting to develop them was presumed to be prohibitively expensive.[73] It came as a genuine shock, therefore, when news filtered through that the French navy had performed proclamation ceremonies at Kerguelen, the Crozets, Saint Paul and Amsterdam islands in the summer of 1892–93, formally annexing them.[74] While some took the view that France had succeeded only in acquiring 'the most barren spot in either hemisphere', others were more concerned.[75] An *Argus* editorial, published after news was received that France had claimed Saint Paul and Amsterdam islands but before news of the annexation of Kerguelen and the Crozets, expressed outrage that the imperial government in London had allowed islands presumed to be British to be seized by another power. Invoking the idea of a sprawling Australian sphere of influence, *The Argus* urged the colonies to

> look about us and see if there are other possible stations that ought to be secured. If the Prince Edward's Islands, the Crozets, and Kerguelen Land are not vested in the British Empire—the Empire of the Seas—why, they ought to be … it would be absurd to have all the islets that dot the vast expanse of the Southern Ocean in alien possession. It is not too much to say that the Southern Ocean between the Cape and Australia should be essentially a British sea.[76]

As it became clear that France had also annexed Kerguelen and the Crozets, a letter to the *West Australian* warned that this was 'solely for strategic purposes … against the commerce of Australia'.[77] Victoria and Western Australia led the colonies' political response to the annexations, issuing formal protests to the British Government.[78] These protests earned a rebuke in the French press for their 'surprising piece of impertinence' and were rebuffed by Britain.[79] With few options left, the restive premiers reluctantly accepted the loss of these Southern Ocean islands.

This was the world in which the Australian Antarctic Exploration Committee operated. There were, of course, many differing visions of what Australia's future might look like in the 1880s. An Australian republic had its advocates, as did diametrically opposed proposals for an imperial federation that would integrate the United Kingdom and the British settler colonies into a single world-spanning federal superstate.[80] Yet the vision that surged to greatest prominence and exercised the greatest influence was of an Australia that would be both federal and imperial—federal in the sense that the colonies were expected to unite in some form to create a self-governing nation; imperial in the sense that a united Australia was expected to control a sphere of influence far beyond the limits of the Australian continent. This control might be exerted through the direct annexation and administration of territories, as ultimately occurred when Britain transferred control of what became the Territory of Papua in south-eastern New Guinea to Australia in 1902, but might also be exercised simply through the exclusion of other powers from a perceived Australian sphere. For those who supported the idea of the Australian colonies taking the lead in exploring and developing the Antarctic, the southern frontier was an integral part of this future.

‹ ›

Charles Sprent's advocacy secured the Royal Society of Tasmania's backing for an Australian Antarctic expedition, and the society's backing in turn secured the first firm offer of financial aid. The offer was modest—Tasmania's newly installed premier, Philip Fysh, offered £1 or £2 for every £1 raised from private donations in Tasmania—but it was a step towards the evidence of intercolonial support that would unlock Victorian Government coffers.[81] At the same time, the committee's proposal was starting to make waves overseas. Graham Berry, Victoria's agent-general in London, was able to report back about two promising leads. The first was interest in the proposal among Scotland's Arctic whaling firms, though the catch was that one of the most prominent Scottish whalers, David Gray, had previously estimated that an experimental Antarctic whaling voyage would cost £64,800 up-front. The second was that Sir Allen Young, a merchant mariner with extensive experience in the Arctic, was interested in taking command of an Australian expedition, but would require a £10,000 premium to protect him against financial losses if whaling proved unviable.[82] News of Young's willingness to lead the proposed expedition was a significant boost to the committee's credibility, and led *The Herald* to openly call for the Victorian Government to grant the entire £10,000 required given that 'larger sums have been squandered with far less hope of any profitable return'.[83]

Soon, the committee was inundated with a mix of offers and advice. A letter from the Dundee whaling firm David Bruce & Co. tentatively offered two ships for an expedition. Another from Norwegian whaling magnate Christen Christensen urged the committee to abandon its plan to combine whaling and scientific research, pointing out the many drawbacks to a hybrid voyage. Having provided this frank advice, Christensen quoted a price of between £3,500 and £6,500 to charter a Norwegian whaling ship and a crew with Arctic experience for a purely scientific voyage. Alternatively, he was open to undertaking a whaling voyage on his own account if the committee would agree to pay a bonus of between £2,500 and £4,500. David Gray shared this view, advising the committee to establish a whaling company of its own rather than trying to combine science and commerce, while still expressing an interest in undertaking a whaling voyage 'if suitable terms were offered'. Another whaler, HF Dessen, offered a ship and crew for £6,500 for twelve months. Applications to join the expedition flowed in, including from a Dundee whaling captain, an Adelaide meteorologist, a Queensland entomologist, and a Royal Navy officer turned Fijian plantation owner.[84]

As these offers reached the committee in Melbourne, it became clear that chartering a suitable ship and crew, whether for a scientific expedition, a whaling voyage or a hybrid, was likely beyond the colonies' means. The committee's solution was to make a small concession to the critics of a hybrid mission, planning now to send two ships with instructions for one to remain in the waters north of Victoria Land to hunt whales while the other pushed onwards to land a party of Australian scientists. The ships' owners would be compensated by a complicated bonus system, with payments for things like each degree of latitude reached beyond 70°S, establishing an observation camp on shore, travelling at least 100 kilometres inland, and harvesting 90 tonnes of whale oil or the equivalent value of 'any merchantable commodity'.[85] This suite of bonuses would require them to raise approximately £10,000.

Early signs were promising. Young offered £2,000 to get the expedition off the ground, while a Victorian businessman offered £1,000. Antarctic enthusiasts had aggressively lobbied NSW premier Henry Parkes, and his responses had been sufficiently positive that the committee was confident it could count on grants from New South Wales as well as Tasmania and Victoria. Berry was instructed to apply for a grant of £5,000 from the imperial government in London, conditional on the committee raising the same amount. This application was endorsed by the Geographical Society of Australasia and in Britain by the Royal Society, Royal Geographical Society, Royal Colonial Institute, BAAS and *The Times*.[86] By December 1887 it was apparent that there would be no expedition that summer, as had initially been hoped, but it was generally felt that 'public opinion is decidedly in favour of the venture, and in such cases time and persistence always effect the end'.[87]

While progress on an Australian Antarctic expedition was slow, Australian interest in the Antarctic continued unabated. GS Griffiths reprised his paper on the history of Antarctic exploration for a public lecture at the Royal Society of Victoria's conversazione.[88] In Hobart, all this talk of Antarctic expeditions and steam whalers spurred a group of shipowners, businessmen and former whalers to attempt to form a company for whaling in Antarctic waters. A public meeting was held, £500 worth of shares were sold, and attempts were made to purchase and outfit a ship to make a preliminary whaling voyage before the enterprise collapsed.[89] Rumours circulated about possible American or German expeditions surging ahead in the race to explore the Antarctic, sparking feverish discussion.[90] Even more potent were rumours that Adolf Nordenskiöld, the Swedish aristocrat and scientist best known for leading the 1878–79 *Vega* expedition through the Northeast Passage, was planning his own expedition to the Antarctic. Some of these rumours held that

Nordenskiöld's scheme was being funded by the king of Sweden and Oscar Dickson, Sweden's wealthiest businessman and a prolific patron of Arctic exploration. Others suggested that Nordenskiöld could be, or perhaps already had been, invited to lead a British or Australian expedition. Still others reported that he was fully occupied working up the scientific results of his work in the Arctic and would not contemplate new projects until 1889 at the earliest.[91] Even the committee was caught up in the rumours, reportedly inquiring through Gillies whether Nordenskiöld would join forces with them, Sweden and Australia each supplying a ship for a joint expedition under Nordenskiöld's supreme command.[92]

There was a feeling of optimism about the whole project in December 1887, but from this high point the Antarctic Exploration Committee's fortunes declined precipitously. Despite an endorsement from the Colonial Office, Britain's chancellor of the Exchequer refused Berry's request for a grant on the grounds that a commercial expedition was not worthy of government support, while a scientific expedition with a budget of just £10,000 could not accomplish anything worthwhile and would merely be a precursor to a later, costlier expedition.[93] The chancellor's wariness extended to that later, costlier and purely scientific expedition proposed by the BAAS. Despite boasting the most influential figures in British polar exploration on its own Antarctic committee, the BAAS scheme failed to attract government support and was abandoned in 1888.[94] Given the Australian committee had chosen to focus its efforts on a small, preliminary voyage to pave the way for a larger British expedition, this was a near-fatal blow for Australian ambitions.

This dashing of the committee's hopes led to public criticism and recriminations. The president of the Linnean Society of New South Wales, William Stephens, rebuked his colony for being so preoccupied by its centenary celebrations that it had failed to support 'an enterprise of such importance', calling its failure to fund the proposed expedition 'deplorable'. He argued that one-fiftieth of the money the colony had wasted on statues, celebrations, unemployment relief and rabbit extermination could have 'secured to New

South Wales an enduring renown worthy of the completion of her century'. To make amends, Stephens urged his colony's government to take responsibility for organising an Antarctic expedition of its own.[95] The Anglican bishop of Tasmania had a similar response, calling for Tasmania to mount its own expedition before it could be forestalled by Germany.[96]

Some supporters blamed the lack of unity between the colonies, a view endorsed by Gillies, who insisted that Victoria would still contribute liberally to an expedition provided it was 'an enterprise of all Australia in a truly federal spirit'.[97] Others blamed the committee's approach rather than the colonies' parsimony. The *Adelaide Observer* agreed that such an unambitious proposal was unworthy of government support, while *The Argus* criticised the decision to combine whaling and scientific exploration when 'there is no reason why wealthy countries like our own should not carry out both projects' individually.[98] The *Brisbane Courier* warned that Australia had now drawn the attention of other countries to the value of the Antarctic, meaning that 'an important geographical and scientific enterprise, which should of right belong to Australia and to the British race by which it is being peopled, is in danger of passing into other hands'.[99] The *Leader*, ever the bastion of the Antarctic enthusiasts, was more optimistic, saying simply that 'the mooting of the idea has nevertheless raised a widespread interest, which is likely ere long to bear fruit'.[100]

The committee responded to the collapse of its proposal by instructing Berry to make it known among Britain's whalers and shipowners that a more modest bonus would still be available to any who were willing to send two steam whalers to the Antarctic.[101] In a progress report to the Geographical Society, Crawford Pasco said he was confident that this approach would still bear fruit. Indeed, he remained optimistic that an expedition might still be organised in time for a barrel of Antarctic whale oil to be added to the colony's displays at the Melbourne Centennial International Exhibition over the summer of 1888–89.[102] Berry's efforts did lead to an opportunistic final offer from Dessen to send a ship to the Antarctic for a payment of £5,000, but this was declined. Dessen's proposed voyage would not depart from Australia, instead sailing directly to the South Atlantic and visiting Melbourne only on its return. There would only be one ship with no scientists and no Australians, and the £5,000 would be a premium rather than a bonus contingent on geographical or scientific achievements. Finally, if the expedition resulted in the development of a significant whaling or sealing trade out of Melbourne, then Dessen's fleet would be entitled to 'the same privileges and exemptions as shall be accorded to vessels owned by subjects of the colony' in perpetuity.[103] Desperate as the committee members were to sponsor an Antarctic expedition, these conditions were unpalatable.

‹ ›

The Antarctic committee's failure to successfully organise an Australian expedition after three years of effort can largely be blamed on the decisions to combine the scientific and commercial objectives into a single expedition, and to fund it through a convoluted bonus system. The committee was hamstrung by the fact that it could not afford to outfit a purely scientific expedition, while Australia's scientific societies would not support a purely commercial venture. The system developed was a creative attempt to circumvent this problem, but bonuses of up to £10,000 were insufficient to persuade any whaling firm to take the risk of combining whaling with tasks like exploring and surveying.

The committee's reams of correspondence with Arctic whalers therefore amounted to nothing in the short-term. They did, however, help to popularise the enthusiasts' vision of the Antarctic's importance—to science, to industry, and to Australia's future. Internationally, they drew attention to the possibility that the Southern Ocean might become a valuable whale fishery. Christen Christensen eventually despatched the finest and most expensive of the ships he had offered the committee on an experimental whaling voyage to Graham Land in 1892. That same year, Dundee whaler

Robert Kinnes, who had served as an adviser to the short-lived Tasmanian whaling company, despatched a fleet of four whalers to the same region.[104] And domestically, it helped to promote and popularise the idea that Australians had a special interest in the Antarctic, perhaps even a 'destiny' to explore and exploit this southern frontier. This was not enough to persuade colonial governments to prioritise the small and idiosyncratic exploring expedition promoted by a bunch of Melbourne enthusiasts over other demands for public funds, but it ensured that political leaders, scientific associations and the press were aware of the possible role the Antarctic might play in Australia's future.

4

'ANOTHER KLONDYKE'

Australia and the Renewal of Antarctic Exploration in the 1890s

On a warm summer evening in December 1890, James Cook, a polar bear and the ghost of Sir John Franklin entered Melbourne's Royal Exhibition Building. What sounds like the start of a bad joke was, in reality, an extravagant fundraising effort by the indefatigable Antarctic Exploration Committee. Eighteen months on from the collapse of the committee's first attempt at organising an expedition, its secretary had received a letter from the foreign minister of Sweden. News of the committee's efforts had reached the Swedish Academy of Sciences, prompting them to make an offer: if the committee could raise £5,000 in Australia, local magnate Oscar Dickson would match this sum to outfit a joint Swedish–Australian Antarctic expedition. Here was the opportunity the committee members had been waiting for. They set about raising funds immediately, opting this time to solicit private donations before approaching the colonial governments for grants. Most of the committee's fundraising efforts were decidedly orthodox—public lectures, open letters to the press and so on—but there were also experiments with more creative schemes. One such experiment was an elaborate costume ball.

For one evening, the Exhibition Building's cavernous main hall was transformed into an (admittedly low-budget) Antarctic scene. The committee acquired 3 tonnes of ice and formed it into icebergs, caves and grottos. Sets were borrowed from a comedic theatre company and painted to evoke polar scenes. Stuffed seals were liberated from scientific collections for the night and placed strategically throughout the icy tableau. A group of men, sweltering beneath several layers of real furs, posed (peculiarly for an Antarctic-themed event) as indigenous people of the Arctic. A program had been printed, depicting a ship sailing towards the South Pole and listing the names of the Antarctic Exploration Committee's members. Attendance was reasonable, with somewhere between 500 and 700 people present, though the dancers were dwarfed by a room that could comfortably hold 3,000. Some of these guests arrived dressed as famous figures in the history of exploration, from Columbus to James Clark Ross. Others adopted vaguely polar-themed costumes, or made do in appropriately snowy suits, dresses or cricket whites.[1]

The 'Antarctic Ball' was viewed, initially at least, as a welcome addition to the city's summer social calendar. As well as raising funds for a popular cause, it was scheduled for 'a time when Melbourne is generally inclined to be dull'.[2] But the event itself was a disappointment. The decorations, especially the stuffed seals, were applauded, but reviews in the social pages agreed that the committee had erred by staging its event too late in the year's social calendar and in too large a venue.[3] Other commentators lamented that the committee had been forced to resort to such an 'undignified medium' to raise funds at all.[4] In any case, it seems unlikely that the event was a financial success. Despite ample press coverage at the time, the Antarctic Ball was not mentioned in the committee's progress reports or subscription lists. It seems to have been neither success nor scandal, but rather an attempt to prove to the governments of the Australian colonies that there was mass support for the dream of an Australian Antarctic expedition. When it failed to demonstrate the level of public enthusiasm the committee had hoped for, it was quietly forgotten.

In many ways, this damp squib of a fundraiser is emblematic of the place of the Antarctic in Australian life at the turn of the twentieth century. The idea of a sprawling sphere of influence that included the Southern Ocean, and that would enrich, empower and protect the future Australian nation, had become increasingly widespread and influential. Yet the suggestion that active steps be taken to explore and secure this southern frontier was one made predominantly by a much smaller group of rusted-on enthusiasts and boosters. The zeal of these true believers was often irreconcilable with the views of those who considered unravelling the remaining mysteries of the Antarctic to be a lower priority than other projects or causes.

The incredulity of one Tasmanian newspaper is illustrative. Commenting on the mooted Swedish–Australian collaboration, *The Colonist* could not understand why, when the Antarctic was 'so immediately at their threshold as to make the enterprise a National duty', Australians seemed 'content that strangers should slip in and deprive them of the distinction they should be so proud to win'.[5] For those who sincerely believed Australians had a duty and a destiny to explore and exploit the world to their south, anything less than wholehearted support for the committee's projects was baffling.

This chapter traces the story of attempts to bridge this divide. In the 1880s, Australia's Antarctic enthusiasts and boosters sought to convince leading figures in politics, business, science and the press to support their schemes. In the 1890s, they sought to build a much wider platform of support. To do this, the proponents continued to assert that the Antarctic offered remarkable opportunities for Australians, from lucrative new industries to the chance to elevate the colonies' reputation on the world stage. However, they also increasingly argued that Australians had a duty to understand and explore the world that lay to their south.

‹ ›

The assorted enthusiasts who made up the Antarctic Exploration Committee might have been forgiven for going their separate ways when their plans for an Australian expedition collapsed in January 1888. Instead, they changed tactics, turning their attention to cultivating wider public enthusiasm for exploring the Antarctic and attempting to build stronger intercolonial support for the idea of an Australian expedition. A key pillar of this new strategy was to influence the agenda of the newly formed Australasian Association for the Advancement of Science (AAAS). This organisation, modelled on its British counterpart, was the brainchild of Sydney University chemistry professor Archibald Liversidge, who called on the scientific societies of Australia and New Zealand to send representatives to a meeting in Sydney in 1888 with a view to forming a new federal body.[6]

The association that emerged from this meeting was divided into eight sections, each dedicated to a branch of science, engineering or the arts. Section E was devoted to geography, and boasted WA surveyor, explorer and politician John Forrest as its inaugural president. Forrest, who had dedicated much of his life to the exploration and development of the Australian interior, saw the section's role as supporting the 'great national work of scientifically examining the whole of the continent'.[7] This jarred with the more expansive vision articulated by the Geographical Society, which had stressed from its foundation that Australian geography encompassed the investigation and development of the Antarctic and Pacific as much as the Australian continent.

To influence Section E's agenda and win AAAS support for the Antarctic Exploration Committee's work, GS Griffiths reprised his paper on Antarctic exploration. After giving his usual summary of the likely scientific and commercial benefits, Griffiths drew more overtly than ever before on nationalist sentiment to justify the exploration of the Antarctic. This was, he argued, 'a task which, by our geographical position and our wealth, is thrown on Australia as a duty which we cannot evade if we have any adequate conception of our great position in the southern seas'. Mounting an expedition would secure 'universal attention, and the approbation of the entire civilised globe' for Australia; failure to do so would see Australia forestalled, 'to our mortification and disgrace'.[8] These words clearly had the desired effect. At the suggestion of James Barnard, the old Tasmanian printer who had once assisted Ross with magnetic observations on term days, a new AAAS Antarctic Exploration Committee was appointed 'to consider the question of Antarctic exploration'. Yet, aside from Forrest, every member of this committee had either championed the earlier attempt to mount an Australian expedition or, in one case, been set to join the stillborn expedition. The result of the AAAS committee's consideration was never in doubt.[9] This was confirmed at the second AAAS meeting in Melbourne in 1889, when Section E president WH Miskin declared that it 'behoves us, as Australasians' to explore the Antarctic.[10]

Ensuring that Antarctic exploration was on the agenda of the AAAS geographical section was a significant victory for the enthusiasts. Importantly, it meant that future requests for funding could come from an explicitly federal body. It also generated publicity and helped to place the enthusiasts' ideas before a wider audience. One report on the AAAS meeting in *The Australasian*, for instance, resoundingly endorsed Griffiths' belief that Antarctic exploration was 'of more importance to Australia than to any other country' and hoped that the colonial governments would unite for a 'healthy assertion of the Monroe doctrine' by mounting an expedition.[11]

With one victory secured, the original committee in Melbourne set about building grassroots support through a series of lectures. Melbourne lawyer Thomas McInerney, a recent addition to the committee's ranks, gave the first of these lectures on the prospects of Antarctic whaling and sealing industries to the Melbourne Eclectic Society, a liberal debating club.[12] Another lecture was hosted by a branch of the Australian Natives' Association, a mutual benefit society for men born in the colonies which had become a leading proponent of federation and of Australian nationalism. This lecture persuaded members of the Richmond, Victoria, branch of the merits of Antarctic exploration, and they in turn persuaded the entire Victorian association to formally endorse the idea of an Australian expedition.[13] Other institutions hosted similar lectures or magic lantern exhibits on 'The Marvels of the Antarctic'.[14]

Outside of these self-conscious efforts to cultivate public interest in the Antarctic, rumours continued to attract substantial press interest. One had it that a Norwegian resident of New Zealand had returned home to recruit a Norwegian crew for a whaling expedition to Victoria Land. Others declared that a German–American expedition was imminent, that Nordenskiöld had either abandoned his interest in the Antarctic or was still planning to mount an expedition with Australian support, that Arctic explorer Fridtjof Nansen was planning a Norwegian expedition, and that Nordenskiöld was organising an expedition but had chosen Nansen to lead it in his stead.[15] Such was the growing ubiquity of the idea in the press that an Australian Antarctic expedition was even used as a plot device in newspaper serials.[16]

Just as the committee was focusing its efforts on influencing the AAAS and cultivating wider public enthusiasm for the Antarctic, the Swedish Academy of Sciences floated the possibility of a joint Swedish–Australian expedition.[17] After some discussion, the committee accepted the offer and resolved to begin raising the £5,000 required through public subscriptions.[18] Griffiths, who had been due to give the Bankers' Institute of Australasia's annual address on his favourite topic, agreed to use this lecture in August 1890 as an opportunity to launch the fundraising campaign. Accordingly, the lecture, which deployed the familiar arguments about the benefits of an Antarctic expedition to science, commerce and Australia's international reputation, was shifted to a larger venue and thrown open to the public. At its conclusion, a resolution was passed that the meeting 'recognises a national duty in the scientific exploration of the Antarctic zone, particularly that portion lying nearest Australia', and a subscription list was opened.[19]

The first wave of subscriptions came from old supporters. The Victorian branch of the Geographical Society donated £200, while committee member WC Kernot and the Royal Society of

Victoria added £100 each. Despite opposition from one member opposed to working with Swedes, the Royal Society of Tasmania added another £50. Geographical and scientific associations in other colonies agreed to coordinate local subscription lists, and by the end of the year roughly £500 had been pledged.[20] Soon, other institutions rallied behind the project too. The Australian Natives' Association, attracted by the promise of enhancing Australia's status and reputation abroad, collected £50 in small donations from its members.[21] An eclectic range of groups arranged similar collections, including clubs, local councils, department stores and trading companies.[22] Some individuals took it upon themselves to rouse their fellow citizens to action. Tasmanian librarian Alfred J Taylor offers a good example of this kind of response, arguing that the expedition could be a defining moment for Australia. Whereas other nations had 'been born in the strong throes of Revolution and strife', Australia would be created amidst the 'triumphs that come of knowledge attained in the cause of science, and sacrifice in the cause of truth ... unstained with blood'.[23] Others saw in the expedition a chance to 'enhance the national honor', to 'shed lustre on the land of ... [their] birth', or to improve the safety of Southern Ocean sailing routes.[24] Journalist Laura Suisted collected £21 in small donations in New Zealand.[25]

In this manner, the committee slowly and incrementally accumulated a fund of £1,450 by March 1891. While this fell well short of the total required, it was a reasonable sum in a rapidly deteriorating economic context. The colonies had experienced an economic boom for much of the 1880s, fuelled by land speculation, British investment and a dramatic expansion in bank lending. Melbourne had been the epicentre of this boom, but the bursting of Victoria's financial bubble in 1888 had fuelled a slow-burning catastrophe. By 1891, the colonies were on the cusp of an economic depression that would span much of the 1890s, peaking with a series of bank crashes and failures in 1893. The committee's fundraising drive therefore overlapped with the colonies' steady descent into the most severe and traumatic economic crisis they had experienced.[26]

There was still an air of optimism, however, when the AAAS met in January 1891 in Christchurch. The Antarctic dominated the Section E agenda, with Griffiths devoting thirteen of the nineteen pages of his opening address as section president to the topic.[27] CW Purnell, the Ashburton lawyer who had been one of the earliest proponents of an Australasian expedition in 1878, agreed in his own paper that an expedition was of the utmost importance (including ascertaining, once and for all, if the Antarctic was inhabited by humans). Yet he criticised what he saw as the unambitious scope of the committee's proposal and urged them to settle for nothing less than a full-scale, fully Australasian voyage of discovery.[28] Another New Zealander, Captain Crutchley, used the section's meeting to advance his own idea for an iceberg mapping and early warning system for the Southern Ocean. He drew on familiar themes to justify his notion, arguing that exploring the Southern Ocean was a task 'imposed specially by Nature for the inhabitants of the New World to accomplish, lying as it does at what may be termed the very doorstep of Australasia', and that its realisation 'would win for their new world a peaceful victory which would outshine in splendour many of the warlike achievements of the old'.[29]

Despite Purnell's reservations, the AAAS Antarctic Exploration Committee used its first progress report to throw its endorsement behind the Melbourne committee's plans for a Swedish–Australian expedition. The report itself added remarkably little, a reflection of the AAAS committee's lack of activity. Indeed, the only original ideas it included were two eccentric suggestions proffered by Ferdinand von Mueller: that the expedition use homing pigeons to convey updates from the Antarctic back to Australia, and that it be equipped with balloons for ascending the Great Ice Barrier that had barred Ross's way south.[30] Nonetheless, endorsement by Australasia's peak intercolonial scientific association carried some weight. And with this endorsement secured, Melbourne committee members Crawford Pasco and William Potter made their way to Sydney to lobby the various influential figures in colonial politics who were gathering there for a federal convention in March 1891.[31]

Pasco and Potter's efforts, which followed persistent lobbying by enthusiasts and scientific societies throughout the colonies, persuaded several colonies to offer grants. Queensland premier Samuel Griffith pledged £1,000, while his Tasmanian counterpart Philip Fysh promised £300. NSW premier Henry Parkes took a different approach, promising a grant of £1,266 if the people of his colony donated £634 privately.[32] When SA wool magnate Thomas Elder pledged £5,000, the expedition's future seemed secure. Yet Elder's offer coincided with news from Sweden that the Australian contribution would need to be doubled to £10,000 if the venture was to proceed.[33] Melbourne businessman Robert Reid—a man with a keen interest in Southern Ocean safety, having survived a collision with an iceberg off Kerguelen in 1855—offered £1,000 to save the scheme, bringing the committee's total to roughly £8,000.[34] Progress was promising, and the committee gleefully reported that Australians increasingly 'looked upon this Expedition as peculiarly the duty of Australia'.[35]

Hans Jørgen Gundersen, the consul for Sweden and Norway in Melbourne, had become thoroughly enamoured by the idea of exploring the Antarctic. By 1891, he was attending every Antarctic committee meeting and was a trustee of the expedition fund. He had even reportedly applied to join the Swedish–Australian expedition as photographer and balloonist. While the committee launched a fresh public appeal to try to secure the final £2,000 required, Gundersen wrote to his foreign minister to attest that the fundraising effort was on track and request a copy of Nordenskiöld's detailed plans for the expedition. A series of replies from Sweden revealed that Nordenskiöld's preparations so far amounted to attempting to procure books relating to the Antarctic; he had no plan, no ships, no staff, and would not countenance departing before the middle of 1893. The committee, which had believed the expedition would leave Melbourne in time for the summer of 1891–92, reluctantly accepted this delay, but requested that a formal contract be sent so that the sum raised so far could be wired to Stockholm.[36]

This was the first of several setbacks. Samuel Griffith failed to get the £1,000 grant he had promised through parliament.[37] Then, Elder insisted on a series of impossible new conditions before he would transfer his £5,000 donation, demanding that the intended scientific expedition now conduct whaling operations, that it reach Australia within a year, and that it depart for Antarctica from Adelaide. When told these conditions were impossible, Elder withdrew his offer.[38] The committee continued to maintain that the expedition had only been delayed, and that it had £4,210 in its Antarctic fund even without Elder and Griffith's donations, but rumours began to circulate that the project had collapsed.[39] Rumour soon gave way to criticism. The most cutting reproach came from the London *Times*. In an article that was syndicated widely in the colonies, the *Times* declared the whole enterprise 'sadly mismanaged' and the colonies' approach to the Antarctic 'ridiculous'.[40] For an expedition that had been framed so explicitly as a way to elevate international perceptions of Australia, the notion that it was instead a source of ridicule was crippling. The committee members were finally put out of their misery when, in June 1892, Gundersen forwarded letters from Sweden. As the Australian funds had not been provided by 1 January 1892—a condition never stipulated in any previous correspondence—Dickson's offer had lapsed. The cooperation between Sweden and Australia was at an end.[41]

The committee members made a few last-ditch efforts to salvage, if not the expedition, then at least their reputations. GS Griffiths wrote to *The Argus* to rebut the mounting accusations of mismanagement, pointing out that the committee had raised the £5,000 requested, only to be asked to double its contribution; that Nordenskiöld had failed to provide even a basic plan for the expedition; and that the Swedes had never replied to the committee's request for a contract.[42] There had always been a vein of scepticism among some of the project's supporters about relying on other nations to fit out an expedition, resulting in calls for the committee to go it alone. The *Leader*, for instance, insisted that 'the Australian colonies are able, if they could only see it, to do all that is requisite without European assistance'.[43]

The committee made a final effort to do just this, despatching Potter to Sydney to meet with Parkes's successor as premier, George Dibbs. Dibbs was willing to honour Parkes's grant provided the committee claimed it by the end of the year and evidence was provided that £634 in private donations had been raised in New South Wales. Potter came up with an elegant solution. Despite the depression, Robert Reid remained willing to donate £1,000. Potter suggested this be funnelled through the Geographical Society's NSW branch, allowing the committee to claim Dibbs's grant and put the funds towards a purely Australian expedition. Dibbs was willing to go along with this scheme, but the society's treasurer, HSW Crummer, objected to 'Victorian interference' and the grant lapsed.[44] This dispute drove something of a wedge between the branches, with the NSW branch soon turning its attention to a rival project to promote the establishment of an Antarctic whaling company headquartered in Sydney.[45] Yet even with these final nails in the coffin, committee members continued to defend their dream. Alexander Cameron Macdonald, long-serving committee member and Section E president for the 1893 AAAS meeting, blamed the failure on the depression rather than mismanagement and insisted that the committee would continue to explore the possibility of subsidising an experimental whaling voyage. Despite the many setbacks and disappointments, Macdonald still urged AAAS to ensure that 'the glory of making discovery and explorations in these Southern Seas be not borne from us by others, to our everlasting disgrace'.[46]

‹ ›

Just as the dust was settling on the doomed Swedish–Australian Antarctic expedition, a Norwegian expatriate was trying to muster support for his own idea to unlock the potential of Australia's southern frontier. Henrik Johan Bull hailed from Tønsberg, one of the centres of Norwegian whaling, but migrated to Melbourne in 1886 and found employment as a shipping agent. Living in Melbourne at this time, Bull was exposed to the regular discussions of the Antarctic that characterised this period. And of the many ideas that circulated—about science, industry and Australia's future—it was whaling that captured his imagination. He was inspired by press reports to read Ross's account and became convinced that a profitable industry could be carried out off Victoria Land. He tried to find backers in Melbourne to start a whaling company, penning a series of letters to *The Argus*, meeting with Mueller, and promoting his scheme to investors.[47] But 1892 was not, as the Melbourne Antarctic committee also found, an ideal time to be soliciting investment. For all that Melbourne was the centre of Antarctic boosterism in the 1890s, there were few investors with the capital to spare for the expensive and risky project Bull envisaged.

Recognising this, Bull returned to Norway and pitched his idea to 84-year-old whaling magnate Svend Foyn. Foyn was the grand old man of Norwegian whaling, having pioneered the use of new technologies, such as steam-powered whaleboats and exploding harpoons, and new techniques, such as hauling whale carcasses ashore to be processed at large, modern factories. Foyn's innovations made it possible to hunt, for the first time, the largest and fastest rorqual whale species, including minke, humpback, fin and blue whales, and had catapulted Norway to the forefront of the global whaling industry. Foyn viewed the development of new whaling grounds anywhere in the world as a matter of 'national importance' for Norway, a country that was controlled by Sweden but, like Australia, was popularly presumed to be on a path towards independence. He therefore agreed immediately to fund a voyage to Victoria Land.[48]

Bull departed Norway in September 1893 in a steam whaler christened the *Antarctic*. After calling at Kerguelen to hunt whales and seals there, the *Antarctic* made its way to Melbourne. Intriguingly, Bull was riddled with anxiety when he arrived. He had no idea who owned the Kerguelen archipelago and suspected (as many Australians had done before the French annexation in 1892) that it might be Britain or Australia. He therefore worried that his cargo might be confiscated in Melbourne due to poaching. His fears were unfounded of course, and Melbourne's Antarctic enthusiasts instead celebrated the expedition's arrival. The *Antarctic* was granted a berth at Yarraville, where the blubber from Kerguelen could be boiled down.

The Antarctic Exploration Committee and the royal and geographical societies hosted an official welcome, and Bull was invited to give a paper to the latter. He and Gundersen were also invited to address a meeting of the Victorian Chamber of Manufactures about whaling and sealing at Kerguelen. In turn, Bull hosted members of these associations aboard the *Antarctic*, culminating in the firing of an explosive harpoon across Port Phillip Bay.[49] Such was the enthusiasm for the expedition that a consortium of Melbourne businessmen was hastily organised to try to buy out the expedition and continue it at their own risk. Foyn was open to this offer but set a price of £10,000—double what the consortium could afford—and the deal fell through. Despite this, an erroneous claim that the expedition was 'an enterprise of Victorian capital combined with Norwegian appliances, experience, and skill' circulated widely, further fuelling local enthusiasm for what was still a purely Norwegian enterprise.[50]

Bull and Foyn would soon regret this failure to agree a buyout price. When Bull tried to sell the Kerguelen sealskins in Melbourne, he found no merchant would take them. Unfamiliar with Southern Ocean sealing seasons, the *Antarctic*'s crew had slaughtered seals during moulting season, rendering the skins virtually worthless. To recover from this loss, Bull sent the *Antarctic* under its captain, Leonard Kristensen, to try whaling and sealing around the Auckland and Campbell islands while he tried to get something for the Kerguelen cargo in Melbourne. This proved disastrous. Tasmania and New Zealand had been at loggerheads over the subantarctic islands for the better part of two decades. New Zealand had introduced restrictions to conserve seal populations on its islands, while Tasmania did nothing for Macquarie. This had allowed poachers to evade the NZ regulations by claiming their catches were from Macquarie. By 1894, though, relations between the colonial governments over the subantarctic issue had thawed, and when reports of Bull's intentions reached the Tasmanian Government, officials promptly alerted their

NZ counterparts. The New Zealand Government steamer *Hinemoa*, which had been visiting the subantarctic islands every six months or so since 1876 to inspect and re-provision a network of depots for the use of shipwreck survivors, was despatched to the Aucklands to warn off the *Antarctic*. The encounter between the two ships was tense, with *Hinemoa* shadowing *Antarctic* around the islands before an irate Kristensen gave up and made for the Campbells. There he was intercepted by a British naval vessel and again barred from sealing. Things got even worse when Kristensen ran his ship aground during a storm. When the damaged *Antarctic* limped back into Port Phillip Bay in August 1894, it carried only 5.4 tonnes of oil from a single whale but needed £2,000 worth of repairs.[51]

While the *Antarctic* was overhauled, the Antarctic committee sprang into action. After eight years of frustration, here was the opportunity they had sought. Before departing Norway, Bull had given permission for Norwegian explorer Eivind Astrip and Scottish oceanographer William Speirs Bruce, just returned from a position with the Dundee whaling expedition to Graham Land, to join the *Antarctic* in Melbourne. In the latest blow to Bull's plans, word arrived that neither man would make it to Australia in time. The committee therefore tried to find two Australian scientists who could join the expedition. When this proved impossible, they donated books, charts and instruments in the hope that some useful data might still be collected. Then, days before departure, a Norwegian expatriate who had worked as a surveyor and science teacher in New South Wales since migrating in 1888 applied to join the *Antarctic* as its scientist. Thirty-year-old Carsten Borchgrevink had, like Bull, had his interest in the Antarctic piqued by the committee's campaigns. Borchgrevink's credentials were insufficient to justify the position he requested, but Bull allowed him to sign on as a general hand and devote his leisure time to scientific work.[52] Mired in difficulties as the voyage was, when these Norwegian whalers and their freshly recruited science teacher left Melbourne on 26 September 1894, it marked the first attempt to explore the region south of Australia in half a century.

Despite Kristensen's disastrous attempt at whaling and sealing earlier in the year, Bull resolved to make a second attempt at hunting on and around the Campbell Islands. Once again, though, the Norwegians' attempt at sealing was curtailed by the presence of a NZ ship and a stern reminder that sealing was currently prohibited under New Zealand law. The *Antarctic* therefore plunged southwards, only to be forced back almost immediately when its propeller was damaged by ice. Another £100 was required for repairs, and nine of the crew deserted in New Zealand, before the *Antarctic* finally resumed course for Victoria Land in November 1894.[53] When it returned to Melbourne the following March, it was revealed to have been yet another disaster. The vast numbers of right whales Ross had reported were nowhere to be found, and while they did encounter plenty of blue whales, they lacked the equipment needed to hunt them. The commercial results of an ostensibly purely commercial voyage amounted to 3.6 tonnes of whale oil, 5.4 tonnes of elephant seal oil and 150 low-value seal skins, together valued at £300. The expedition's scientific and geographical results were also, given they had essentially followed in Ross's tracks, largely unimpressive, though they did go one step further than Ross by briefly setting foot on Cape Adare at the northernmost tip of Victoria Land. Borchgrevink's scientific work was mainly limited to basic meteorological observations, though he did collect geological samples that hinted at a continental origin for Victoria Land, and a few lichen specimens that constituted the southernmost vegetation ever discovered.[54]

The voyage of the *Antarctic* was a spectacular failure. Yet, as Bull observed, 'colonial enthusiasm for our expedition remained as great as ever'.[55] Borchgrevink and Bull were invited to address the Geographical Society on the expedition's scientific results and the prospects of Antarctic whaling respectively, then to repeat these addresses at a public lecture, while Kristensen was asked to give an account of the voyage for the society's conversazione. Borchgrevink and Bull then made their way to Sydney, where they repeated their lectures, gave interviews to the press, and gave evidence on the prospects of Antarctic whaling and fishing to a Royal Commission on Fisheries.[56] The depth of interest shown in the colonies helped to reshape the narrative around the expedition, so that by the time of the 1898 AAAS meeting, this hapless Norwegian whaling venture was remembered rather as a bold pioneering enterprise 'largely guided and assisted by the Melbourne branch of the Geographical Society of Australasia'.[57] Buoyed by the undimmed enthusiasm they encountered, both men also began floating the possibility of organising further expeditions with colonial support.[58]

Bull's travails could—and perhaps should—have been read as a cautionary tale, a warning that neither exploration nor commercial development of the southern frontier would be as straightforward as Australia's Antarctic boosters imagined. Instead, it reinforced and re-energised older ideas. Discussions of the expedition in press columns and meeting halls abounded with calls for Australians to recognise their 'responsibility' to explore and exploit the world to their south. A report in the *Sunday Times* is indicative: after lauding Bull and Borchgrevink, it asked: 'why should not Australia despatch an expedition, which will do even greater things than the good men of the whaling steamship *Antarctic* have done'?[59] Bull himself parroted the ideas he had been exposed to during the Antarctic committee's long campaign, declaring that 'to Australians should belong the honour of making further discoveries' in the Antarctic, and that whaling in the seas south of the colonies could 'be made a great national industry'.[60]

Bull's conspicuous attempts to use Australian ideas to solicit Australian funding for another expedition or a whaling company were unsuccessful. He and Borchgrevink fell out and parted ways in Sydney, returning separately to Europe to promote their individual ideas for further Antarctic work.[61] Bull focused on publishing a vivid account of the voyage and attempting to raise funds privately in Tønsberg and Melbourne for further expeditions.[62] Borchgrevink, meanwhile, raced to London in time for the 1895 International Geographical Congress and talked his way onto the program. There, he both presented an account of the *Antarctic*'s voyage and outlined his vision for a new expedition under his own command. This new expedition would construct a base and overwinter at Cape Adare. From there, Borchgrevink would lead a party up 'a gentle slope' he had seen leading from the peninsula up to the Victoria Land plateau and travel roughly 300 kilometres via dog sledge and skis to the magnetic pole.[63] Many of those in the audience were veterans of previous campaigns to organise British and German Antarctic expeditions and were already thoroughly committed to the idea, but Borchgrevink's proposal prompted them to reaffirm this position. In the aftermath of this paper, a resolution was passed declaring 'that the exploration of the Antarctic Regions is the greatest piece of geographical exploration still to be undertaken', and calling on scientific associations around the world to 'urge, in whatever way seems to them most effective, that this work should be undertaken before the close of the century'.[64]

While the long depression of the 1890s meant purse strings remained tight in Australia, one man was inspired by the voyage of the *Antarctic* to organise a modest project of his own. Hans Jørgen Gundersen, consul for Sweden and Norway and staunch supporter of the Antarctic committee, partnered with Ceylon tea planter Charles Rowlands to outfit a sealing expedition to Kerguelen. Gundersen provided the ship—his own ninety year-old Norwegian sailing brig—and recruited a crew from among Melbourne's community of Norwegian sailors. He also took leave from his consular duties to lead the expedition himself, accompanied by Melbourne ornithologist Robert Hall and Rowlands' cousin Hugh Evans to act as a volunteer scientific staff. After outfitting his expedition for only £1,500, Gundersen returned from a five-month voyage over the summer of 1897–98 with a cargo of 900 seal skins, 72,000 litres of elephant seal oil, a large collection of geological, botanical and zoological specimens, and even a live baby elephant seal that became a star attraction at Melbourne's aquarium. This cargo was enough for the partners to make a small profit and for Hall to publish his ornithological findings and share specimens with other specialists.[65]

Gundersen's project was exceedingly modest in its scope and achievements, yet it adds another example to an intriguing phenomenon. Bull, Borchgrevink and Gundersen were all influenced by the ideas and the rhetoric about the Antarctic they encountered in Australia, to the point that they each, in their own ways, became actors in the exploration of the Antarctic and the investigation of its commercial prospects. The Antarctic committee, and the colonies' wider community of enthusiasts and boosters, plainly failed in their efforts to mount an Australian Antarctic expedition. Yet in failure they remain historically significant. The ideas they drew on, articulated and deployed took on a life of their own, defining what was imagined as possible or desirable for the future of Australia and its southern frontier. That three Norwegians were provoked into action by these ideas offers a reminder that the enthusiasts, for all that they were unable to get boots on the ground, shaped the discourse in the Australian colonies around the Antarctic in fundamental ways.

‹ ›

By 1896, the challenge posed by the International Geographical Congress to mount a full-scale scientific expedition to the Antarctic before the turn of the century had resulted in four separate proposals. One came from those associated with the earlier movement by the BAAS for what would eventually become the British National Antarctic Expedition (NAE). Another came from one-time Melburnian Georg von Neumayer and the Commission for South Polar Exploration he had established in Germany. The third was being promoted and organised by an undistinguished Belgian naval officer, Adrien de Gerlache, with support from his country's geographical society. The fourth was for an expedition organised by Borchgrevink and primarily funded—he hoped—by the Australian colonies.[66]

In September 1895, Borchgrevink wrote to his only political contact in the colonies, NSW lands minister Joseph Carruthers, to ask if there might be funding available for a 'purely Australian expedition' under his command.[67] When this amounted to nothing, Borchgrevink cabled the colony's premier, George Reid, with an offer to lead an expedition if New South Wales provided £15,000. This was nearly twelve times greater than the largest sum previously offered by a colonial government for Antarctic work, and it was unsurprisingly declined. In a final effort to win colonial support for his plans, Borchgrevink arrived in Adelaide in January 1897 to embark on a lecture tour. While in Adelaide he received some encouragement from the local branch of the Geographical Society and premier Frederick Holder, but both refused to commit funds to Borchgrevink's smaller private proposal given the rumours that an official British expedition would soon be launched. At Holder's suggestion, Borchgrevink made his way to Hobart, where a conference of colonial premiers was being held. As in Adelaide, his proposal generated ample good will, including a public meeting that issued a resolution calling on the colonial governments to fund it, but no grants. A few final efforts in Sydney and Brisbane, including persuading the governor of New South Wales to join his expedition's 'Honorary Council', had the same result.[68]

Throughout his abortive fundraising trip, Borchgrevink drew on the same key ideas that had by now underpinned Australian interest in the Antarctic for decades. In articles and interviews, he framed his expedition as an opportunity to 'show that the country is willing and eager to accomplish a task which its geographical position claims that it ought to do, and add a glorious page to the chronicles of the Commonwealth of Australia'—four years before there was a Commonwealth of Australia to speak of. He insisted that Australians 'must no longer leave the surrounding lands blindly to the enterprise of foreigners'. He vowed to staff his expedition with 'as many Australians as possible, young men educated at Australian universities'. He swore to construct his ship in Hobart and entirely from Australian timber. And he promised to return with samples of whales, seals and guano to properly illustrate the commercial prospects of Victoria Land.[69] It is impossible to know whether Borchgrevink's invocation of these fundamental ideas of geographical proximity, national prestige and unbridled commercial opportunity was cynical or sentimental. Perhaps, through long exposure to these ideas and debates during his time in New South Wales, he had come to sincerely believe them. Or perhaps he had simply observed that *others* sincerely believed them and he hoped to exploit this to win support for his scheme. Either way, Borchgrevink was clearly aware of how Australians thought and talked about their southern frontier.

Undaunted by his failure to raise a single pound, Borchgrevink returned to England and persuaded publisher George Newnes to stump up the expedition's entire £40,000 budget.[70] By the time he returned to Hobart in November 1898, Borchgrevink's transformation from regional science teacher to bona fide explorer was complete. Two years earlier he had travelled to Hobart to plead with the assembled premiers for support. Now, he sailed up the Derwent in command of *Southern Cross*, a twelve-year-old Arctic whaler designed by Norway's finest shipbuilder and specially adapted for Antarctic service. Like the earlier generation of explorers who had used Australian ports as bases for their voyages south, Borchgrevink was inundated with social invitations and gifts. As Tasmanian-born, Melbourne-based astronomer Louis Bernacchi, the expedition's physicist, later recalled, 'the whole town appeared to us to have but one occupation—entertaining the members of the Expedition'.[71] Or, as the *Sydney Mail* put it, 'though we have given little towards helping Antarctic exploration, it has a special interest for Australians'.[72]

Upwards of 800 people turned out for a reception organised by the Royal Society of Tasmania to welcome Borchgrevink to the colony, while the colonial government organised a farewell on the eve of his departure. The explorers received many gifts, including whaling gear presented by a Hobart alderman who noticed the *Southern Cross* had none—it is telling that this scientific expedition was seen as incomplete without the means to hunt whales. During the expedition's final days in Hobart, Borchgrevink led his men in a series of ad-hoc rituals. They laid a wreath at the foot of a statue of John Franklin, then visited 83-year-old James Agnew, who had danced on the *Erebus* and dined on the *Terror* half a century before. A group associated with the old Antarctic committee, including Gundersen, travelled down from Melbourne to join the crowd that swarmed the docks to farewell the *Southern Cross*.[73] Commenting on these scenes, one local paper observed that it had been 'many years since the departure of a vessel from a Tasmanian harbour, or an Australian one for that matter, has aroused such widespread interest'. The only comparison the author could recall was the departure from Sydney of a military contingent bound for Sudan in 1885. But whereas 'the interest on that occasion centred more in the departing soldiers than in the cause which drew them forth', in this case 'the greater amount of enthusiasm was displayed in the mission upon which the hardy Norsemen were embarked'.[74]

Of the four Antarctic expeditions either in the field or in development in 1898, Borchgrevink's generated the most interest in Australia. The expedition was essentially Anglo-Norwegian in character, with a London publisher providing the funds and Norway most of the staff and equipment. Aside from Borchgrevink's six-year stint in New South Wales, the recruitment of Bernacchi and choice of Hobart as the port of departure were the expedition's only Australian connections. Yet Borchgrevink had consistently emphasised his colonial connections and the benefits of Antarctic exploration to the colonies, and this rhetoric served to stimulate Australian enthusiasm for the project. This was in stark contrast to how Borchgrevink was viewed in Britain, where his fundraising efforts saw him characterised as an upstart rival to the NAE.

In Britain, a coalition of scientists and Arctic veterans had been pushing for another government-backed expedition since the 1880s. Their campaign flagged after a string of disappointments, but was relaunched by biologist and *Challenger* veteran John Murray in a paper to the Royal Geographical Society in 1893.[75] This call was taken up by Clements Markham, the society's newly elected president and another prominent proponent of polar exploration. Markham led a relentless campaign for government backing, eventually securing a grant of £45,000 conditional on the organisers—a joint committee of London's royal and geographical societies—raising another £45,000 themselves.[76]

Markham was aware that there was substantial interest in the idea of exploring the Antarctic in Australia and sought to capitalise on this interest by making repeated public and private appeals for aid. In 1895, he approached all the Australasian colonies' agents-general in London about the possibility of the colonial governments providing grants to the NAE, and asked the AAAS to lobby the governments in support of this proposal. When the colonial premiers descended on London for the Queen's Diamond Jubilee celebrations in 1897, Markham invited them to attend the grandiloquently titled 'Anglo-Australasian Antarctic Conference' to repeat his request.

When these private approaches failed, Markham went public, issuing a press appeal to the colonial governments and scientific associations to fund the NAE in 1898.[77] In response, the old Antarctic committee, diminished by Griffiths' resignation and the deaths of Pasco and Mueller, but still meeting on occasion after twelve years, pledged £250 to the NAE fund, while AC Macdonald supported Markham's call both in the press and at the 1898 AAAS meeting. Despite these efforts, the only other substantial donation that came from Australia was a £1,000 grant by Queensland.[78] Sufficient funds were ultimately subscribed in Britain and the NAE got underway in 1901, but it is notable that the call to aid a metropolitan British venture openly committed to geographical discovery and science was even less successful in raising funds than the earlier campaigns for an Australian or Australian–Swedish project, or even the hasty movement to buy out Bull's whaling voyage. There was plenty of interest in the NAE in Australia, but Australian governments, organisations and individuals seem to have been less willing to financially support a metropolitan project that made no grand claims to be enhancing Australia's prestige, commerce or security.

Borchgrevink's expedition returned to Hobart in April 1900. Having been the first to spend an Antarctic winter on land (the Belgian expedition had endured a torrid winter trapped on their ship amidst sea ice in the Bellingshausen Sea in 1898),

Borchgrevink's party had obtained the most complete set of meteorological, magnetic and geological data yet collected in the Antarctic. They had also proved that a party could pass an Antarctic winter in relative safety and comfort. Their geographical discoveries, though, were modest. Cape Adare had been a poor choice for a base. Contrary to Borchgrevink's expectations, there was no way to scale the surrounding cliffs, leaving the party effectively stranded on the peninsula and unable to make journeys inland. When the *Southern Cross* returned to collect the party, Borchgrevink resolved to visit and land on Ross's Great Ice Barrier and made a rapid dash a few kilometres inland to at least set a new farthest south record.[79]

Despite a lack of spectacular results, Borchgrevink was once again feted on his return to Australia. And once again, Borchgrevink played to the ideas he was familiar with. Having sold the press and book rights to Newnes, Borchgrevink remained coy about many details of the expedition while still stoking interest in it. At a civic reception organised by the Tasmanian Government and the state's Royal Society, for instance, he shared few details but declared this expedition would come to be seen as a 'bright intellectual landmark in the history of the culture of the nations of the Southern Hemisphere'.[80] On another occasion, he donated sledges and other equipment to the Tasmanian Museum so that it could create an exhibit dedicated to the expedition, and on yet another he vowed that his account would 'strike the astonished world like a streak of lightning'. This led some to conclude that right whales had been found in large numbers, opening the way for the long-awaited Australian Antarctic whaling industry.[81] There was a bidding war for the rights to syndicate Borchgrevink's story, and when it was finally published in June 1900 it was serialised across eight illustrated instalments.[82] Particularly prominent was Borchgrevink's claim to have discovered gold on an island near Cape Adare and his prediction that Victoria Land would prove to be 'another Klondyke'. Borchgrevink's 'gold' was later found to be pyrite, but his invocation of the Klondike gold rush that had drawn tens of thousands of prospectors to far northern Canada captured the imagination of many Australians and became an enduring part of how the southern frontier was discussed and portrayed in Australia over the next thirty years. Having been so influenced by the ideas about the Antarctic he had been exposed to in Australia, here was Borchgrevink's own contribution to the intellectual tradition of Australian Antarctic boosterism. In an early indication of the influence of his Klondike comparison, the Adelaide *Advertiser* declared that Borchgrevink had made the Antarctic 'annexable and exploitable'.[83]

Enthusiasm for Borchgrevink's adventures continued with the publication of his book *First on the Antarctic Continent*, which was widely advertised, discussed and reviewed in Australia.[84] The *Brisbane Courier*, for example, emphasised the book's relevance to Australians, making special note of the possibility of goldmining in Victoria Land and suggesting that

> to Australians the importance of a knowledge of the great Antarctic continent is assuredly much more manifest than to those on the other side of the equator, and for that reason if for no other Mr. Borchgrevink's account of his voyage of exploration ... should be widely read on this continent.[85]

There were occasional criticisms too—Tasmanian newspaper *The Clipper* published a particularly scathing review of Borchgrevink's self-aggrandising narrative—but the overwhelming response to Borchgrevink's expedition in Australia was laudatory.[86] In this, Australian attitudes diverged sharply from those in Britain. Markham and others associated with the national expedition viewed Borchgrevink as a vainglorious interloper who had accepted a single £40,000 donation that could (and they felt *should*) have gone to the NAE fund. This personal hostility ensured that Borchgrevink and his expedition were widely excoriated in Britain.[87]

‹ ›

This divergence in attitudes towards a single eccentric Norwegian reflects a wider divergence in thinking about the Antarctic and the wider Southern Ocean world. Over the course of the nineteenth century, a set of distinct and coherent ideas had developed in the Australian colonies. Foremost was a belief that the colonies had an especial interest in the Antarctic by virtue of Australia's geographical proximity to this region. Closely related to this was an assumption that Australia's southern frontier offered remarkable opportunities, those envisaged being mainly commercial, including revitalising lapsed industries such as whaling and sealing, and opening new ones like guano harvesting and goldmining. Yet other kinds of opportunities were imagined too, such as improving the safety and reliability of Australia's Southern Ocean shipping routes and enhancing Australia's reputation on the world stage.

In the 1880s, these ideas about interest and opportunity became entangled with wider discussions about Australia's future. In the context of heightened anxiety about the potential annexation of various islands in the Pacific by expansionist European powers and a growing belief that a federation would soon be necessary to ensure Australian concerns and interests were not sidelined, the idea that Australia had a natural sphere of influence that extended far beyond the boundaries of the continent surged to prominence. The island of New Guinea dominated this conversation, but there were regular indications—most notably an explosion of frustration at the annexation by France of subantarctic islands that had been presumed to be British—that many Australians envisaged a natural sphere of influence that extended into the Southern and Indian oceans as well as the Pacific.

Amidst swelling discussions of interests, opportunities and rights in the Antarctic, a more contested idea emerged in colonial discourse: that these interests, opportunities and rights brought with them responsibilities. In the 1880s and 1890s, this conception of particularly Australian responsibilities in the Antarctic zeroed in on the idea of exploration. Despite a brief burst of exploratory activity in the 1830s and early 1840s, the Antarctic remained poorly charted and poorly understood. Fundamental questions, such as whether the patchwork of coastlines sighted and visited by explorers were part of a massive Antarctic continent, remained uncertain. A smaller group of Antarctic enthusiasts and boosters therefore promoted the idea that the exploration and scientific investigation of the Antarctic was a particularly Australian responsibility. While the proponents of the Australian-led exploration of the Antarctic failed in their immediate goals of fitting out expeditions and testing the waters for the commercial development of the southern frontier, they did much to promote and popularise these entangled ideas of interest, opportunity, rights and responsibilities. These ideas would, in turn, shape how Australians and their newly federal government thought about and engaged with the Antarctic as it became a site of escalating international interest and competition over the first decades of the twentieth century.

5

'THE READING OF YESTERDAY'S MENU TO A HUNGRY MAN'

Antarctic Fever in the Early Commonwealth

Federation, the formal union of the six Australian colonies, was celebrated with remarkable gusto on 1 January 1901. Across the newly minted Commonwealth of Australia, there were parties and parades, fireworks and picnics, sports days and light displays. Sydney was the centre of festivities, with an estimated 250,000 people lining an 8-kilometre parade route. The streets were decorated with a series of commemorative arches erected by business and community groups, culminating in an ornate plaster pavilion at the site of the official inauguration ceremony at Centennial Park.

Yet once the crowds had dispersed and the federation day souvenirs had been packed away, the Commonwealth's provisional Cabinet had to immediately begin the work of assembling a functioning government for the new nation. Foremost among the concerns of inaugural prime minister Edmund Barton, his chosen ministry and the governor-general was the urgent need to organise elections for the first federal parliament by the end of March. At the same time, they needed to commence the work of building a federal civil service and find a new defence minister, Barton's first pick having died within ten days of taking office. And they needed to do all of this with an eye to the future, articulating their visions for the Commonwealth's legislative priorities and mounting their own election campaigns.[1] Alongside these more prosaic concerns, one item on the agenda for Barton's ministry during the Commonwealth's first chaotic weeks stands out: the annexation of the Kerguelen archipelago.

Two years earlier, NSW politician Henry Copeland had published a pamphlet entitled *Kerguelen Island and Australian Commerce*. In it, Copeland argued that Kerguelen was Australia's 'natural half-way house', an island destined to become either a naval station for the protection of Australian shipping or a base from which it could be attacked. To Copeland, the solution to this looming threat was obvious: Kerguelen must be annexed and occupied by Australia. That France had already proclaimed sovereignty was unimportant, since proclamation alone meant little until steps were taken to occupy a territory. Copeland therefore called for the full-scale colonisation of the archipelago. A band of hardy settlers would be tasked with setting up the colony: introducing crops and livestock, establishing a coal depot for steamships, prospecting for minerals, establishing whaling and sealing stations, and fortifying the best harbours for use as naval bases. In only a short time, Copeland predicted, 'a cheerful radiance would emanate from the windows of snug little cottages, dotted here and there in the sheltered valleys'.[2]

Soon after publishing his pamphlet, Copeland headed for London to take up a position as his colony's agent-general. He had no qualms about taking advantage of his new position to advance a cause he considered to be of the utmost national importance, and therefore broached the Kerguelen question with both the Admiralty and colonial secretary Joseph Chamberlain. When he learnt that Barton had been commissioned as prime minister, Copeland implored his old parliamentary colleague to confer 'an eternal benefit on the Commonwealth' by purchasing the remote archipelago.[3] Barton was sufficiently persuaded by Copeland's arguments about strategy and geopolitics to share copies of the pamphlet with his ministers and take the proposal to a Cabinet meeting. Out of this meeting came a firm resolution to pursue the acquisition of

Kerguelen, with the governor-general asked to communicate the Cabinet's decision to Chamberlain.[4]

This audacious decision to acquire an uninhabited archipelago in the Southern Ocean from a European power was widely discussed in the Australian press. One paper noted that the Cabinet had received an early taste of 'the cares which come with greatness'.[5] *The Sydney Morning Herald* collated political figures' responses to the news. While a few thought 'Mr Barton and his colleagues were rather too Imperialistic in their ideas', the majority view was that possession of territories like New Guinea, New Caledonia and Kerguelen by any non-British imperial power was 'a menace to the wellbeing of these States' and that these islands should gradually be acquired by the Commonwealth.[6] *The Argus*, which had led the chorus of outrage when France had proclaimed sovereignty over the islands two decades earlier, welcomed the news. Indeed, it suggested that the Commonwealth should go further and request the transfer of all the Southern Ocean islands between South Africa and Australasia, since if they were 'ever to be utilised it must be by Australia'.[7]

Chamberlain considered the Australian request seriously but ultimately accepted advice from the Admiralty that French control of Kerguelen posed no threat.[8] With the Colonial Office unwilling to open negotiations with France on the Commonwealth's behalf, both the request and Copeland's eccentric vision of an Australian colony in the Southern Ocean faded into obscurity. Yet the fact remains that, for a brief period in 1901, the legal status of a subantarctic island group was deemed to be an urgent issue for Australia's fledgling federal government.

Historian Marilyn Lake has argued that the 'Commonwealth of Australia was founded in dreams of a Pacific empire'.[9] This was certainly the case—the early federal movement was entangled with the popular idea of an Australian Monroe Doctrine, and another of Barton's priorities in 1901 was to arrange for the transfer of the British colony in south-eastern New Guinea to Commonwealth control. Yet Lake's formulation does not quite capture the full extent of Australia's foundational imperial aspirations. When politicians dreamt of an Australian empire, their imaginations wandered south and west as well as north and east, to the Southern and the Indian Oceans as well as to the Pacific. An article published in the *West Australian* newspaper in November 1901 neatly captures the multidimensionality of this expansionist vision. News that the federal government had arranged for south-eastern New Guinea to be transferred to the Commonwealth was welcomed, since this showed that Australia had committed to 'her own Monroe Doctrine'. With this first step taken, it was now only a matter of time until Fiji, the New Hebrides, New Caledonia, Saint Paul, Amsterdam and Kerguelen were all brought 'into the Australian fold'.[10]

Barton's attempt to acquire Kerguelen may have amounted to nothing, but the attempt itself was significant. It offers an important reminder that the ideas that circulate in the public domain are essential for defining what is possible and desirable in the political domain. The Southern Ocean had been firmly positioned as part of Australia's natural sphere of influence since the 1880s, and Australians as the coming citizens of not only a continent but of a vast region in the Southern Hemisphere. This way of imagining Australia's rights and responsibilities, threats and opportunities, and above all the nation's destiny, fundamentally shaped the kind of Commonwealth that was created in 1901. As the precocious attempt to acquire control of Kerguelen indicates, the Commonwealth was, from its foundation, an expansionist polity engaged and concerned with a sphere of interest far beyond the limits of the Australian continent. This chapter considers how Federation altered the dynamics of the southern frontier. It will argue that the Commonwealth created a political apparatus to assert and promote Australian perspectives and interests to an unprecedented degree, but that the requirement to work within a British imperial framework continued to be a moderating factor.

‹ ›

It did not take long for Antarctic exploration to be placed on the new federal government's agenda. In May 1901, the organisers behind the NAE wrote to Barton to request a government grant. The expedition was already well funded, but Clements Markham and his colleagues anticipated further expenses, such as chartering a second ship to ferry supplies, and hoped that Australia would contribute. Despite sustained lobbying from Markham and his local ally, AC Macdonald, Barton declined this request, explaining that he was personally supportive of the expedition but had reservations about the constitutionality of a grant.[11] Federation had taken place against a backdrop of devastating droughts, economic depression and stalling population growth. Quite deliberately, therefore, the early Commonwealth was a lean and frugal operation, and its powers were circumscribed by the Constitution.[12]

It soon transpired that the NAE did indeed require further funds. The plan devised by the organising committee and Markham's handpicked commander, naval officer Robert Scott, entailed allowing the expedition's fabulously expensive, purpose-built ship *Discovery* to be frozen into the sea ice near Ross Island from March 1902 to serve as a base for scientific observations and for journeys inland. The drawback to this plan became apparent when the relief ship *Morning* arrived at Ross Island with its cargo of fresh supplies in January 1903 only to find *Discovery* still firmly stuck in the ice. The NAE therefore remained in situ for a second winter, leaving the organisers to scramble for funds to send two relief ships in the summer of 1903–04 to evacuate the explorers if *Discovery* could not be released. Abandoning the ship seemed a very real possibility, but after six weeks of ramming, blasting and sawing, wind blew the remaining ice out to sea and the ship was able to sail for New Zealand on 16 February 1904.[13]

Though it never translated into financial support, there had been considerable interest in the fortunes of the NAE in Australia from the time it was first mooted. In a practice that would become increasingly common over the following decades, Lauchlan Mackinnon, manager of the Melbourne-based *Argus* and

Australasian newspapers, attempted to capitalise on this interest by acquiring the first publication rights for the NAE's story.[14] As well as press accounts, the NAE's adventures and achievements were communicated through two books—Scott's official account and a popular narrative by second-in-command Albert Armitage—and an Australasian lecture tour by expedition member Reginald Ford. Books and lectures alike received rave reviews, including being described by one reviewer as rivalling 'the best adventure of fiction', helping to keep the expedition in the public eye.[15]

There were also plenty of other stories to satiate Australian readers' appetite for Antarctic news. A Swedish expedition organised by Otto Nordenskjöld—nephew of the Antarctic committee's erstwhile collaborator Adolf Nordenskiöld—was duly reported. It only truly became a major news story in Australia, though, when the expedition was first reported overdue, then rescued in a daring operation orchestrated by the Argentine navy.[16] In similar fashion, a German expedition under Erich von Drygalski and a French venture under Jean-Baptiste Charcot were consistently reported on but generated the greatest interest when they appeared to be missing.[17] A Scottish expedition was likewise chronicled in Australia without ever becoming a subject of particular fascination.

The Scottish National Antarctic Expedition (SNAE) may not have been a major news story in Australia, but it does offer an intriguing comparison to Australian ideas and attitudes about the Antarctic. Oceanographer William Speirs Bruce, who had previous experience in both the Arctic and Antarctic, applied to join the NAE in 1899 but was ignored. Bruce then began raising funds in Scotland for his own expedition, earning him the eternal enmity of Markham. The SNAE was an avowedly nationalist enterprise. Funds were raised exclusively in Scotland, the expedition members were Scottish or Scottish-educated, the explorers flew the Royal Banner of Scotland above their base, and they lamented that there was no way for them to legally proclaim Scottish sovereignty over the South Orkneys. Even its name was a self-conscious assertion of Scottish nationhood, and Bruce corrected anyone who dropped 'national' from the SNAE's title.[18] Both Scotland and Australia occupied awkward positions as national communities within the British Empire, and in both places a movement developed that positioned Antarctic science and exploration as a way to achieve international recognition and acclaim for the national community. Just as Australian enthusiasts had insisted that an Australian expedition would 'increase the respect and esteem in which Australia is held', so too did Bruce suggest that his expedition had 'shown that the nationality of Scotland is a power that must be reckoned with'.[19]

It is notable, then, that the dynamics of Australia's interest in the Antarctic were out of step with wider international trends. Antarctic boosterism flourished in Australia during a long period of relative international disinterest in the region from the 1840s to the early 1890s. Two of the expeditions that helped to reinvigorate international interest, Bull's and Borchgrevink's, had their intellectual origins in Australia and stimulated intense interest locally. Yet during the unprecedented burst of Antarctic exploration between 1901 and 1906, when British, French, German, Scottish and Swedish expeditions were all active in the region, Australian enthusiasm, while discernible, was more muted than it had been for the previous twenty years. The period 1901–06 was therefore a time of escalating worldwide interest in the Antarctic but with no corresponding boom in Australia. For all that the expeditions of this period undertook objectively significant work, they each emerged from their own distinct intellectual and historical milieu that differed from the ideas that had developed in Australia. None of these projects vowed to elevate Australia's status and reputation on the world stage, or unlock a new hinterland for Australian commerce and industry, or guarantee Australian interests and security in the Southern Ocean. They were imagined and justified in different terms to appeal to their own core constituencies, and the engagement of Australian governments, institutions, businesses, media and individuals was therefore less than organisers like Markham expected based on the colonies' prior enthusiasm for less-ambitious projects and less-qualified explorers. To elicit more passionate and more practical forms of support in Australia, organisers needed to engage more fully with Australian traditions of thinking about the Southern Ocean world.

This is not to say that Australians were uninterested in the Antarctic in this time. They remained avid consumers of tales of Antarctic adventure and images of Antarctic wildlife (especially penguins).[20] They remained as willing as ever to entertain ideas, however eccentric, about how to use their southern frontier, including separate proposals for a summer tourist cruise to the Antarctic and a health cruise for tuberculosis sufferers.[21] Ideas about Australia having a Southern Ocean destiny continued to circulate, such as a claim by NSW politician Ned O'Sullivan that the Commonwealth occupied 'the most advantageous position in the world' at the confluence of the Indian, Pacific and Southern oceans, the latter of which offered 'great possibilities in the way of whaling, sealing, fishing, and perhaps another Klondyke'.[22] And rumours about future expeditions, from an immediate follow-up by Charcot to an idea from two veterans of the disastrous 1898 Belgian expedition to drive to the South Pole by motor car, were reported far and wide.[23] The most notable rumours, however, concerned a former NAE officer who was said to be planning a small, privately funded expedition to claim the South Pole for Britain.

Ernest Shackleton had distinguished himself as *Discovery*'s third officer during the early stages of the NAE and was one of two men chosen by Scott to accompany him for an attempt on the pole in November 1902. The party surpassed Borchgrevink's farthest south mark by nearly 4 degrees but was badly affected by frostbite, snow blindness and scurvy. When they made it back to the expedition's base at Ross Island, Shackleton was invalided home on the relief ship *Morning*. Back in England, Shackleton acted as the NAE committee's expert adviser as it developed plans for evacuating the expedition if *Discovery* could not be freed, and he advised the

Argentine navy on its preparations to rescue the missing Swedish expedition. This restless and ambitious young merchant navy officer then stood unsuccessfully for parliament and tried his hand at jobs with the *Royal Magazine*, Royal Scottish Geographical Society, and shipbuilding firm William Beardmore & Co. By 1906, however, he had begun preparing to return to the Antarctic in command of his own expedition.[24]

As with Borchgrevink and Bruce before him, Shackleton alienated the Royal Geographical Society by launching an expedition that was seen as a rival, in this case to an as-yet-unannounced follow-up expedition by Scott to finish the NAE's work in the Ross Sea region.[25] Shackleton was therefore forced to raise funds without government or institutional support in Britain, relying instead on donations and loan guarantees from friends, including his employer William Beardmore, Australian pastoralist Rupert Clarke, and twenty-year-old aristocrat Phillip Brocklehurst, who donated £2,000 in exchange for a place in the shore party.[26] As Shackleton's plans firmed, he was able to generate a frenzy of press coverage by floating a series of novel ideas: using a motor car for polar travel, taking the first cinematographic and phonographic recordings in the Antarctic, using Manchurian ponies rather than dogs, and even using homing pigeons to send updates back from the Antarctic.[27]

Shackleton's expedition was organised at a fraction of the cost of the NAE and was narrower in its scope and ambition. Where the NAE had boasted the brand-new, purpose-built *Discovery*, for instance, Shackleton made do with the dilapidated Arctic sealer *Nimrod*, less than half the size and purchased for a tenth of *Discovery*'s £51,000 cost. Yet, soon after *Nimrod* departed England in August 1907, it became apparent that this shoestring endeavour would capture Australian interest in a way the NAE had never been able to. The key to unlocking mass enthusiasm and financial support turned out to be fifty-year-old Sydney University geology professor Edgeworth David.

Welsh-born, Oxford-educated David had migrated to New South Wales in 1882 to take up an assistant geological surveyor position. His surveying work led to the discovery of a major new coalfield in the Hunter Valley, earning him a distinguished local reputation that helped secure the geology professorship in 1891. His star rose still further when he organised an expedition to Funafuti in Tuvalu that produced the first firm evidence to support Charles Darwin's theory of coral atoll formation, earning him international plaudits and sparking a sideline as a prolific public lecturer.[28] By 1907, he was an internationally renowned expert on glaciation, a beloved geology teacher, and one of Australia's most respected public intellectuals. He also had an established interest in the Antarctic, having taken charge of the analysis of Borchgrevink's geological samples from the voyage of the *Antarctic*.[29]

In September 1907, it was revealed in the Australian press that David would be joining *Nimrod* for its first voyage south. The plan was for David to mentor Shackleton's youthful scientific staff (the expedition's twenty-year-old geologist, Raymond Priestley, was still in the final year of his undergraduate degree) and do some brief geological field work before returning with the ship for the start of the university term. This announcement was widely celebrated in Sydney. *The Sydney Morning Herald*, for instance, declared that 'it has always been a reproach to Australia that she has neglected to take practical interest in her extreme southern neighbor', so it was to be welcomed that someone 'so thoroughly competent to represent the State has been asked to accompany an expedition to the great Antarctic continent'.[30] David's students organised a dinner to congratulate their professor, at which they noted that 'Shackleton had conferred a great honor on the University of Sydney'.[31] David's involvement led to an offer from the City of Sydney to supply all the coal the *Nimrod* required for its voyage free of charge if it could call at Sydney en route to Shackleton's intended departure point of Lyttleton, New Zealand. When this proved impracticable, it was instead arranged for first the expedition's business manager, Alfred Reid, and subsequently Shackleton himself to give lectures in Sydney during their brief stopovers in Australia, and for *Nimrod* to visit when the expedition returned.[32]

When Shackleton arrived in Australia in late November 1907, he was mired in debt and still £5,000 short of the minimum required to finish outfitting his expedition. He was fortunate, then, that awareness and enthusiasm about his project had exploded in Australia since David's involvement was announced. A barrage of cablegrams welcomed him to Australia, and a desperate journalist cornered him for an interview during a brief stop in Fremantle. During another stopover in Adelaide, he was whisked away to a formal welcome by the mayor, governor, premier, various naval and military officers, and the local Geographical Society. When he reached Melbourne the following day, he was immediately taken to the Town Hall for another official welcome, at which he was assured that 'Australia had always taken the keenest interest in the Antarctic'.[33] This was followed by another lengthy press interview, in which Shackleton revealed his funding shortfall and expressed a hope that there might be 'ten men in your prosperous Commonwealth who will contribute £500 each'.[34] Shackleton concluded his whirlwind Melbourne stay by attending a meeting of the Geographical Society in the afternoon and lecturing to a sold-out audience in the evening.[35] Inspired by Shackleton's lecture, the Geographical Society orchestrated a fundraising drive that collected £66 in small donations, with all Victorians urged to contribute since they had been 'the first to initiate the revival of further exploration and research in our little known Antarctic region'.[36]

Shackleton enjoyed a similar reception in Sydney, going straight from Central Station to the city's Town Hall for still more formalities. His lecture the following day was highly anticipated, to the extent that doors were barred thirty minutes early when the hall filled beyond capacity, resulting in unprecedented scenes of the crowd outside attempting to 'lay siege to the doors'.[37] Shackleton again explained his precarious financial situation, and a committee was formed on the spot to coordinate fundraising in Sydney.[38] In a public call for donations, this committee stressed that the Antarctic was Australia's 'great sister continent', that the expedition boasted three Australian scientists now that David's former students Douglas Mawson and Leo Cotton had signed on, and that Australia stood to benefit more than any other country from the expedition's research into Antarctic meteorology and its search for valuable minerals.[39] In this way, the expedition was absorbed into the older rhetorical traditions of Australian Antarctic boosterism.

The notion of Australia having a direct stake in the expedition was constantly repeated in the press. The proposed benefits of supporting Shackleton's venture were eclectic, ranging from the discovery of workable gold reefs to dramatic improvements in Australian weather forecasting, to gaining collections of biological and geological specimens for Australian museums, and obtaining live seals for Sydney's zoological gardens at Moore Park.[40] *The Sydney Morning Herald* neatly summarised this argument by declaring that Australians 'stand to benefit most if the expedition is successful, wherefore it behoves us to do everything in our power to ensure its success'.[41] This argument proved influential. Sydney University and the city's two largest newspapers subscribed £100 each, while various figures in business, science, politics and education donated smaller amounts, all of which brought the 'Antarctic Exploration Fund' to £491.13.0 by 21 December.[42]

Realising that the small donations being steadily collected in Melbourne and Sydney would not raise the £5,000 required in time, David put his extensive personal connections to use and asked the Commonwealth Government to save the expedition. Home affairs minister William Lyne and prime minister Alfred Deakin agreed to provide the entire sum. They were more confident than Barton had been that the Commonwealth could dole out grants in this way, but felt they needed at least semi-official approval from parliament.[43] Deakin accordingly introduced a motion without notice on the final sitting day of the year, asking for approval to advance £5,000 to Shackleton. He argued that the expedition's work would have 'special value to Australia' and that aiding it would 'do us credit abroad, and advance the cause of science ... without making any undue demand upon us'.[44]

Deakin's proposal received cross-party support. Joseph Cook, deputy leader of the opposition Anti-Socialist Party, agreed that 'we owe a duty to ourselves and to posterity to explore the antarctic regions'. Labor leader Andrew Fisher agreed it was 'the duty of this Parliament to provide the requisite funds'. Indeed, the only dissenter was Labor's Charles Frazer, who did not object to the grant but rather to discussing the proposal without notice, but his procedural protest was shouted down with cries of 'Shame!' by his colleagues.[45] The decision proved popular outside parliament, too, with the *Daily Telegraph*'s prediction that it would 'prove an inestimable advantage to the Commonwealth' indicative of public sentiment.[46]

With the financial question resolved, the expedition members convened in Lyttleton, where they benefited from further practical support. Supplies of New Zealand produce, including dried milk, butter, cheese and thirty-two live sheep, were gifted to the expedition, while the NZ Government granted another £1,000. Prime minister Joseph Ward also agreed to resolve a second issue that threatened the expedition's viability. The tiny *Nimrod*, with its maximum speed of 6 knots, could not physically carry both the supplies needed for the expedition and sufficient coal for a return voyage. Shackleton's radical solution was to ask for a steamer to tow *Nimrod* as far as the icepack. Ward duly opened negotiations with the director of New Zealand's largest steamship company, who offered to cover half the cost of providing the steamer *Koonya* for this unusual mission if the government covered the other half. To round out his gifts to the expedition, Ward gave Shackleton a NZ flag to take to the South Pole, had him sworn in as a NZ postmaster, and presented him with 24,000 NZ stamps overprinted with the name of the expedition's intended destination, King Edward VII Land.[47] The accoutrements of a post office were a practical gift in one sense, giving the expedition a way to prepare mail during the long Antarctic winter, but were also a way to coopt the expedition to advertise New Zealand's role.[48]

With these arrangements made, and with messages of encouragement flowing in from Australia, *Nimrod* departed Lyttleton on

New Year's Day 1908. The farewell was considered 'the greatest ever bestowed on any vessel leaving a New Zealand port', with as many as 30,000 said to have been in attendance, and the passenger steamers then in port listing heavily as crowds thronged to one side to watch the laden *Nimrod* leave.[49] And while Shackleton had abandoned the idea of pressing pigeons into service, the expedition did continue to provide an unusually steady stream of media content to an eager audience in Australia and around the world. When the *Koonya* returned, its captain Frederick Evans and Ashburton pastoralist George Buckley (who had sailed with the *Nimrod* as a tourist as far as the pack ice before transferring to the *Koonya*) shared vivid details of the steamer's harrowing voyage, having remarkably towed the *Nimrod* through the turbulent Southern Ocean for nearly 2,800 kilometres—farther south than any iron-hulled ship had ever travelled.[50]

The *Koonya* also brought word that Edgeworth David had agreed at the last minute to join the shore party as its chief scientist and remain for the duration of the expedition. Reactions to this announcement were universally positive. The *Daily Telegraph*, for example, said that David's continued involvement 'gives Australia distinction' since 'the exploration of Antarctica is as emphatically Australia's work as anything can be which is of universal significance, and it is fortunate, indeed, that the Commonwealth has in the expedition a man so rarely qualified scientifically and temperamentally'.[51] David's decision to remain was as unsurprising as it was popular. Prominent feminist Cara David had even foreshadowed it in an interview, suggesting that her husband was 'praying that the *Nimrod* will be iced in, so that he will have some excuse to stay'.[52]

As well as a brazen application for leave from his university duties, David sent back a lengthy account of the expedition so far via the *Nimrod*. This account, blending details of the voyage, vivid descriptions of the scenery and wildlife, humorous anecdotes and scientific observations into a coherent narrative, was published as a popular thirteen-part series by the *Daily Telegraph* and *Sydney Morning Herald*.[53] Even after the press had exhausted the potential of David's copy, the expedition remained a prominent topic of conversation and media coverage. Everything from the make-up of the crew for *Nimrod*'s second voyage to collect the shore party to how the explorers were faring was speculated on in the press.[54] One of David's colleagues, anatomist James Wilson, later recalled that wherever he went in Sydney during the expedition's absence, someone stopped him to ask, 'How do you think David is getting on?'[55] The Antarctic was clearly in the zeitgeist. Sydney University students organised celebrations around the theme of 'Professor David's Odyssey', resulting in a parade that included a polar bear driving a trolley down George Street towing replicas of *Nimrod* and Mount Erebus.[56] Attempts were even made to organise a three-week polar cruise for December 1908, the £25 tickets to include photographic excursions and seal shooting under the midnight sun. While nothing ultimately came of the project, the seriousness with which it was discussed is indicative of the renewed prominence of the Antarctic at this time.[57]

‹ ›

The return of Shackleton's expedition to Australia in early 1909 was a bona fide cultural phenomenon. Shackleton had fallen just 180 kilometres short of his goal, but had set a new farthest south record of 88°23'S that was within 100 geographical miles of the pole before dwindling supplies and the impending Antarctic winter forced the four-man party to turn back. This record-breaking southern journey, which shaved more than 6 degrees off the previous mark, was the expedition's headline achievement, but the party could also claim to have made the first ascent of the world's southernmost volcano, Mount Erebus, and to have been the first to physically reach the south magnetic pole. These latter accomplishments had particular resonance in Australia, as David had been in command of both journeys and had been joined in both by 26-year-old Adelaide University mineralogist Mawson. That Australians had not only contributed financially to and participated in Shackleton's expedition but had been instrumental to its achievements was a spur for Australian pride and enthusiasm. One of Shackleton's first acts when the *Nimrod* returned to Lyttleton was to cable Deakin's successor Andrew Fisher to offer the expedition's meteorological data to the Commonwealth, and to renew his promise of geological and biological collections for whichever Australian museums Fisher nominated. All these factors contributed to a bubbling sense of enthusiasm about the expedition and its Australian connections, sparking calls for public receptions to be held in Sydney to allow people to demonstrate 'our appreciation as Australians' for the polar exploits.[58]

David was the first to arrive in Sydney, in March, having travelled by steamer ahead of the slow-sailing *Nimrod*, and was greeted by a throng of friends, family, journalists, students and admirers who had gathered on the dock from midnight to await his arrival. His daughter and a university colleague were among the crowd, and they swiftly bundled the professor into a waiting motorcar to take him to his second welcome, hosted by botanist Joseph Maiden, then to a third with Sydney's lord mayor, then a fourth with the chancellor of Sydney University. By lunchtime he was at a fifth welcome hosted by the university's staff and students. Nominally a university event, some enthusiasts resorted to subterfuge to gain entry—Cara David was initially turned away by an exasperated doorkeeper who explained she was the seventh Mrs David he had admitted.[59] In the afternoon, David boarded a train to his home in the Blue Mountains and was greeted by crowds lining the entire route from Woodford Station to his house as part of yet another welcome organised by the local council.[60]

The most thoroughly welcomed man in the Commonwealth was then the guest of honour for an event at Sydney Town Hall on 1 April. The lord mayor bowed to public pressure to democratise proceedings by offering tickets to hear David speak to those who arrived first rather than by invitation. While this was a popular move, it resulted in a crowd of thousands outside the building and the start was delayed for thirty minutes when David was stranded outside the locked doors. When the pandemonium that greeted his belated arrival finally subsided, David gave a speech that was steeped in firmly established ideas about Australia's relationship with the Antarctic: it should 'have a special interest to Australia', it was Australia's 'sister continent', it 'abounded in economic minerals', and it would soon become a destination for Australian tourist cruises.[61]

Even after this event, Sydney's obsession with David and the expedition continued. His office at the university attracted a steady stream of visitors desperate to see the polar equipment he had stowed there, which was 'handled with curious awe'. Curious awe also described the reaction to David going shopping for new clothes in the city—a fattening diet of seal and penguin blubber necessitated a new wardrobe—when shop assistants and customers alike 'flocked to gaze at him'.[62] A full-page sketch of David graced the cover of the *Sydney Mail*.[63] He recounted the full tale of his adventures in a public lecture at the university, which proved so popular that he was asked by the University Extension Board to teach an entire course about the expedition for 750 continuing education students.[64] Another series of lectures was organised by the Royal Society, followed by an exhaustive nationwide lecture tour over 1909–10 to raise funds for the publication of the expedition's scientific reports.[65] While recounting his Antarctic experiences, David always had an eye on the future, reminding his audiences that it was Australia's 'bounden duty' to establish a permanent meteorological observatory somewhere in the Antarctic, suggesting that valuable radioactive minerals could be mined there, and reiterating that a lucrative Antarctic fishing industry was available on Australia's doorstep.[66]

David's return to Sydney was followed by that of Mawson and five other shore party members on 16 April, Shackleton on 20 April, and the *Nimrod* later that day. This sparked another flurry of Antarctic events, with 3,500 people cramming into the Town Hall's basement for a civic reception before the expedition members drifted off to be feted at a variety of welcomes, conversaziones and lectures.[67] Shackleton declined offers from commercial promoters to embark on a lucrative Australian tour but did agree to a one-off lecture in Sydney. There were over 7,000 applications for tickets, convincing Shackleton to offer a second lecture. Again, demand for tickets rapidly outstripped physical spaces, so much so that the council was forced to issue a public plea for those without tickets not to go to the venue.[68] With additional seats crammed into spaces beneath the galleries and behind the screen, Shackleton was thought to have attracted 'probably the largest audience that ever attended to hear a lecture in Australia'.[69] Despite the expedition still being thousands of pounds in debt, Shackleton impulsively donated the £512 he earnt from these lectures to a local charity.

Encouraged by the success in Sydney, Shackleton continued to give lectures on an ad-hoc basis. In Melbourne, he gave another sold-out Town Hall lecture, again donating the proceeds to charity, then repeated his talk for an audience of schoolchildren. In Adelaide, he gave another pair of lectures and again donated the proceeds. And during a brief stopover in Fremantle, he agreed to come ashore and deliver one final lecture before continuing on to England. In every case, Shackleton's lectures were sold out and received effusive reviews.[70] Discussing his final lecture in Western Australia, for instance, the *Western Mail* declared that no lecture 'has made, or ever will make, more of an impression upon an audience here', while the *Daily News* declined even to describe it, saying only that 'those who heard it will never forget it—but to offer those who did not hear it a synopsis or a list of slides would be as unsatisfactory as the reading of yesterday's menu to a hungry man'.[71] Such was Shackleton-mania that 'Shackleton' was even submitted to a 1909 competition to pick a name for Australia's new federal capital.[72]

The *Nimrod* itself arrived in Sydney on 20 April. The state government waived all port fees and provided an anchorage at Neutral Bay, but this otherwise quiet spot on the harbour was soon deluged with viewers and visitors.[73] Many prominent Sydneysiders secured coveted invitations to tour the ship, but since these were few and far between, a majority of interested onlookers took to the water. Harbour ferries were seen listing heavily as passengers swarmed to one side to look at the famous little ship, while a few savvy entrepreneurs chartered a vessel to take passengers to the bay, where they 'merely cruised round and round the *Nimrod*'.[74] Eventually, it was announced that, once the necessary repairs had been completed, the ship would be berthed at Circular Quay and thrown open to the public on 3 and 4 May. To avoid overcrowding, tickets were sold as a charity fundraiser. Some 2,000 people descended on the *Nimrod* on the first day, and somewhere between 5,000 and 6,000 on the second. Expedition members were on hand to offer tours of the ship, and accordingly found themselves besieged with requests for autographs and souvenirs.[75] Geologist Raymond Priestley later recalled that demand for souvenirs was so great, and the remuneration for supplying them so lucrative, that 'every scrap of spare wood and rope was disposed of; every scrap of penguin skin or sealskin; every penguin and skua egg; every small piece of erratic rock, found their way into the pockets of enthusiastic sightseers'. When the supply of these souvenirs was exhausted, visitors resorted to cutting apart the rigging, while one enterprising sailor came up with the idea of collecting rocks from the quayside to sell as 'genuine specimens of Erebus lava' at half-a-crown each.[76]

Another highlight of the *Nimrod*'s open days were the sledge dogs housed on the bridge. Puppies born in the Antarctic were given as gifts to prominent local supporters, while David, Shackleton's first and most influential advocate, was permitted to take home his favourite dog, Ambrose.[77] The last of the puppies was intended to be a gift to the Queen when the expedition returned to England, but such was the insatiable demand for polar souvenirs that the dog was stolen by a visitor, sparking an unsuccessful police search.[78]

Despite some suggestions that the Commonwealth purchase the *Nimrod* to undertake further meteorological work in the Antarctic, Shackleton instructed his young first officer, John King Davis, to return the ship to England via a circuitous Southern Ocean route, departing Sydney on 8 May. This final voyage would, said Shackleton, complete the expedition's work by determining whether reported subantarctic islands such as Dougherty, Emerald, Nimrod and the Royal Company's Islands actually existed. If the islands were found, there was a possibility they might harbour untouched fur seal populations that could be exploited by Australia and New Zealand, while if they proved to be phantoms, the voyage would improve the accuracy of ocean charts and collect valuable oceanographic data.[79] In incorporating this work into the *Nimrod*'s homeward voyage and couching it in terms of possible economic benefits and improved maritime safety, Shackleton again demonstrated his understanding of Australian conceptions of the Commonwealth's interests in the Southern Ocean world.

‹ ›

The degree to which the *Nimrod* expedition was reimagined as a quasi-Australian endeavour is remarkable. There were regular references to 'Australia at the Pole', to the 'British–Australian' or 'Shackleton–David' expedition, and to the 'commercial value to Australia' of the expedition's work.[80] The contribution of the Australian members—David, Mawson and Cotton, as well as Victorian pony-handler Bertram Armytage and the Sydney-born captain of the *Koonya* and later *Nimrod*, Frederick Evans—was a major focus of the blanket press coverage. The explorers were commended for 'representing Australia on such an historical occasion' and for doing work that was expected to prove 'of much subsequent value to the country'.[81] The expedition was heralded as a coming of age for Australian science and universities. Australians had excelled in the field, with Mawson proving himself to be 'an Australian Nansen'.[82] Just as significantly, the expedition's scientific reports were primarily produced by Australasian scholars.[83]

Shackleton's expedition marked a significant transformation in Australia's relationship with its southern frontier. By the time the debt-laden explorer arrived in Australia, decades of exploitation, interest, boosterism and lobbying had created an ideological consensus that the Antarctic was a region of especial interest to Australia, that it would become a commercially valuable hinterland in the future, and that Australia's proximity to the region made its exploration both especially beneficial to, and particularly incumbent on, Australia. That these ideas were broadly accepted did not, as the likes of the Melbourne Antarctic committee and the organisers of the NAE found, automatically translate into blank cheques from Australian institutions. Reservations around both the capacity of various projects to advance Australian interests and the capacity of Australian governments and institutions to support them had undercut many proposals in the past.

Unlike his predecessors, however, Shackleton was able to lean on Edgeworth David. A universally respected figure with extensive political contacts, David mediated between Shackleton's objectives and Australian ideas and interests to persuade the federal government to set aside any lingering reservations and ensure the expedition could depart. The Commonwealth therefore became the expedition's largest financial supporter, the shore party became one-quarter Australian, and Shackleton made changes to his program to cater to Australian interests, such as handing over his meteorological data to the Commonwealth's newly established Bureau of Meteorology and instructing David and Mawson to search for signs of valuable minerals in Victoria Land. Shackleton was only too willing to cater to Australian ideas and interests to ensure his oily-rag operation could proceed and he could chase his dream of being the first to reach the South Pole. Australians were only too willing to co-opt an expedition and reimagine it as essentially Australian. The result was that the Antarctic was catapulted to mainstream attention, laying the foundations for a far more active and expansive role for the Commonwealth in the world to its south.

6

'A GOLDEN EL DORADO DOWN SOUTH'

Australia and the Race for the Pole

The Arctic forests and tundra of Yukon and Alaska had, Edgeworth David told a packed audience at Sydney's Town Hall, at one time been universally considered 'useless'. Yet since 1897 these territories had produced something like £40 million worth of gold. The goldfields clustered around the Yukon River were, at 64°N, virtually as close to the North Pole as the coast of the Australian Antarctic was to the South Pole. And yet, despite the remote location and Arctic conditions, tens of millions of dollars worth of gold had been extracted within twelve years from territories barely a sixth the size of the Australian sector of the Antarctic continent. Drawing on every ounce of his authority as a geologist and the discoverer of the south magnetic pole, David reminded his audience that the Antarctic was riddled with geological markers that indicated the likely presence of gold. When NSW lieutenant-governor William Cullen took to the stage to give thanks for David's address, he issued a final rallying cry to the crowd: 'Professor David has offered you a golden El Dorado down south. Let us see if Australia cannot have some share in it.'[1]

Cullen's evocative turn of phrase—'a golden El Dorado down south'—perfectly captures the idea that, by 1911, had permeated Australian discussions of Antarctica and the wider Southern Ocean world for the better part of a century. Belief that this region on Australia's virtual doorstep, overlooked and undervalued by other nations, could be developed into a source of unimaginable wealth had underpinned how and why Australians engaged with the Antarctic. There had always been other factors, of course: geopolitical concerns, improvements to the safety of sea routes, a greater understanding of Australian weather, the international status that came with investing in geographical discovery and scientific research, nationalism, and simply an interest in drama and adventure. But the dream of a golden El Dorado had always been at the core of the assumption that the southern frontier offered enormous opportunities, and that by virtue of proximity and history those opportunities should naturally fall to Australia. Now, in June 1911, David, Cullen and others were mobilising this idea to raise funds for the first expedition organised, funded and staffed primarily in Australia.

David took to the Town Hall stage at a relatively low ebb in the campaign to get the Australasian Antarctic Expedition (AAE) off the ground. After an early burst of substantial donations from wealthy individuals, momentum had slowed and the expedition's leader, Douglas Mawson, had decamped to London to solicit aid and obtain supplies. Mawson's allies in Australia had therefore deployed the familiar language of opportunities, rights and responsibilities to rally popular support and persuade governments and individuals to get behind the AAE. And these arguments struck a chord. Mawson raised the funds he needed to outfit his expedition and recruit an extensive scientific staff, primarily from among the young graduates of Australasian universities. The expedition that eventually departed Hobart in December 1911 was, as Tom Griffiths has argued, 'a distinctively Australian endeavour, driven by nationalism, a Southern Hemisphere sensibility about the need to know one's own backyard, and a keen sense of Australia's distinct geopolitical interests'.[2]

This was not, however, a sudden burst of Australian sentiment. The distinctly Australian sensibilities and interests noted by Griffiths and others were products of the ideas, the proposals and the relentless boosterism that had circulated for decades, experiencing both moments of enormous influence and spells of irrelevance. And, importantly, these ideas had proved malleable as well as durable. The idea that the Antarctic was a sphere of special interest, influence and opportunity for Australians was remarkably flexible. It could justify significant investment, both public and private, in Mawson's self-consciously Australian expedition. Yet it could just as easily allow ventures organised overseas (often with little awareness of, or concern for, how Australians imagined their own Antarctic interests) to be, through some Australian connection or another, reimagined as somehow Australian too. This chapter, then, explores the influence of these ideas on how Australia and Australians engaged with the myriad expeditions that headed south between 1910 and 1912, a period commonly known as the 'race for the pole'.

‹ ›

When it was revealed in 1909 that Shackleton had fallen 180 kilometres short of his goal, there was interest from many quarters in mounting another expedition to finally reach the pole. Shackleton almost immediately entered negotiations with the *Daily Mail* to fund a fresh attempt. In Scotland, William Speirs Bruce was working on a plan of unprecedented ambition, a transantarctic journey from the Weddell Sea to the Ross Sea via the pole. In the United States, Robert Peary, just returned from the North Pole, was rumoured to be working with the National Geographic Society on an Antarctic journey. In Norway, Belgian Antarctic Expedition veteran and Fridtjof Nansen protégé Roald Amundsen had been planning an attempt on the North Pole but, after hearing reports it had been claimed, began work on an expedition to the south. In Germany and Japan, army officers Wilhelm Filchner and Nobu Shirase respectively were actively preparing national expeditions of their own. And finally, Shackleton's former commander Robert Scott, having long harboured plans for a follow-up to the NAE, seized the opportunity presented by Shackleton's misfortune to officially announce his own plans.[3]

One of Scott's key concerns was to assemble a party capable of simultaneously surpassing Shackleton's farthest south mark and outstripping his expedition's scientific achievements. At the top of his list was the 'Australian Nansen' Douglas Mawson, who had proven himself an exceptional polar traveller and field scientist. Scott saw Mawson as someone who could virtually guarantee the success of the polar journey, though it cannot have escaped his notice that the appointment of prominent Australians had also opened the door for the Commonwealth's £5,000 grant to Shackleton. When Mawson visited London in January 1910, Scott used the offer of a place in his final polar party to try to recruit him. Mawson, however, was far more interested in exploring the region directly south of Australia that he and David had visited briefly during their journey to the magnetic pole. He therefore offered to join the new expedition if Scott would place him in command of a second four-man party based in Adélie Land. Scott refused, so Mawson resolved to organise his own project and approached Shackleton for assistance in fundraising. Scott, meanwhile, harboured hopes that Mawson would change his mind, and kept the Australian's name on the list of expedition members until the last possible moment.[4]

Even without Mawson, Scott hoped to receive similar support from Australia and New Zealand to Shackleton. Scott therefore invited the Commonwealth's official secretary in London, Muirhead Collins, to represent Australia at a meeting of the committee he had formed to oversee his expedition. The secretary of Australia's Department of External Affairs, Atlee Hunt, barred Collins from attending in an official capacity to avoid committing the Commonwealth to contributing financially but encouraged him to attend privately and report back. Undeterred by this lukewarm reaction, Scott wrote personally to NSW premier Charles Wade to ask him to press the expedition's case to the federal government. This request, essentially asking the Commonwealth to fund a venture following the same route to the South Pole as Shackleton while undertaking the same scientific work in the same part of Antarctica, was also declined.[5] Much like the NAE a decade earlier, Scott found himself in charge of an expedition that was generating enormous interest and enthusiasm in the Australian press yet struggling to persuade government officials of its merits.

Just as Shackleton had done in 1907, Scott's expedition departed Britain in June 1910 on the refurbished Arctic whaler *Terra Nova* with its finances under a cloud. Scott made his way to South Africa, where he raised £1,274 in grants and donations, while his wife, renowned sculptor Kathleen Scott, and the expedition's chief scientist, Edward Wilson, headed to Melbourne. On arrival, Scott and Wilson made it abundantly clear in press interviews that the expedition needed to receive at least £5,000 in Australia to proceed as planned.[6] This plea seemingly sparked Australia's Antarctic enthusiasts into action, with the tenor of the press coverage promptly shifting from description to advocacy. *The Sydney Morning Herald*, for instance, urged the Commonwealth to again come to the rescue, noting that Shackleton's expedition had proved 'a splendid advertisement for Australian science', that Australia would be represented in Scott's party by geologists Griffith Taylor and Frank Debenham, and that Australia would benefit practically from research that might, among other things, identify minerals that would see the Antarctic become 'a southern Klondyke'.[7] Similar arguments were made by AAAS and by the man who had fast-tracked Shackleton's grant through parliament, former prime minister Alfred Deakin.[8] By the time Scott and *Terra Nova* reached Melbourne in October, public sentiment was clearly in favour of government intervention. Bowing to the pressure, acting prime minister WM Hughes announced a grant of £2,500.[9]

The decision to offer only half of the required sum attracted criticism, with *The Argus* notably lamenting the 'niggardly treatment of a British–Australian expedition' by the Commonwealth.[10] Some supporters in Sydney organised a public meeting to begin lobbying Hughes to double the grant. The letter produced by this committee was steeped in familiar ideas about Australia's Antarctic interests, urging the federal government not to 'shirk its obvious responsibility' and dwelling on the notion that the expected economic benefits of Antarctic exploration would 'naturally belong' to Australia, and thus 'should be secured by the Commonwealth'.[11] Other supporters rallied to provide in-kind donations. The Powell Wood Process Company in Sydney, for instance, agreed to provide the treated timber Scott needed for sledges, and invoked the belief that this British expedition's work 'was of so important a character to Australia' that they would do so free of charge.[12] Still others set about trying to raise the remaining £2,500 themselves. A local subscription list was opened, while the AAAS council invited Scott to give a fundraising lecture at the newly constructed Glaciarium, Sydney's largest venue. An estimated 5,000 people crammed into the cavernous ice rink, forcing Scott to deliver his lecture from atop a table in the centre of the room to ensure he was heard. As calls for Australians to step in and save the expedition reached fever pitch, Samuel Hordern, owner of a prominent Sydney department store, saved the day with a £2,500 donation.[13]

As Scott, funding secured, made his way to Christchurch and then onwards to Ross Island, *The Sydney Morning Herald* reviewed the expedition's prospects. 'If it is humanly possible,' the paper declared, Scott would 'annex the Pole for England—and the Commonwealth. For it will be our Pole, too, since part of the cost of the expedition is being borne by Australia'.[14] This comment reflects a peculiar feature of Australian thinking about the Antarctic. By relying on Australian support or Australian staff, projects organised elsewhere could be reimagined as at least partly Australian in character. Even a small stake in an expedition was sufficient for its victories and—as the reaction to Scott's demise would soon demonstrate—its failures to be understood as Australian victories and Australian failures. This helps to explain how the idea of Australia having a special interest in the Antarctic could be sustained and replicated over several decades, even as effort after effort to launch an actual Australian expedition fell apart.

As with Shackleton three years earlier, the fortunes of Scott's expedition were a subject of relentless press coverage. Griffith Taylor followed in the footsteps of his mentor, David, by penning an evocative account of the voyage to satiate the demand for Antarctic news.[15] Even more significantly, controversy erupted on the eve of *Terra Nova*'s departure over a decision by Roald Amundsen to challenge Scott in what was now turning into a race to the South Pole. Amundsen, veteran of the first expedition to overwinter within the Antarctic Circle and commander of the first ship to navigate the North-West Passage, had received significant backing from the Norwegian Government, monarchy and private donors to lead an expedition to the North Pole. His preparations had been stymied by news that the Americans Robert Peary and Frederick Cook had independently claimed to have reached the pole first in 1909, but Amundsen publicly insisted there was still valuable work to be done in the Arctic and continued making arrangements for a five-year voyage. He departed Norway in August 1910, but announced on departure from Madeira a month later that he would first attempt to reach the South Pole before continuing to the Arctic.[16]

The secretive nature of Amundsen's entry into the race for the South Pole was controversial enough; his decision to establish a base at the Bay of Whales, an inlet on the Ross Ice Shelf only 670 kilometres east of Scott's base at Ross Island, was potentially incendiary. Thus, as Scott sailed south and simmered, the ethics of Amundsen's actions were debated in Australia. One view was that Amundsen's conduct was in 'bad taste and unsportsmanlike', but this sentiment was far from unanimous.[17] Others deemed it 'ridiculous to even infer that Amundsen has taken an unfair advantage of his rival'.[18] Scott insisted the news didn't change his plans, but he was forced into one alteration. After initially rejecting Mawson's suggestion of a second party, Scott had returned to the idea and arranged for a six-man party to establish a second base in King Edward VII Land. However, after encountering Amundsen at the nearby Bay of Whales, this party instead established its base at Cape Adare, which Mawson had informed Scott was to be one of the bases for his planned Australasian expedition, sparking further controversy over Scott's intrusion into the Australian sphere. Mawson personally weighed into this escalating debate, suggesting that both Amundsen and Scott's actions were a breach of 'polar etiquette' and warning that, in Scott's case, 'some dissatisfaction in the Commonwealth is inevitable'.[19]

It might be expected that Australians would have rallied around Scott and roundly condemned Amundsen. They were, after all, 'Australian Britons'—British subjects with close imperial ties to, not to mention a moderate financial stake in, Scott's British expedition.[20] That discussions around the 'race to the pole' were considerably more nuanced, and even extended to criticism of Scott's infringement of Mawson's rights, is indicative of the complexity of Australian attitudes towards the Antarctic at this time. The belief that any extension of Antarctic knowledge would bring considerable benefits to Australia had become a truism, leading to a convention of offering at least some support to anyone venturing south from an Australasian port. There was some tension between this convention and the emerging belief, articulated most ardently by Mawson, that Australia had a discrete sphere of influence in the Antarctic. For the most part, though, these attitudes did not come into outright conflict, a fact seen most clearly in how the Japanese and Norwegian expeditions were received when they made their way to Sydney and Hobart respectively.

‹ ›

Like Amundsen, Japanese army lieutenant Nobu Shirase had harboured dreams of Arctic exploration before turning his attention southwards when the North Pole was claimed in 1909. Echoing claims about the potential for Antarctic exploration to enhance Australia's international standing, Shirase argued that a Japanese expedition would be a boon to that nation's status. This argument failed to win government funding but it did secure backing from former foreign minister Shigenobu Ōkuma, who agreed to serve as president of the expedition's supporters' association, and from the *Asahi* newspaper group, which solicited donations through the popular press. This approach helped Shirase secure sufficient funds to proceed, but political and institutional rivalries meant that the expedition alienated Japan's government, navy, universities and scientific societies. One result was that Shirase struggled to recruit a single reputable scientist to join the Japanese Antarctic Expedition (JAE).[21]

The JAE's ship, *Kainan-maru*, left Tokyo on 29 November 1910. Little was known of the venture outside Japan, and the tone of the press coverage in Australia was dismissive. Mawson was particularly critical, castigating Shirase for breaching the 'unwritten laws of etiquette regarding scientists making for the same ground' and speculating that the expedition was merely cover for a sealing venture.[22] Australian commentators' low expectations for the JAE were seemingly confirmed when *Kainan-maru* appeared unexpectedly in Sydney Harbour on 1 May 1911, having come within sight of Antarctica in March before being forced back by ice and storms. Shirase had decided to winter in Sydney before making a fresh attempt in the summer of 1911–12, but admitted that his decision was tinged with concern given Australia's reputation as a 'country where anti-Japanese sentiments were widespread'.[23] Contrary to his expectations, however, local and federal authorities were overwhelmingly supportive, including agreeing to treat *Kainan-maru* as a diplomatic vessel to ensure it was exempt from the terms of the Immigration Restriction Act.[24] Crowds of Sydneysiders flocked to see the ship when it arrived at its anchorage at Double Bay, with many onlookers invited on board for a tour. Soon, Shirase received permission to establish a winter camp on shore at a site at Parsley Bay owned by Vaucluse Council.[25]

The explorers erected the prefabricated huts and tents intended for their Antarctic base and settled into the routines of camp life.[26] There was a degree of xenophobic anxiety about their presence, including a protest by nearby residents and concerns raised by military officials about the proximity of the camp to fortifications at South Head. Yet these were swiftly set aside, with Vaucluse Council voting down the protest and the Sydney press ridiculing the idea that the Japanese might be spies, pointing out that spies would hardly use an Antarctic expedition as cover when such an expedition was guaranteed to 'attract the attention not only of Australia but of the whole world'.[27]

Any lingering resentments about the camp were diffused by the positive relationships that developed between explorers and locals. The camp became a tourist attraction, with the crowds of up to 300 people visiting each day on weekends eventually forcing Shirase to implement visiting hours and a receiving area. Perhaps the most enthusiastic visitor was 21-year-old actress Dot Miller, who visited six times to collect signatures, messages and even watercolour paintings in her autograph book.[28] Some of these visitors proposed initiating a public fundraising campaign for Australians to support the expedition, but the offer was politely declined by the Japanese consul-general, who promised that sufficient funds were available in Japan and that the expatriate community in Sydney would provide any necessary assistance in the interim.[29] Local families struck up especially strong relationships. Publican Alexander Hilliar offered his services as guide whenever the explorers wanted to travel into the city, while his son Robert recalled having free run of the camp with the other young children of Parsley Bay families.[30]

In June, Shirase hosted an elaborate party for around 300 Vaucluse locals and Japanese expatriates to celebrate the coronation of King George V. The following week, the Vaucluse Debating Society hosted the expedition members and expatriates for a lecture by the expedition's scientist, Terutarō Takeda.[31] Even more significantly, Edgeworth David took Shirase and Takeda under his wing, hosting them at Sydney University, visiting them at the camp, introducing them to Mawson, giving them advice on polar navigation, and supplying them with charts, books and scientific instruments. At David's urging, Shirase abandoned his quest for the South Pole, recasting the JAE's second voyage as a scientific expedition to explore King Edward VII Land, where no expedition had ever landed.[32]

Fresh supplies and two new recruits arrived from Japan in October, and by 19 November the explorers were clearing away the final traces of their camp and preparing to depart. Press interest was intense, and public enthusiasm was on clear display when crowds gathered at Circular Quay four hours ahead of *Kainan-maru*'s departure. Wellwishers came on board to farewell the explorers personally, including David and a party from the university, the Japanese consulate's entire staff, several Japanese expatriates, and many of the regular camp visitors. As well as being greeted by large crowds at Circular Quay and Vaucluse, the ship was escorted by a flotilla of small boats. David remained on board until the last moment, when Shirase presented him with a remarkable gift. A sponsor had given Shirase a sword, forged in 1644 by a revered swordsmith, to take to the pole. In a rare instance of such a culturally significant sword being presented to a foreigner, Shirase gave it to David as a mark of respect and gratitude.[33]

The JAE's achievements were modest, although they did become the first party to make a landing at King Edward VII Land and claimed a smell stretch of land for Japan. The expedition did not deliver the boost to Japan's international reputation that Shirase expected. Indeed, when Takeda wrote to the Royal Geographical Society with a description of the JAE's discoveries in King Edward VII Land and a request for names such as *Yamato Yukihara* ('Japanese Snow Plain') to be added to maps of the Antarctic, secretary J Scott Keltie ignored him, believing the Japanese discoveries had all previously been mapped by Scott.[34] Furthermore, Shirase's own government, opposed to the expedition from its conception, refused to affirm his territorial claim.[35]

‹ ›

The JAE was potentially the greatest challenge to the idea that Australia should support any kind of Antarctic research. In an era of profound anti-Asian sentiment in Australian politics and discourse, and with the Commonwealth's foremost Antarctic scientist warning that the JAE could be a front for sealing in the seas to Australia's south, it would have been unsurprising if Shirase was met with the hostility he anticipated. Instead, Australia's Antarctic enthusiasts sought to aid the JAE and to celebrate its connections to Australia. The same phenomenon was evident in the treatment of Scott's bitter rival Amundsen when he arrived in Hobart on the morning of 7 March 1912. A restless crowd formed around the wharves, hoping for news, while a group of reporters clubbed together to hire a steam launch to take them out to Amundsen's ship *Fram*, only to hastily turn around when they spotted Amundsen sneaking ashore. Amundsen went about his business, visiting Norway's consul and stopping by a post office to send telegrams, without answering questions. He was amiable and apologetic, but he and his staff steadfastly refused to reveal anything.[36] Amundsen's reticence was described as 'aggravating' by one paper, which pointed out that 'the world is waiting to fall at his feet, and acclaim him a hero'.[37] But silence also generated rumours, such as an erroneous claim that Amundsen's mysterious cable had read 'Scott discovered Pole'.[38]

It was not until 11 March that Amundsen's account of his discovery of the South Pole, sold exclusively to London's *Daily Chronicle* and *The New York Times*, was finally published in Australia.[39] There was little resentment evident in the Australian reaction to the news. For example, *The Sydney Morning Herald*, which had proudly proclaimed that if Scott claimed the pole it would 'be our Pole, too', showed little bitterness towards the Norwegian interloper for snatching the pole from Britain and Australia. Instead, it observed that Amundsen had scrupulously avoided infringing on Scott's intended route and forged his own path, meaning that he did not breach the explorer's 'code of honour'.[40] Even the more critical responses were mild. The *Brisbane Courier*, for instance, commented rather churlishly that while Amundsen had discovered the geographical pole, David had discovered the magnetic pole, 'which may prove of even greater importance'.[41]

As news of his achievement spread, Amundsen was feted in Tasmania. There was the now standard welcome by the state government, local council and Royal Society, though there were also calls for a bigger ceremony that would allow the public to celebrate this 'epoch-making event'.[42] There was even talk of renaming Murray Street, where the explorer had stayed, 'Amundsen Street', and of *Fram*'s anchorage becoming 'Fram Cove'.[43] The *Fram* itself became a popular attraction, and a cameraman travelled from Sydney to film the ship.[44] Amundsen, meanwhile, signed copies of a map of Antarctica produced by a local bookseller, which were sold as souvenirs.[45]

Carlyle Smythe, an enterprising lecture agent best known for organising Mark Twain's 1895 Australasian tour, had contacted Amundsen's brother Leon in Christiania as soon as he heard of the Norwegian's Antarctic plans. They had struck a deal for a short Australasian lecture tour, then sent the contract south with *Fram*, making it the 'first contract ever made in the continent of Antarctica'.[46] In accordance with this agreement, the 'most widely-talked-of man in the world' made his way to Adelaide on 20 March 1912 to share his account, photographs and even some breathtaking colourised films of the polar journey for the first time. While there were complaints about Smythe charging extortionate admission fees, Amundsen's lectures, especially the films, were said to have held audiences 'spellbound'.[47] After popular lectures in Adelaide, Melbourne, Geelong, Sydney, Brisbane and New Zealand, Amundsen headed for Buenos Aires and then Europe.[48]

‹ ›

While Scott, Shirase and Amundsen all captured substantial interest in Australia, the most significant expedition of this period, as far as Australians were concerned, was Mawson's AAE. Having rejected Scott's offer, Mawson turned to Shackleton for assistance in organising an expedition to explore 4,000 kilometres of unmapped coast west of Cape Adare. Shackleton offered to lead the expedition himself, with Mawson as chief scientist, and secured vague promises of £10,000. Despite his initial enthusiasm, however, Shackleton's interest waned as he turned his attention instead to some risky investment schemes. When Mawson returned to Australia in

May 1910, he left with an agreement that if Shackleton decided not to command the expedition, he would support Mawson to lead it instead.[49] Thus, when Mawson arrived in Sydney, he outlined his vision for an Australian expedition to Adélie Land. This region, he explained,

> is the nearest part to Australia, and it should be Australia's special duty and her obligation to contribute to the world at large whatever store of secrets this land holds. Whatever material of economic value—gold and mineral wealth, whale oil, seal oil, or anything else it may contain—will of course be to the advantage of Australia.[50]

Commenting on Mawson's proposal, *The Argus* made the familiar case that 'from an economic, scientific, and ethical point of view, it is surely the duty of Australia to undertake further exploration in this great sister continent that lies so near to our shores'.[51] The *Daily Telegraph* was similarly positive, openly describing it as a 'chance to acquire a new territory'.[52] FE Du Faur, an Antarctic booster since the 1880s, declared that 'the time has arrived when the Commonwealth should recognise its duty, and take an active part in Antarctic research'.[53] Mawson, careful not to jeopardise Scott's fundraising, did not actually appeal for donations, but he did continue promoting the idea that it was Australia's 'moral duty' to explore the Antarctic, including giving lectures in his full *Nimrod* sledging outfit to generate interest.[54]

By December 1910, with Scott gone and Shackleton confirming he wouldn't be taking command, Mawson was finally free to begin the arduous task of raising the £40,000 the AAE would require. He travelled to Sydney the following month to launch his fundraising campaign at the annual AAAS meeting, promoting his proposal in a series of press interviews en route. In these interviews, Mawson emphasised the political dimensions of his proposition. He explained that he hoped to take possession of the entire region lying south of Australia 'and hoist the Australian flag upon it', took to calling this area 'Australian Antarctica', and warned that if the expedition did not depart in 1911, 'the unique object may have to be abandoned to a foreign nation, several of which are already pressing upon the Australasian Antarctic'.[55]

Arguments about territory, sovereignty, economic development and Australia's international standing were also central to Mawson's argument in the paper he presented to the AAAS's geographical section, which broke attendance records when the other sections postponed their sessions to allow all delegates to attend.[56] He insisted that the region south of Australia should be 'cherished by Australians' both because of its proximity and because no other stretch of the Antarctic 'held forth such advantages for the collection of scientific data and for industrial pursuits'. He also reiterated his warning that if Australia did not act soon, 'foreign nations will step in and secure this most valuable portion of the Antarctic continent for themselves, and for ever from the control of Australia'.[57] In closing the paper dubbed 'a stirring appeal to Australians', Mawson asked:

> Can our scientific societies remain content to allow distant countries to poach on their inherited preserves? Can Australians remain heedless of this land of great potentialities lying at our doors? Can our national conscience remain unstirred in the face of achievements to be accomplished, achievements such as have ever formed girders in the constitution of nations.[58]

The response to Mawson's proposal was almost universally positive. A *Daily Telegraph* leader declared that 'there may be pecuniary possibilities, but whether they are present or absent the obligation to explore and classify and know is Australia's'.[59] *The Mercury* focused more on the opportunity to 'alter the impression which exists of the aims and ideals of Australians internationally by despatching an all-Australian scientific venture'.[60] The AAAS pledged an unprecedented grant—£1,000, a third of its savings—and assembled an influential committee to oversee Mawson's fundraising, including David, Adelaide University historian GC Henderson, and Melbourne University chemist Orme Masson.[61] They swiftly persuaded Hordern, tobacco magnates Hugh Dixson and Hugh Denison, Melbourne philanthropist Roderick Murchison and SA businessman Robert Barr Smith to make substantial donations.[62] Masson and Mawson met with federal defence minister George Pearce to request government support, assuring him that the expedition would not only do important scientific work but would also 'make the occupation of this land profitable to Australia'.[63] Expanding on this idea of occupation in an interview as he left Melbourne, Mawson suggested it was 'fairly certain that settlement in a limited way will be made upon this coast during the next few years'. Whaling, sealing, tourism, and mining coal, gold and tin were all mooted as industries that would underpin the imminent occupation of the Australian Antarctic.[64]

Leaving further fundraising in the committee's hands, Mawson decamped to London to collect Shackleton's £10,000 and obtain equipment that could not be acquired in Australia. He soon found, however, that the money Shackleton had promised was mysteriously no longer available. This left Mawson and JK Davis, formerly *Nimrod*'s chief officer and now the AAE's second-in-command, together with Australian high commissioner George Reid, to scramble for donations in Britain. Reid used his connections to secure a £2,000 grant from the British Government, while Mawson aggressively lobbied the many wealthy Australians and New Zealanders who had made their way to London for the coronation of George V, from opera singer Nellie Melba to pastoralist George Buckley, the New Zealander who had impulsively joined *Nimrod* for a trip to the Antarctic Circle with nothing but his briefcase and a summer suit. The Australians' fundraising efforts infuriated Scott's supporters, who were themselves appealing for an additional £15,000 and felt Mawson had blocked the possibility of further Australian donations, but they succeeded in raising £9,000 for the AAE, just enough for Mawson to buy a ship. He had hoped that the Commonwealth might fund the purchase of *Pourquoi Pas?*, purpose-built for Charcot's French Antarctic expedition in 1908, with a view to it becoming Australia's official polar research vessel. But with the federal government unwilling to commit to a polar vessel and Mawson unable to afford either *Pourquoi Pas?* or his second choice, Bruce's *Scotia*, he was forced to settle for the rundown 35-year-old Newfoundland whaler *Aurora*.[65]

After the initial surge of support, fundraising proved more difficult for the AAAS committee. Once again, then, they mobilised the language of rights, responsibilities and opportunities to rally support, securing another influx of small donations.[66] Mawson, though, was the true silver-tongued master of Antarctic boosterism.[67] When he returned to Australia in July 1911, he threw fuel on the fire of expectations that the AAE would finally unlock the potential of Australia's southern frontier. The vision of the Australian Antarctic articulated by Mawson was of an Australian colony administered by the Commonwealth. If the government could guarantee it would 'ratify possession' of the lands he intended to explore and claim, Mawson was confident his supporters would contribute the necessary capital to develop these lands into a profitable Australian territory.[68] If the Commonwealth failed to act, however, he warned that it would 'be a matter for continual regret to Australia if foreign nations opened up the coastline so near our own territory'.[69] Mawson's vision then permeated wider discussions about the expedition's significance, so that *The Argus*, for instance, felt one of the key features of the AAE was 'to pave the way for an economic future for a land which should someday become part of the Commonwealth'.[70]

Mawson continued to add new industries to the list of those he expected to develop, suggesting ice harvesting and fish trawling as possibilities alongside the usual whaling, sealing, mining and tourism.[71] And even when Mawson departed for the Antarctic, the AAE's business manager, Conrad Eitel, continued to stress the centrality of the Antarctic to Australia's future in Mawsonian terms. In October 1912, for instance, Eitel suggested that Perth's proximity to Antarctica would ensure that the Australian Antarctic would eventually outcompete the eastern states to supply Western Australia with coal, adding that 'the advent of such an industry would mean that Antarctica would very soon be brought under the effective administration of the Australian Commonwealth'.[72]

This talk of occupation and effective administration was laden with meaning. In the early twentieth century, the doctrine of effective occupation was the primary way a territory not already under sovereignty could be claimed. Discovering or exploring a territory and proclaiming sovereignty over it might give a state an inchoate claim to that land, but actually occupying and administering it was necessary for the claim to be recognised as legitimate. It was not entirely clear what effective occupation might entail in a hostile or uninhabitable territory like the Antarctic, but discovery followed by a proclamation of sovereignty and the exercise of authority through the regulation of industries, as Mawson urged, would make for a solid and defensible claim.[73] When Mawson and his allies talked of occupation and effective administration in this way, they were advocating for Australian control of a bona-fide Antarctic colony.

Mawson's unabashed boosterism and the sustained lobbying by his supporters ultimately did the trick, unlocking the large public grants the AAE still required. SA premier John Verran announced that his state had 'a duty to support the venture' and granted £5,000. This was followed by news of £7,000 from New South Wales, £5,000 from the Commonwealth (to the outrage of Opposition leader Joseph Cook, who was dismayed that a state government had offered more than the federal) and £6,000 from Victoria.[74] Promises of in-kind support flowed in, too, from the construction of the expedition's prefabricated huts by a consortium of Sydney construction firms, to daily fish donations by Hobart fishers to keep the expedition's dogs fed as they awaited departure.[75]

During these frenetic final days, Mawson also made a relatively late addition to his program. The possibility of establishing wireless contact between Australia and Antarctica for the immediate sharing of meteorological data had been suggested to Shackleton and Scott during discussions about federal grants, but neither had deemed the request practicable. Mawson, however, was willing to establish an additional base at Macquarie Island to serve as both meteorological observatory and wireless relay station. The Macquarie base would make wireless communication with Mawson's main base possible, while also allowing the Meteorological Bureau to assess the value of data from Macquarie Island for weather forecasting.[76] The catch was that Mawson now needed to staff and supply three bases, a task that was beyond the *Aurora*. Hobart's Queen's Pier therefore became a hub of frenzied activity as supplies were unloaded, re-sorted and split between *Aurora* and the steamer *Toroa*, which had been chartered to take people and equipment as far as Macquarie.[77]

With the AAE's departure in December 1911, Australian engagement with the expedition settled into a familiar pattern. When the ships returned, they brought with them accounts of the voyage and of Mawson's establishment of a base at a site he dubbed Commonwealth Bay.[78] Stray remarks were seized on, such as Davis's announcement that he had spotted right whales in the Australian Antarctic, sparking another intense burst of discussion about the prospect of forming an Australian whaling company to exploit them.[79] The *Aurora* was thrown open to the public when it returned to Sydney for repairs in April 1912, including an open day for school groups that aimed to impress upon children 'that this is an Australian expedition making investigations for the benefit of Australians'.[80] And there were opportunities for audiences to become acquainted with the expedition's work through a film based on the voyage and the establishment of the three bases, screened widely under titles such as *Australians to the Antarctic*, occasionally in conjunction with lectures by the likes of David and Davis.[81] As historian Robert Dixon has shown, these kinds of film screenings were in truth complex multimedia events, a blend of verbal and visual, local and international, old and new technologies, reportage and popular entertainment, fact and self-constructed myth.[82] Such events were at the heart of how Australians came to imagine and understand the Antarctic.

The wireless connection between Australia, Macquarie Island and Mawson's base at Commonwealth Bay allowed for other novel forms of interaction. The wireless' main function was to send regular meteorological reports from Macquarie to Hobart, but some enthusiasts saw it as a chance to go beyond receiving multimedia representations of the Antarctic and actually send messages of their own there. For example, the staff and students of Fort Street High School clubbed together to pay for a message to the school's most famous alumnus, Mawson.[83] Eitel, meanwhile, saw the expensively assembled wireless equipment as a press asset, and arranged to sell subscriptions to wireless reports from Mawson about life in the Antarctic to various newspapers for £1,000.[84] But while there was regular contact with Macquarie Island, wireless communication with Commonwealth Bay proved sporadic and unreliable due to the area's exceptionally strong katabatic winds, magnetic interference, and the limitations of the instruments. Then, on 13 October, communication ended completely when the main base's wireless mast toppled in a blizzard.[85]

The AAAS committee was now forced to downplay public fears about the lack of communication from Mawson.[86] Eitel, meanwhile, panicked at the prospect of losing his press deal. After contemplating suing the company that had provided the wireless equipment, Eitel resorted to fabricating a message to preserve his deal, insisting that a very faint message from Mawson had missed its intended target at Macquarie Island and been received in Hobart.[87] As a result of this kerfuffle, when Davis took the *Aurora* back to Commonwealth Bay in December 1912 to collect Mawson's party, he also brought with him new wireless equipment, a new wireless operator, and Conrad Eitel, who felt compelled to join the ship personally to talk to Mawson about the 'important matter' of the press deal.[88] Eitel never got the chance to raise the issue, however. He arrived to discover Mawson and two companions had failed to return from a sledging expedition. With time running out for Davis to collect the AAE's second party, based 2,410 kilometres further west on the Shackleton Ice Shelf, a five-man party agreed to spend a second winter at Commonwealth Bay in the hope of finding the missing men.[89]

Wireless communication did improve during that second winter, and it was by wireless that news of Mawson's remarkable survival and the deaths of his companions Xavier Mertz and

Belgrave Ninnis was shared. This story captured the attention of the Australian press, sparking a debate about whether the gains to science that came from Antarctic expeditions justified such a loss of life, and forcing Mawson's allies to begin raising funds to outfit an unexpected third voyage south.[90]

7

'UNFAIR ADVANTAGE'

Rights and Responsibilities in the Australian Antarctic

In the closing months of 1914, when all eyes were on the war in Europe and the conflicts that were already rippling around the world, a one-eyed man arrived in Sydney and swindled the Commonwealth out of £4,595 worth of goods and services. Aeneas Mackintosh, a former merchant navy officer who had lost his eye to a cargo hook while serving on Shackleton's *Nimrod* expedition six years earlier, had found himself in charge of a life or death mission to mount an expedition to Antarctica. Shackleton's attempt to reinvent himself as a businessman with mining interests in Hungary had fared poorly, and the restless explorer had once again turned his gaze south. Adopting the preposterously ambitious plan to cross the Antarctic continent from the Weddell Sea to the Ross Sea developed and abandoned by WS Bruce, Shackleton set about raising £60,000 for the Imperial Trans-Antarctic Expedition (ITAE) in December 1913. The plan required two parties in two ships. Shackleton would command the main Weddell Sea party and lead the trans-continental journey himself. Mackintosh, who felt he had unfinished business in the Antarctic because his eye injury had cost him a place in Shackleton's shore party in 1908, was given command of the Ross Sea party, charged with laying a string of depots on the Ross Ice Shelf.[1]

Mackintosh's mission was prosaic compared to other polar journeys, but the stakes were high. The trans-continental party could not carry sufficient food to survive the journey, so failure to place the depots correctly would condemn Shackleton and his companions to certain death. Adding to the sense of urgency was the fact that Shackleton had not, prior to his departure from England, decided whether he would attempt the crossing in the summer of 1914–15 or overwinter somewhere in the Weddell Sea sector and cross the following summer. To ensure the depots were ready for an immediate crossing, Mackintosh needed to leave Australia by the end of November. But unfortunately for him, war and funding shortfalls had conspired to leave him with an understaffed crew and limited supplies, and relying on the battered *Aurora*—still unrepaired after the last of its three back-to-back voyages to Commonwealth Bay—to get his party to Ross Island. With no funds available to fix the ship or purchase supplies for the voyage, Mackintosh threw himself at the mercy of the federal government and the Australian public.

Naturally, the war was the Commonwealth's priority, but prime minister Andrew Fisher was nonetheless responsive to Mackintosh's pleas. Knowing that Shackleton and his companions would die if Mackintosh failed, Fisher granted him free use of the naval docks at Sydney's Cockatoo Island and agreed to fund repairs up to a firm limit of £500. By the time *Aurora* finally departed on 15 December, weeks behind schedule, it had undergone repairs to the tune of £3,938. Mackintosh had also helped himself to £657 worth of naval stores and equipment. His ballooning spending had caused concern, but with Antarctic explorers' survival at stake, the chief of the Commonwealth Naval Board, William Creswell, had reluctantly accepted that 'there is no other course but to accept the position of fitting out and deferring the question of payment'.[2]

On its own, this is a moderately amusing story about how a one-eyed sailor chanced his luck and fleeced the federal government and navy. But it is a story that cannot truly be viewed on its own. This was the third time in two years that Australians had been called upon to assist a group of Antarctic explorers in some form of peril.

Within a year, the Commonwealth would again be asked to step into the breach, this time to orchestrate a rescue mission to save Mackintosh's party when it became stranded in Antarctica itself. Thus, between 1912 and 1916, Australian governments and private donors donated over £30,000 to projects dedicated to aiding the families of dead Antarctic explorers or rescuing living ones—a figure that does not include in-kind donations or the tens of thousands of pounds donated to fit out the Scott and Mawson expeditions in the first place.

This chapter tells how and why Australian individuals and institutions repeatedly stepped in to support and coordinate these projects. This burst of aid offers a window into the development of a new way of thinking about Australia's southern frontier in this period. As one appeal after another was made, an idea began to emerge ever more clearly that Australia's proximity to the Antarctic, its right to claim Antarctic lands and exploit Antarctic resources, and the benefits it stood to gain from Antarctic exploration, brought with them certain responsibilities, chief among them a responsibility to aid those who sought to unlock the mysteries of the Australian Antarctic.

‹ ›

In February 1913, the Australian press was filled with debate and speculation about two missing explorers: the Englishman Robert Scott and the Australian Douglas Mawson. Scott had been expected to return by April 1912, but when the *Terra Nova* reappeared there was no sign of Scott or the four companions he had chosen for the final polar journey. It did, however, bring back Scott's account of the expedition up to his departure for the pole, a comprehensive photographic and cinematographic record, and enough expedition members to satiate the press's desire for interviews.[3] The films in particular, captured by photographer Herbert Ponting and edited into *With Captain Scott to the South Pole* by staff at the Gaumont film company's Sydney office, helped maintain public interest in the expedition even after it became apparent that Scott had lost the 'race' to Amundsen.[4] Speculation throughout 1912 had therefore focused on whether or not Scott had reached the pole too, and news was eagerly awaited when *Terra Nova* returned from its third and final trip to Ross Island on 10 February 1913.[5] Mawson, meanwhile, had similarly failed to return from a sledging journey in time to rendezvous with his ship. News that Mawson had made it back to Commonwealth Bay alive while his two companions had perished reached Australia only a fortnight after the *Terra Nova* returned with news of Scott. These two overlapping stories ultimately had very different outcomes, but both mobilised the Australian public.

Contradictory accounts of Scott's fate began circulating on 11 February 1913. All agreed that *Terra Nova* had arrived unannounced in Oamaru, a small port between Christchurch and Dunedin chosen to avoid the scenes of the previous year when journalists had tried to break the news before it could be sent to the expedition's publication rights holders.[6] Little else was known with certainty. Some reports insisted Scott had been seen catching the train to Christchurch, leading *The Sydney Morning Herald* to publish an editorial thanking Scott for his efforts and congratulating him on a safe return.[7] Down in Melbourne, *The Age* published a darker version of events, saying that Scott and his four companions had reached the pole but had 'perished in a blizzard' during the return journey.[8] By the time the afternoon dailies were printed, it was *The Age*'s version that had been confirmed.[9] Over the following days, further details emerged and tributes were offered by those who had known the explorers, such as Edgeworth David and Griffith Taylor.[10]

Australian reactions to the news were immediate and unrestrained. Condolences were issued on behalf of the nation via the governor-general. In New South Wales, flags were flown at half-mast on public buildings. Huge public memorial services were held at St Andrew's Cathedral in Sydney and St Paul's in Melbourne, with dozens of smaller services in churches across the country, from Hobart, Adelaide, Perth and Brisbane, to Bendigo, Benalla, Longreach and Nowra. Sydney schools ceased work at noon on 17 February so that an account of Scott's death and his final 'message to the public' could be read to the pupils. On the fifteenth, work was suspended for five minutes at noon at many workplaces across South Australia to allow workers to reflect on the tragedy. The letters pages of newspapers became logbooks of grief.[11]

In among the various expressions of sorrow, from the performative to the private, was a growing sense that Australia should be doing something to help. One suggestion, picked up by the *Daily Telegraph*, was to equip an Australasian expedition to go to Antarctica to collect Scott's remains so they could be reinterred at St Paul's Cathedral in London.[12] Others suggested various forms of public memorial.[13] A consensus swiftly emerged, though, that Scott's dying wish had been 'to see that those who depend on us are properly cared for'.[14] This request became a focal point for the public reaction, leading to a proliferation of funds collecting donations to aid the explorers' families. In Sydney alone, three newspapers, the Chamber of Commerce and the lord mayor all launched their own funds.[15] At the national level, prime minister Andrew Fisher vowed that Scott's final request would 'not go unheeded' by the Commonwealth, with the federal government ultimately donating £2,000 on behalf of Australia.[16]

The Scott appeal organised by Sydney tabloid *The Sun* offers a glimpse into the diversity of Australians who felt affected by this event. *The Sun* argued that 'men and women of humble means, as well as the rich, make up the nation to which Scott directed his appeal. Their sympathy is as deep, though their power to aid is less.' It therefore organised a 'Shilling Subscription List', accepting donations of no more or less than 1 shilling to allow 'everybody to help in a great national movement'.[17] Hundreds of readers donated individually, while others organised collections in schools, workplaces, streets, hotels, apartment buildings and local councils. For example, thirty-two residents of an apartment building in Potts Point donated a shilling each, as did ninety guests at the Surry Hotel, the Hotel Australia's kitchen staff, the staff and students of various schools, staff and patients at hospitals, staff at the Bank of New South Wales, and Auburn, Hurstville and Kogarah councils. Others hosted events, charging a shilling for entry. Sara Collins raised 232 shillings by organising a theatrical performance at Randwick Town Hall. The New York Picture Theatre at Circular Quay screened Ponting's film all day on 23 February, the one-shilling admission fees going to *The Sun*'s fund. Bronte Palace Pictures raised 366 shillings through its own memorial show. By the time it closed on 13 March, *The Sun* had raised £143, 13 shillings—representing 2,873 one-shilling donations.[18]

And *The Sun*'s was only one of the myriad fundraisers and subscription lists that cropped up in one city. Elsewhere in Sydney, the customs officers, ambulance corps, public works department, Odd Fellows club, Women's Patriotic Club, the petty officers from Rushcutters Bay naval depot, the state associations for everyone from commercial travellers to billiards players, and dozens of businesses, churches and schools organised their own fundraisers.[19] Children were urged to give their pennies to the children of the dead explorers as 'a lesson to them on self-sacrifice', while entertainment companies hastened to organise charity concerts and vaudeville shows across Sydney and the Blue Mountains.[20] A 'Scott Memorial Concert' was held at Sydney Town Hall on 1 March—for reasons lost to time, a bulldog called Barry was stationed in the vestibule to collect donations, ultimately raising £107, 9 shillings.[21] Australasia's largest theatrical agency, JC Williamson, organised its own series of memorial concerts in Auckland, Christchurch, Sydney and Melbourne, and a sports event in Sydney, raising £3,000 for the Scott appeal. When asked why the company was devoting so much to the appeal, organiser Hugh J Ward explained that 'Australia … is the country that would chiefly benefit by south polar exploration', and the eyes of the world would be taking notice of how Australians responded.[22]

By June 1913, the multitude of collections across New South Wales had been amalgamated into a single sum of £7,000 to be remitted to the expedition's organisers in London.[23] Such was the fervour associated with fundraising that there were recriminations against those seen to not be doing enough. One concerned citizen of Bathurst demanded to know why the town had not yet started a collection list and called on the proceeds of the Bathurst picture shows to be donated. Cricketers were another target, accused of being behind their fellow sportspeople in supporting the cause. *The Sun*'s preferred target was the 'niggardly English response', in contrast to the generosity shown in Australia.[24] And while there were some criticisms of the excessive sum raised—Sydney lord mayor Arthur Cocks was disparaged for refusing to retain any funds to build a local memorial to Scott, while the state Labor Council questioned the relative lack of support for the families of forty miners killed in the Mount Lyell disaster in Tasmania—such concerns represented a small minority of responses.[25]

Though New South Wales was the most active fundraiser, the pattern was similar around the country. In total, Australia contributed over £10,000 to a fund that raised £74,509 internationally to provide pensions for the explorers' families, settle the expedition's debts, publish its scientific reports, and construct memorials.[26] Yet even this outsized contribution did not mark the end of Australasian enthusiasm for Scott memorialising. Within four years, New Zealand had a memorial oak tree, boulder, bust, essay prize and a full-scale marble statue. Australia held its own in the race to memorialise the explorers, though: a portrait for a school in Sydney, a tablet for a naval base in Newcastle, a fountain for a garden in Melbourne, and a window for a church in Hobart all cropped up.[27] There was even a short-lived suggestion that the Commonwealth's future capital be named 'after the great man of the present, Captain Scott, our lost hero', or perhaps 'Bowes' (an acronym for the five dead explorers: Bowers, Oates, Wilson, Evans, Scott). These proposals, along with the idea of a Scott monument for the capital, faded during World War I, but their brief popularity offers a window into how Scott's death was imagined not only as an imperial but as an Australian tragedy.[28]

Public reaction to Scott's death has been chronicled by several scholars, notably Max Jones and Stephanie Barczewski. But while these studies recognise the global nature of the reaction to Scott's demise, they do so from a metropolitan perspective that overlooks how Australians responded to and took advantage of this event in distinct and hitherto unremarked on ways.[29] It is true that the disaster was seen locally, as it was in Britain, as an imperial tragedy, one that could assuage fears of British racial or civilisational decline by proving, in the words of Sydney's *Daily Telegraph*, that 'British blood has lost none of its quality'.[30] Yet it was simultaneously experienced as a distinctly *Australian* event, one that could actuate a sense of Australian pride. In some cases, this meant emphasising Australian connections to the expedition—including occasionally tenuous links, such as the fact that the memorial cross erected in Antarctica by Scott's companions was made of Australian jarrah.[31]

The dominant theme in the discourse surrounding the Scott appeal in Australia, though, was the idea that the exploration of Antarctica that Scott had been involved in at the time of his death was a peculiarly Australian concern. Cutting through the language of mourning, celebration and mythologisation were phrases that captured this idea—that Australians were 'bound by strong ties to the inhospitable coast of that white continent in the south' and that 'Australians are particularly interested in the exploration of the Antarctic'.[32] Permeating the discourse around Scott's death was the familiar idea that Australians stood to benefit more than any other people in the world from the investigation of the Antarctic. This notion had long been used to argue that Australia had an obligation to support expeditions bound for the Antarctic; now it was used to explain why Australians felt a duty to rally in support of the dependents of men who died on those expeditions. The idea of Australia having political and economic rights in the Antarctic had been articulated since the mid-nineteenth century, reaching a crescendo with Mawson's invocation of a dream of an Australian Antarctic colony. The reaction to Scott's death, though, reveals a crystallising understanding of how a claim to Australian rights in the Antarctic also engendered Australian *responsibilities*.

‹ ›

This conception of Australian obligations in the Antarctic similarly infused discussions of the AAE. Two members of Mawson's party were dead; six were stranded at Commonwealth Bay. As news of Mawson's ordeal spread, the possibility of allocating some of the funds raised in Australia for the Scott appeal to the families of Ninnis and Mertz was canvassed. A letter to the *Daily Telegraph*, for instance, suggested that some of the Scott funds be reallocated since the expedition was 'primarily of Australian origin, and as the data obtained will probably be of immense service to the Commonwealth'.[33] The *Telegraph* endorsed this suggestion in an editorial, arguing that the men's families deserved support because the expedition was Australian, the data it was accumulating was of greater value to Australia than to any other country, and ultimately 'it was in the service of Australian effort and adventure that Mertz and Ninnis died'.[34]

No dedicated fund was ever created for the families of Mertz and Ninnis, perhaps because they were both young, unmarried men from wealthy families, perhaps because unlike Scott they left no poignant final messages. There was also the fact that six living, breathing Australians remained at Commonwealth Bay and needed rescue. Where Scott's supporters turned their focus to the dead in 1913, Mawson's needed to raise £11,000 to equip *Aurora* for a third Antarctic voyage that had never been budgeted for. This forced the AAE's organising committee to launch its own 'Mawson Relief Appeal' that emphasised both the value of the expedition's work and the idea that Australians had a duty to their explorers.[35] Coming immediately after the Scott appeal though, this call raised only £600 in Sydney and a miserly £80 in Melbourne. John King Davis managed to secure £1,000 from Anglo-Australian businessman Robert Lucas-Tooth during a trip to London, while George Reid persuaded the British Government to part with another £1,000.[36] By July, Scott's second-in-command, Teddy Evans, was telling Australians that sufficient funds had now been raised for the Scott appeal and urging them to instead contribute to the AAE, backing his words by donating £100 himself.[37] With funds trickling in, prime minister

Joseph Cook offered £5,000, saying that 'the Government deems it both a duty and a pleasure to assist further'.[38]

This combination of public and private funding was sufficient for *Aurora* to head south and retrieve the six men, though there remained a £4,000 deficit for Mawson to deal with when he returned in February 1914. The expedition caused some surprise by returning to Adelaide, though Mawson explained that it was because South Australia had been the first state to offer the AAE a grant and had never before hosted a polar vessel.[39] While the surprise arrival meant nothing had been planned, a familiar pattern soon emerged: a formal welcome at the university, an overcrowded public reception, and the *Aurora* opened to public inspection for three days.[40] From Adelaide, Mawson travelled on to Ballarat, Melbourne and Sydney, where he was greeted by a large crowd at Central Station and whisked away to the usual welcome event at the Town Hall.[41] Over the coming days, Mawson enjoyed the celebrity status of an Antarctic explorer, feted by the likes of the University Union, Royal Society and University Club.[42] There were also spontaneous celebrations in other parts of the Commonwealth. David, for example, was aboard a steamer in Fremantle when news of Mawson's safe return was received, and 800 fellow passengers immediately assembled to hear him give an impromptu address.[43]

While Mawson's return was characterised by an outpouring of enthusiasm, enthusiasm alone could not solve the AAE's financial problems. Mawson therefore hurried to London to arrange the publication of a book.[44] Edgeworth David and David Orme Masson endeavoured to raise additional funds in Australia but ran into problems caused by Conrad Eitel's irregular financial management. Masson secured promises from several Melbourne businessmen, conditional on a full statement of accounts being published to show why the expedition was £4,000 in debt.[45] Eitel's accounts were haphazard and included unexplained cheques drawn on the expedition's account.[46] The Australian fundraising appeal therefore stalled, while the outbreak of World War I delayed publication of

Mawson's book, leaving him to return to Australia to gradually raise funds through lectures.[47]

Throughout this period after Mawson's return, even after the war began to dominate public attention, familiar ideas were invoked. To raise funds to clear the AAE's debts and begin staking the ground for further research, Mawson and his supporters continued to emphasise the unique value of Antarctic exploration for Australia, the prospect of the 'Australian Antarctic' being integrated into the Commonwealth, and the international status Australia had gained, and would continue to gain, from Antarctic exploration. For instance, Mawson told *The Age* that the AAE had completed the 'superficial examination of the Australian quadrant', and there was now 'no reason why that area should not be under the control of Australia. We are the nearest country, and it is a kind of heritage for us'.[48] Comments made by Mawson in 1914—that follow-up work in a region of 'special interest to Australia' that 'lies at our very door' was 'a duty which fell to Australia'—could as easily have been made in 1911, such was the consistency in his rhetoric.[49] David, too, was consistent in his boosterism, telling the Royal Geographical Society that Mawson had discovered one of the largest coalfields in the world.[50] The idea that the expedition had elevated Australia to 'the group of nations that have fathered the heroes of Polar exploration' and done 'more to lift Australia to the front rank of science than any other endeavour in the past' was also repeated in news reports and letters around the country.[51]

The plea for aid issued by Aeneas Mackintosh in October 1914 was therefore the third such attempt to invoke the idea of Australian obligations to those who ventured south in the space of under two years. Despite the importance of Mackintosh's Ross Sea party to his own survival, Shackleton had been remarkably blasé about its preparations. The funds he raised were insufficient for the scale of his plans, so Shackleton prioritised his own party. He purchased the two-year-old Arctic yacht *Polaris* for £11,600 for the Weddell Sea party, whereas Mackintosh was assigned the battered and unrepaired *Aurora*, purchased from Mawson for only £1,000.[52] Shackleton's group boasted half-a-dozen Antarctic veterans, whereas Mackintosh had only two: Ernest Joyce, a notoriously difficult character with NAE and *Nimrod* experience, and Mackintosh himself, whose experience was limited to the critical eye injury suffered while unloading *Nimrod* in 1908, and turning a 40-kilometre sledge trip into a harrowing nine-day, near-death experience when he returned to Ross Island in 1909. Other appointments to the Ross Sea party included bank clerk Victor Hayward, schoolteacher-turned-priest Arnold Spencer-Smith, 21-year-old medical student John Cope, Belgrave Ninnis's cousin Aubrey, Frank Wild's brother Ernest, and Glasgow University teaching assistant Alexander Stevens as chief scientist. Positions such as doctor and physicist were not filled, with Mackintosh expected to find volunteers in Australia.

Mackintosh had to operate on the slenderest of shoestrings, trusting to Australians' sense of obligation to get the unseaworthy *Aurora* ready to depart. On arrival in October 1914, Mackintosh told reporters that he hoped that 'the generosity Australians had always displayed would enable the expedition to go away with a complete outfit'.[53] He persuaded the Hobart Marine Board to provide free docking for *Aurora*, and enlisted Edgeworth David to approach Fisher about having the ship overhauled at Cockatoo Island. The NSW Government was convinced to cover the cost of installing a wireless system, while four Australians—physicists Richard Richards and Keith Jack, general assistant Irvine Gaze, and wireless operator Lionel Hooke—were recruited to flesh out the party's ranks, though even Mackintosh's best efforts could not persuade any doctor to forgo the war for an Antarctic sojourn.[54]

The need for more extensive repairs than the £500 worth initially agreed, and a strike by workers at Cockatoo Island, delayed the *Aurora*'s departure significantly. These delays exacerbated concerns that the party would not make it to Ross Island in time to lay the depots Shackleton would need if he was attempting the transantarctic crossing in the 1914–15 summer. These concerns were significant enough that when Mackintosh asked the naval dockyard to provide him with additional stores and equipment, including rations, tools, paint, sails, and even a custom-built collapsible hut, the Commonwealth Naval Board reluctantly authorised additional expenses that ballooned to £4,595. An outraged Fisher later ordered an investigation into the expenditure, with the resulting report both identifying failures of oversight by the Naval Board and blasting Mackintosh for taking 'unfair advantage of the situation'.[55]

Mackintosh never had to answer to the federal government for his actions. Shackleton had instructed him to freeze *Aurora* into the sea ice near Ross Island for the winter to avoid the expense of multiple voyages, but the attempt to do so proved disastrous. The ship was torn from its moorings and trapped in the ice, suffering extensive damage as it drifted with the icepack for 312 days before emerging in New Zealand in April 1916.[56] Mackintosh and nine others were stranded on Ross Island without most of their sledging equipment when the ship broke free, and were forced to seek shelter in Scott's abandoned hut. Unaware that Shackleton had abandoned the transantarctic journey when his own ship was crushed by ice in the Weddell Sea, the ten men improvised sledging gear out of supplies left behind by Scott and Shackleton and set out to establish depots. In the face of colossal challenges, the unheralded and inexperienced group succeeded in laying depots at every degree of latitude along Shackleton's intended route. Mackintosh, Hayward and Spencer-Smith all died in the attempt.[57]

The ITAE had no funds left for a relief voyage, so when *Aurora* reappeared in New Zealand, bringing news of ten men stranded at Ross Island, Shackleton's wife approached Fisher, now high commissioner in London, to ask the Commonwealth to fund a rescue. Putting aside any personal resentments, Fisher agreed, and by May 1916 the British, Australian and New Zealand governments were deep in discussions over two relief expeditions: one to rescue Mackintosh's party from Ross Island, and another to search for Shackleton in the Weddell Sea.[58] Advisory committees were appointed in London, Melbourne and Dunedin, with experienced figures like Mawson, Masson, Griffith Taylor, JJ Kinsey and Davis asked to coordinate the rescues. When Shackleton reappeared at South Georgia and managed, with the Chilean Government's assistance, to rescue the rest of his party, attention shifted solely to the Ross Sea. The British Government offered to cover half the cost of a rescue mission if Australia and New Zealand covered the rest, with the two dominions eventually agreeing to provide £8,645 and £1,950 respectively. *Aurora* was compulsorily acquired for the 'Ross Sea Relief Expedition', with Davis released from war transport work to take command for the summer of 1916–17. The expedition was entirely a government enterprise but drew on the services and expertise of a tight circle of Antarctic veterans. This approach made for a smooth and efficient rescue, with the seven survivors collected after a largely uneventful voyage.[59]

‹ ›

The short period between 1912 and 1916 was a pivotal one in the history of Australia's relationship with the Antarctic. As well as the moment when popular enthusiasm for Antarctic exploration was at its zenith, this was the era of the first unambiguously Australian expedition to explore, survey and claim the land directly to the nation's south. Mawson and his allies justified the expense of the AAE by emphasising that the 'Australian Antarctic' was essential to Australia's national interests, drawing on ideas about Australian rights and opportunities in this region. To its proponents, the AAE would lay the foundation for the acquisition of an Australian Antarctic dependency that would benefit and enrich the Commonwealth through improved weather forecasting, revitalised whaling and sealing industries, and the developing of new industries like coal, gold and perhaps even radium mining. Such benefits and riches should, argued boosters like Mawson and David, belong to Australia by right of proximity, and by exploring and claiming this land Mawson would formalise the Commonwealth's inchoate right to control it.

Yet, as well as a high point for popular interest and for Australian Antarctic optimism and boosterism, this was a period characterised by repeated appeals for Australia and Australians to assist Antarctic explorers in various forms of peril. First it was to aid the families of Scott and his companions when the explorers died on their return from the South Pole. Then it was to rescue Mawson and his companions when they were unexpectedly forced to remain at Commonwealth Bay for an additional year that had never been planned or budgeted for. Finally, it was a plea to bankroll an expedition to lay the depots necessary for the survival of Shackleton's transcontinental crossing party, then a relief expedition to rescue the stranded depot-layers. Yet, despite lingering concerns over explorers' failures to put sufficient contingencies in place, and specific resentment towards Mackintosh and Shackleton over the *Aurora* affair, there was never any real controversy over whether answering these pleas was truly Australia's responsibility. Instead, the burgeoning sense that the Antarctic coastline south of Australia should by rights be a Commonwealth dependency was accompanied by an emerging acceptance that claims to special interests or territorial control in this region would come with obligations and responsibilities. Most notably, it was accepted that Australia was obliged to aid those engaged in exploring or developing the Australian Antarctic.

Within this moment can also be seen the kernel of the transformation of Antarctic science, exploration and commercial investigation from the private to the public sphere. Until this time, Australian governments wrote cheques for Antarctic projects but had little role in their organisation. The Commonwealth Government, however, took a greater role in Mawson's AAE, including taking over the Macquarie Island meteorological station when the expedition ceased funding it, before taking full control of organising the Ross Sea Relief Expedition in 1916. From this moment onwards, Antarctic projects would overwhelmingly be government projects.

8

'THE EQUATOR TO THE POLE'

Performing Sovereignty in the Australian Antarctic

Douglas Mawson was roused from his bed on board *Discovery* around 5.30 on the morning of 13 January 1930. He awoke to news that the cumbersome sailing ship he commanded, built for Scott's NAE in 1901 and now pressed into service for the British Australian New Zealand Antarctic Research Expedition (BANZARE), was nearing a small island spotted the previous day. Mawson summoned the ship's staff—a mix of scientists, photographers and aviators—to prepare to go ashore, though a band of ice meant they spent most of the morning waiting while Mawson and *Discovery*'s captain, JK Davis, bickered about the best path forwards. Eventually they were able to launch a boat, only for the motor to fail immediately. With the ice constantly shifting around them, there was no time to repair the motor, so they broke out the oars and rowed to what they now named Proclamation Island. While two scientists stayed near the boat to take magnetic observations, Mawson led the main party up a steep slope to the pinnacle of the rocky island, travelling lightly without food or gear. They had one urgent objective and would be leaving almost as soon as they achieved it. When they reached the island's peak, they erected a flagpole, held in place by a cairn of rocks. Come noon, they raised the British flag, removed their woolly hats, gave three boisterous cheers, sang 'God Save the King', and posed for photos.

Before rushing back to the boat, Mawson recited a proclamation of sovereignty, and a plaque affirming that the ceremony had taken place was nailed to the flagpole, facing south towards the continental shore. Mawson had brought a written proclamation, taken from a stack given to him by the Australian Government, but on attempting to read from it, found that it had been buried beneath the cairn already. He therefore recited the words from memory, proclaiming sovereignty over not just this one tiny island but the entire stretch of the Antarctic continent between 73°E and 47°E. *Discovery* had been skirting the edge of this land for over two weeks, discovering a new stretch of coastline during a reconnaissance flight in the expedition's small two-man seaplane. Mawson named this new discovery Mac. Robertson Land after the expedition's patron, Freddo Frog creator Macpherson Robertson. Continuing westwards, the party had rediscovered Kemp Land, sighted in 1833 but not seen since, and shown that it was connected to Enderby Land, first discovered in 1831. Throughout this journey, Mawson had been searching for a place to go ashore to proclaim sovereignty over this westernmost stretch of the Australian Antarctic. As it became clear a landing would be impossible, Mawson made do with his brief ceremony at Proclamation Island.

The BANZARE continued exploring further west, sighting another small slice of land at around 45°E before beginning the voyage home. On the morning of 25 January, as *Discovery* neared Proclamation Island again, Mawson and pilot Stuart Campbell took the seaplane up and flew a few kilometres inland. Here, 900 metres above ice-covered Enderby Land, Mawson handed Campbell a flag on a short pole. Campbell stalled the engine so that he could hurl the flag over the side while Mawson recited his proclamation, claiming sovereignty over all of Mac.Robertson, Kemp and Enderby lands. After confirming that the flag had made it to the ice below, they returned to the ship, with Mawson holding onto the signed and dated proclamation on this occasion as evidence of the claims he had made on behalf of his king and Empire.[1]

Why was Australia's most famous Antarctic explorer spending his time mounting plaques on rocky islands and throwing flags from planes? These moments were the culmination of Mawson's commitment over more than two decades to the idea of the Australian Antarctic, a vast swathe of polar land and sea recognised as Australian territory. This chapter tells the story of a significant change in the Commonwealth's attitude towards its southern frontier. Informed by the influential rhetoric of Antarctic boosterism that framed the Antarctic as an impending El Dorado, and the idea that proximity and history gave Australians a special interest in the Antarctic and a natural right to control it, the Commonwealth's approach shifted in the 1920s. Having hitherto imagined the Southern Ocean as part of an informal sphere of Australian influence, the Commonwealth began pursuing formal recognition of this region as Australian territory.

‹ ›

It is often argued that World War I fundamentally changed the way the world viewed Antarctic exploration. The war marks the end point of many accounts of the 'Heroic Era', that period of intense international interest in Antarctica spanning from Bull and Borchgrevink's landing at Cape Adare in 1895 to the return of the Ross Sea party's survivors in 1917. Edward J Larson argues that if Europeans found meaning at the turn of the twentieth century in heroic human struggles against nature and fate, the experience of war 'broke the spell'.[2] Tom Griffiths likewise deems the Heroic Era 'Europe's last gasp before it tore itself apart in the Great War', and suggests that consequently it was Americans, 'less traumatised' by the war than Europeans, who revived Antarctic exploration in the 1920s.[3] This emphasis on discontinuity stems from a common-sense assumption that the mass slaughter of World War I rendered older forms of popular heroism anachronistic if not obsolete. Yet treating the war as a stark divide risks obscuring significant patterns of continuity in how people thought and talked about the Antarctic.

Even as the war dominated attention, Antarctica retained some of its fascination for Australians. Saturation coverage of the war did not preclude, for instance, speculation about Shackleton's whereabouts during the ITAE, nor did it prevent Shackleton from packing out Sydney Town Hall to give lectures about his remarkable survival story in 1917.[4] Indeed, Shackleton even became the face of an Australian enlistment campaign, appearing on a poster as 'one who has carried the King's flag in the white warfare of the Antarctic, and who is going now to serve in the red warfare of Europe'.[5] That military recruiters used an Antarctic explorer to promote enlistment clearly demonstrates that the war did not simply displace older ideas about heroism and adventure. Nor did these older ways of thinking about and engaging with the Antarctic disappear in the postwar period. There was, for instance, a publishing boom for Antarctic stories. As well as official accounts by Scott (1913), Mawson (1915) and Shackleton (1919), books appeared by Scott's companions Griffith Taylor (1916 and 1928), Herbert Ponting (1921), Teddy Evans (1921) and Apsley Cherry-Garrard (1922); NAE veteran Gerald Doorly (1919); *Aurora* captain JK Davis (1919); AAE and ITAE photographer Frank Hurley (1925); and the youngest member of Shackleton's final expedition, James Marr (1923). To these could be added a biography of Shackleton by Royal Geographical Society secretary HR Mill (1923) and two histories of Antarctic exploration by J Gordon Hayes (1928 and 1932).[6] All of these works were sold, reviewed and read in Australia during and after World War I.

As well as a publishing boom, Antarctic films, such as Hurley's *South* (1919) and *Siege of the South* (1930), and Ponting's *The Great White Silence* (1924) and *90 Degrees South* (1933), remained popular in Australia after the war.[7] So, too, did Antarctic lectures. Hurley returned from service as a war photographer in France to embark on a lecture tour in 1919, speaking to his films and photos in 'synchronised lecture entertainments' that demonstrated significant continuity with the multimedia events of the prewar world.[8] Mawson, who still needed to raise funds to publish the AAE's scientific reports, mined his Antarctic experiences for material throughout the 1920s, lecturing on topics such as Macquarie Island, 'the great commercial possibilities in the Antarctic Ocean', and 'life and scenery in the Antarctic'.[9] These lectures continued to be a major drawcard, with police called to one in 1927 to prevent hundreds of disappointed people from rushing the doors to hear Mawson retell his Antarctic adventures and outline Australia's right to control the Antarctic.[10] Edgeworth David still gave occasional lectures, and still emphasised the vast commercial riches waiting to be unlocked.[11] Other AAE alumni such as Davis, geologist Cecil Madigan, meteorologist Morton Moyes and general hand John Close also turned their hand to lecturing in the 1920s, as did *Terra Nova* veterans Griffith Taylor and Teddy Evans.[12] Significantly, the enduring appetite for Antarctic stories was not limited to a nostalgic yearning for uncomplicated tales of prewar adventure. In 1924, 'scores of people were turned away' from lectures by Tasmanian journalist AJ Villiers on his experiences with a Norwegian whaling expedition to the Ross Sea, while a new generation of Australian explorers, such as Hubert Wilkins and John Rymill, drew substantial crowds throughout the 1920s and 1930s.[13]

And while polar exploration was no longer quite the mass culture phenomenon of the immediate prewar period, proposals to further explore, develop and annex the Antarctic continued to capture interest. In 1921, for instance, Shackleton launched his third and final expedition, outfitting the tiny sealing vessel *Quest* for a vague program of oceanographic work that included circumnavigating Antarctica and searching for phantom islands. Sydney's *Sun* newspaper was willing still to purchase the exclusive Australian publication rights for Shackleton's wireless updates about the expedition's progress. This proved a savvy investment when Shackleton died early in the voyage, triggering a flood of tributes and renewed interest in his life and career.[14] Richard E Byrd led three successive US expeditions to the Ross Sea in the 1930s, capturing attention by providing a stream of wireless updates and live radio broadcasts from the Antarctic.[15] Byrd's compatriot Lincoln Ellsworth led a series of four self-funded expeditions to explore Antarctica by air in the 1930s, including the 1935 transantarctic flight that prompted the Commonwealth's dramatic but essentially unnecessary rescue mission.[16] Australian Hubert Wilkins sailed with Shackleton in the *Quest*, worked with Ellsworth, and led two of his own expeditions to Graham Land funded jointly by Australian donors and American news magnate William Randolph Hearst.[17]

As well as projects to continue the exploration of Antarctica and the Southern Ocean, the 1920s saw a surge in schemes aimed at developing Antarctic industries. John Cope, biologist and de facto medical officer for Mackintosh's Ross Sea party, launched plans in 1919 for a project to 'locate exactly, and claim for the British Empire the vast economic resources already proved to exist in the Antarctic Continent'.[18] Cope sought to raise £150,000 to spend six years in the Antarctic, establishing a network of permanent observatories, prospecting for minerals, studying whale populations, and conducting aerial surveys with a view to collecting all the information required for Antarctica's full-scale commercial development. But despite enthusiasm and endorsements from the likes of the Royal Geographical Society's recently retired secretary, J Scott Keltie, Cope's grand plan devolved into the most farcical Antarctic expedition of the twentieth century.[19] He ultimately led a debt-laden four man expedition to Graham Land in January 1921 but decided to return home with his disgruntled second-in-command, Wilkins, six weeks later, leaving two men to spend a year in Antarctica before being rescued by Norwegian whalers.[20]

Unsurprisingly, Cope's talk of unlocking the commercial potential of the Antarctic attracted significant attention in Australia, where a discourse of profitable opportunity had been so influential for so long. Having interviewed Frank Hurley about Cope's proposal, *The Sydney Morning Herald* remarked that 'Australians will wake up some day to the immense possibilities that lay to the south of them', citing the £1,000,000 of whale oil that had been harvested from the seas around South Georgia in the past year alone.[21] *The Sun* sought to highlight that Cope's was a very different proposal to previous public calls for donations, as Cope was seeking to 'mark out a new field for British and Australasian enterprise' in a region with conditions no worse than in Siberia or Klondike but which offered even greater wealth.[22]

Edgeworth David reiterated his long-held optimism, declaring that a project like Cope's would find a vast coalfield and probably gold and copper deposits too.[23] The only notable dissent in Australia came from Griffith Taylor, who was already building a reputation for his pessimistic views on the future settlement and development of central Australia and believed that any new Antarctic expedition should be to advance scientific knowledge rather than commercial gain.[24] Yet Cope seemed fully aware that his boosterish rhetoric would have particular purchase in Australia. He persuaded Andrew Fisher to join the organising committee in London and both Wilkins and Ross Sea Party alumnus Ernest Joyce, who had lived in Australia since 1911, to attach their names to the expedition. The possibility of Hurley joining and of Cope recruiting a majority-Australian scientific staff were also floated in the press.[25]

Cope was not the only Ross Sea party veteran attempting to leverage Antarctic experience into a commercial venture. Joseph Stenhouse, who captained *Aurora* during its long drift trapped in ice, developed the most concrete plans yet for an Antarctic tourist cruise. Stenhouse's plan to take 200 passengers on a five-month round-the-world cruise capped by a summer tour of the Ross Sea, including visits to the Scott, Shackleton and Amundsen bases, dog-sledging excursions, one night camping on the Antarctic continent, a whaling demonstration and tours of penguin colonies, was well received in Australia. He convinced the Holland-America Line to back the proposal, chartered the Norwegian cruise ship *Stella Polaris*, and enlisted New Zealander Frank Worsley, captain of Shackleton's *Endurance* during the ITAE, to co-lead the cruise. At least one Sydney woman booked a £500 ticket, and there was speculation that Australian cricketer Don Bradman and aviator Charles Kingsford Smith would make the trip. Unfortunately for Stenhouse, he planned the cruise for the austral summer of 1930–31. Overtaken by the Great Depression, he postponed it to 1931–32, but the devastating economic downturn foiled that attempt, too. It was not until 1958 that the first Antarctic tourist cruise eventually took place.[26]

Aubrey Ninnis, a British veteran of *Aurora*'s ordeal under Stenhouse, looked to Australia and New Zealand to raise £750,000 capital for his own plan to develop the Antarctic into 'a permanent and important source of production'.[27] Ninnis saw an opportunity to use the reliable profits from Antarctic whaling to subsidise survey parties to search for guano and mineral deposits, and to experiment with other industries, such as fur farming, penguin egg harvesting and deep-sea fishing. Research would be carried out by scientists attached to the survey parties and based at the whaling stations. As well as beginning the full-scale development of Antarctica, Ninnis appealed to Australasian investors by arguing that his company would break the Norwegian monopoly on Antarctic whaling and ensure its profits remained in Australasia, an appeal to the idea that these resources rightfully belonged to them in the first place. Ninnis recruited business partners and sought advice from Antarctic experts like Mawson, Davis and Kinsey before eventually abandoning the scheme, largely due to being unable to find anyone with whaling expertise to oversee the project's crucial first stage.[28]

The same interest in economic development was evident in discussions over utilising Tasmania's most remote dependency. Macquarie Island had been the site of a fur-sealing boom in the 1810s and sporadically targeted by elephant sealers throughout the nineteenth century. Then, between 1889 and 1920, NZ businessman Joseph Hatch had operated a controversial penguin oil factory on the island.[29] The Commonwealth Government briefly maintained a meteorological station from 1913 to 1915 before it was closed amidst difficulties staffing and resupplying it during wartime. Throughout the station's short history, though, the government had one eye on a more productive future for the island.[30] Meteorological staff were charged with overseeing experiments with chickens, ducks and sheep, resulting in a recommendation that the island could be expected to sustain a flock of 18,000 sheep.[31] In 1920, Tasmanian governor William Allardyce, who had overseen the explosive growth of the whaling industry on South Georgia as governor of the Falkland Islands, began promoting the idea that sheep and fur seals could be farmed at Macquarie.[32] Allardyce's successor, Ernest Clerk, campaigned for the occupation and utilisation of Macquarie in the 1930s, variously advocating a wildlife sanctuary, elephant sealing industry, meteorological station and a military base.[33] Mawson made similar arguments throughout the interwar period.[34] Despite warnings by Clerk that the 'absence of an effective occupation by the Australian government' posed a security risk, these kinds of development projects were seen as too expensive for the speculated returns and did not eventuate.[35] Yet, while these plans amounted to little, they offer another perspective on the serious interest in Antarctic and Southern Ocean development that characterised this period.

It is clear, then, that there are significant continuities in how the Antarctic was imagined and discussed in Australia either side of World War I. Forms of popular engagement with the Antarctic, and ideas about Australian rights, responsibilities and opportunities in the region, had proven remarkably durable. It is also clear that these continuities are significant. Within fifteen years of the war ending, the Commonwealth had formally asserted sovereignty over the Australian Antarctic Territory, the 5.896 million-square-kilometre region between Enderby and Victoria lands that comprises roughly 42 per cent of the Antarctic landmass. Conventionally, scholars of Antarctic history and politics have seen the acquisition of the AAT as a product of British imperial policy, with Australia simply a passive recipient of its Antarctic territory. As historians such as Marie Kawaja have shown, however, this interpretation is untenable. Annexation of the AAT was the culmination of extensive negotiation and manoeuvring by Australian political actors in the 1920s and 1930s.[36] The Australian position in these negotiations—that Commonwealth control of this region was vital to Australian interests—was in turn shaped by the ideas traced in this book.

Established ideas about Australia's relationship with the world to its south had a profound influence on Australian objectives and policies regarding its relationship to the Antarctic. The Commonwealth's shift in strategy, however, from treating the Antarctic informally as part of an Australian sphere of influence to assertively pursuing formal recognition of its control of the AAT, stemmed from a set of changes that occurred in the 1920s. One key factor in this shift was a fundamental change in the organisation of the Antarctic whaling industry.

This industry had its origins in the establishment of a shore whaling station at Grytviken, South Georgia, in 1904. Norwegian Carl Anton Larsen, who had spent time in the Antarctic with a Norwegian whaling reconnaissance voyage in 1892 and the Swedish Antarctic Expedition in 1901–04, returned to South Georgia backed by Argentine capital to establish a whaling station. Larsen's station was immediately profitable, and by 1917 there were six stations operating at South Georgia and another further south at Deception Island. This Antarctic shore whaling industry, in which whales were slaughtered at sea and hauled ashore for processing, peaked in 1925–26, when 7,825 whales were killed in a single season.[37]

While the shore stations at South Georgia would remain in use until 1966, in the 1920s Larsen switched his attention to pelagic or open-sea whaling on the other side of the Antarctic. Technical innovations, such as the development of slipways that allowed whales to be hauled on board a factory ship, obviated the need for a shore station and opened up new whaling grounds. Larsen therefore applied to the British Government for a licence to hunt whales in the Ross Sea, presuming that it was a British-claimed territory. A five-year licence was granted in 1922, but the surprise application spurred the British Government to clarify the extent of its Antarctic sovereignty claims. Accordingly, the entire region between 160°E and 150°W south of 60°S was, in 1923, officially proclaimed the Ross Dependency and placed under the governor-general of New Zealand's administration.[38] Larsen's new company again reaped remarkable profits. By 1927–28, it took only nine weeks to fill the company's three factory ships, their combined cargo of oil amounting to 171,311 barrels from 2,012 whales. And as had occurred at South Georgia, other companies followed Larsen's lead, so that by the summer of 1929–30, one British and three Norwegian companies were operating in the waters of the Ross Dependency.[39]

The rapid expansion of Norwegian whaling into a region many Australians saw as part of an Australasian sphere of influence caused no little consternation in the Commonwealth. When rumours of Larsen's intentions emerged, JK Davis, now Commonwealth director of navigation, asked JJ Kinsey to persuade New Zealand's government to assert its control of the Ross Sea before whaling could commence.[40] When whaling *did* begin, acting prime minister Earle Page cabled prime minister Stanley Bruce, then in London, urging him to request that the sector south of Australia be placed officially under Commonwealth control, since Norwegian whalers would likely move into this area if Larsen's Ross Sea experiments proved successful.[41] Upon duly raising the matter with the Colonial Office, Bruce was informed—in an echo of previous showdowns over New Guinea and Kerguelen—that there was 'no urgency for Australian action'.[42] This did little to assuage Davis's concerns and he continued to implore Bruce to assert Australia's claim.[43] Others were airing similar concerns publicly. Morton Moyes, veteran of the AAE and Davis's Ross Sea Relief Expedition in 1916–17, warned in a 1929 lecture that Australia was 'steadily being pushed out of the Antarctic continent, in which geographically and scientifically it should have so great an interest'.[44] Mawson was even more belligerent, accusing other nations of 'reaping the harvest of the Australian Antarctic' and sparking a minor diplomatic incident by openly criticising Norway.[45]

One response to these concerns was a renewed barrage of attempts to develop an Australian Antarctic whaling industry. In 1920, *The Argus* argued that it was time to both formally claim the Australian Antarctic and revive 'what was once Australia's greatest industry'.[46] As Ross Sea whaling boomed throughout the 1920s, with some Norwegian companies offering 45 per cent dividend yields, *The Sydney Morning Herald* bemoaned that 'Norwegian enterprise has discovered and exploited a field of industry that is Australian by right of proximity'.[47] Similar complaints were regularly aired in the letters pages of the country's press: that Australia had made 'absolutely no attempt to avail herself of the excellent opportunity presented … while foreign countries take from the Ross Sea'; that the Antarctic whaling industry was 'one that rightly belongs to Australia'; that 'Norwegians and others have established profitable industries in … areas which rightly belong to the Australian continent'; and that it was 'very regrettable that so much wealth lies practically at our back door, and no attempt is made to procure it for our own revenue'.[48] Mawson feared that whales might soon be exterminated, and therefore used the press to call for Australian companies to enter 'this lucrative field of enterprise, before it is too late'.[49] And in 1933, Perth's *Daily News* urged the government to support Mawson's efforts to get a company off the ground, describing Antarctic whaling as 'virtually a national industry for Australia'.[50]

There was no shortage of would-be whaling magnates ready to heed these calls. As well as Aubrey Ninnis's ambitious, multifaceted Antarctic development scheme, the Australian Whaling Company was formed in Sydney in 1929 with plans to raise £750,000 capital to acquire a factory ship and five catchers.[51] This company was envisaged as simultaneously a nationalist and commercial enterprise. Its prospectus, for example, proudly trumpeted that it was 'a TRULY AUSTRALIAN INVESTMENT' that would secure a place in the Norwegian-dominated industry for 'the VIRILE YOUNG AUSTRALIAN and NEW ZEALANDER'.[52] Mawson was brought on as the company's expert adviser, but even with his talent for boosterism and substantial early investment, the Australian Whaling Company never managed to get a ship in the water and was dissolved in 1933.[53] The Pacific and Ross Sea Whaling Company was also founded in Sydney in 1929, with former AAE committee chairman Orme Masson as a director. It avoided the overtly nationalist framing of its rival, instead partnering with Larsen's former business partner Magnus Konow, reserving 10 per cent of its 500,000 £1 shares for Norwegian investors, and planning to rely on Norwegian crews.[54] Ultimately, though, the company suffered the same fate as its rival, collapsing amidst the Great Depression.

‹ ›

Mounting concerns that Australia had fallen behind in the exploitation of Antarctic resources on its doorstep were a key factor in the Commonwealth's shift to a more assertive and expansionist policy in the 1920s. Two other factors contributed to this shift: a changing political context in the Antarctic, as other states increasingly asserted their own territorial rights; and a changing political context in Australia, as territorial expansion was increasingly looked to as a strategy for advancing the national interest. The interwar period was an expansionist moment for Australia. An enduring concern during the war, both diplomatically and in wider discourse, had been the question of what was to become of Germany's colonies in the Pacific. German New Guinea and Nauru had been occupied by Australian troops since the war's early stages, and prime minister Billy Hughes stridently advocated for both to become Australian territories.[55] Hughes openly drew on the idea of an Australian Monroe Doctrine to justify his bellicose position, declaring in April 1919, for instance, that 'Australia is committed to a Monroe Doctrine of the Southern Pacific, and its integrity must be maintained'.[56]

Hughes's bullish insistence on permanent Australian control of former German colonies in the Pacific was generally popular, with responses falling into three broad camps. Sydney journalist and author E George Marks summed up the first, saying that 'national and strategic reasons must impel Australia to keep the firmest grip on islands which are inevitably linked with her future greatness and expansion'.[57] The second camp was similarly supportive of Hughes's reassertion of an Australian Monroe Doctrine, but, rather than a prerequisite for greatness and expansion, it saw the acquisition of territories like New Guinea and Nauru as a modest preventative measure to ensure the Commonwealth's 'peace and security'. As Sydney's *Daily Telegraph* insisted, 'it would not matter to Australia who owned the Pacific islands, so long as we were in no danger from them. All we are concerned to fight for is that they shall not come under the control of any enemy or potential enemy Power'.[58] The third camp agreed that Australia's interests demanded that foreign powers be prevented from controlling territories in the South Pacific but felt this objective could best be achieved by placing the former German colonies under international authority rather than annexing and administering them as Australian territories.[59] Hughes's demands would ultimately be decided at the Paris Peace Conference, arranged by the Allies in 1919–20 to determine terms for the end of World War I and reorder the postwar world in pursuit of a more lasting peace. The solution that ultimately emerged from the conference was a compromise of sorts: the Commonwealth was not permitted to simply annex the territories it had occupied since 1914 but rather was granted a mandate to administer and develop them on behalf of the League of Nations—individually in the case of New Guinea, jointly with Britain and New Zealand in the case of Nauru.[60] In practice, Australian administration of these mandate territories centred on the development of resources, most notably Nauruan phosphate, and was little different to if they had been annexed directly.[61]

While the Pacific dominated the Australian agenda at Paris, Mawson called on the Peace Conference to also 'deal definitely with the allocation of the Antarctic lands'.[62] The question of sovereignty in the Antarctic was becoming more urgent as the commercial value of the region became clearer, Mawson argued, and it was vital that the Australian Antarctic be under Commonwealth control. Mawson had already privately urged Hughes to use the end of the war as an opportunity to claim the Australian sector, saying that 'The Commonwealth would then stretch from Pole to Equator' and could 'supply every possible climate for the production of every possible material'.[63] Despite Mawson's best efforts, however,

Antarctic sovereignty was not resolved at the conference, though Germany's renunciation of its rights to all overseas territories was interpreted as a renunciation of any claim to an Antarctic territory.[64]

In the absence of international agreement on the future of the Antarctic, Britain, Australia and New Zealand reached an agreement of their own. British colonial secretary Viscount Milner, seemingly unaware of the importance already attached to the issue in Australia, concluded in 1919 that control of Antarctica and the Southern Ocean 'might become of serious interest to the British communities in the southern hemisphere', and that a policy of gradually bringing the entire region under the empire's control should be adopted.[65] Milner's undersecretary of state, Leo Amery, drafted a proposal along these lines in 1920, leading to a meeting between Amery, Australia's repatriation minister, and New Zealand's defence minister in London in February 1921. The result of these discussions was an agreement that, just as the Antarctic Peninsula and a sweep of subantarctic islands were administered via the Falkland Islands as dependencies, Australia and New Zealand should each take control of a swathe of adjacent Antarctic territory. The question of how to actually implement this objective, though, was deferred pending legal advice.[66]

The federal government invited David, Davis and Mawson to comment on the proposal. True to form, David focused on the commercial benefits Australia would derive from controlling an Antarctic territory, reiterating that the region explored by the AAE was likely to contain coal and gold and potentially smaller amounts of rare minerals like molybdenum. Davis similarly endorsed the prospect of claiming 'the Antarctic hinterland south of Australia'.[67] Mawson made it three from three, agreeing that 'this region will have a great economic value to Australia', and predicting that it would be profitable for the Commonwealth in the short term through whaling and in the longer term through mining or even wind-powered nitrogen fixation plants to take advantage of controlling Commonwealth Bay, the windiest place on earth.[68]

Both Davis and Mawson also raised fears about the possibility of rival claims. Davis was concerned that France and the United States might claim areas within the Australian sector based on discoveries by d'Urville and Wilkes in 1840. Mawson dismissed this possibility, pointing out that the only significant exploration of Adélie Land had been undertaken by the AAE, and suggesting that Australia should not only claim Adélie Land but seize the opportunity to acquire the French-claimed subantarctic and southern Indian Ocean islands as well, since these were of little value to France but might be rendered useful as wireless or naval bases for Australia. As far as Mawson and Davis were concerned, the biggest risk to Australian control was New Zealand. Mawson warned that the British and New Zealand governments would likely try 'to allocate the best of the Australasian Quadrant to New Zealand', and both men recommended that care be taken to ensure New Zealand did not receive any territory west of 160°E.[69]

The Australian position was clear: recognition of Australian control of its Antarctic sector was a priority. The Colonial Office, however, resolved to first proclaim the creation of the Ross Dependency and its transfer to New Zealand in 1923, thus resolving the question of responsibility for regulating Ross Sea whaling. Only then would they 'proceed more cautiously in the case of the Australian sphere'. This was due to concerns over the possibility of a French counterclaim, concerns which proved prescient.[70] France responded to the proclamation of the Ross Dependency by asserting French sovereignty over Adélie Land, the Crozets, Kerguelen, Saint Paul and Amsterdam Island in 1924.[71] Predictably, this caused consternation in Australia.[72] The federal government's immediate response was to express concern that Adélie Land would form a 'serious enclave' in the Australian Antarctic, particularly since the French proclamation had not specified any boundaries to its claim. The Commonwealth also openly dissented from Milner and Avery's policy of quietly and gradually shoring up sovereignty, informing the Colonial Office that 'it would be advisable to assert rights over these regions at the earliest opportunity'.[73]

In response to the news, Orme Masson led an Australian National Research Council deputation to protest the annexation to prime minister Stanley Bruce, saying that France's claim had 'surprised and alarmed those who have the interests of Australia at heart'.[74] The deputation worried that 'Australia will lose not only Adélie Land, but all that much larger southern region, of which it is a part and which, on geographical and historical grounds … should belong to Australia'. Masson handed Bruce a detailed memorandum that sought to provide the information needed to demolish France's claim, including evidence that d'Urville had completed only the most perfunctory of surveys along perhaps 280 kilometres of coastline, whereas the AAE had actually mapped, explored and occupied the region. Additionally, Masson argued that proximity—the fact the Antarctic was barely 2,500 kilometres distant from Hobart, closer than Hobart was to Perth—supported Australia's claim over France's, and cited the precedent set by Canada in the Arctic. Canada had recently invoked the 'sector principle', a contested idea in international law, to claim that its western and eastern borders continued uninterrupted to the North Pole, making all land and seas to Canada's north Canadian territory.[75] Finally, Masson reiterated the economic and meteorological value of the Australian Antarctic to the Commonwealth, before concluding the meeting by expressing his hope that 'Australia, which already extends its government over such a wide range of latitude and climate, will go still further to the south and thus definitely claim control from the Equator to the Pole'.

Bruce sought to assuage these fears, insisting that his government 'had not the slightest intention of allowing any rights accruing to Australia from the splendid exploration work carried on by Australians in the Antarctic to be overlooked'.[76] He also forwarded the memorandum to Amery with a note explaining that the Commonwealth was anxious to prevent 'the establishment by any other country of a considerable enclave in the Australian quadrant'.[77] Bruce's frank recommendation was that France's claim should be contested and Australia's rights over the rest of the sector be proclaimed immediately. This recommendation was considered at the 1926 Imperial Conference, attended by ministers from each of the British Empire's self-governing dominions, but a subcommittee concluded that France's claim to Adélie Land was 'indisputable' and that France was unlikely to agree to any exchange of territory.[78] The Australian suggestion of applying the sector principle to determine sovereignty over polar regions was also rejected, since a policy that would strengthen the Commonwealth's claim to the Australian Antarctic would simultaneously strengthen Argentina's claim to the Falkland Islands Dependencies.

Instead, a dedicated Committee on British Policy in the Antarctic developed a cautious three-stage plan. First, Britain would advise other states of its intentions by publishing a summary of the conference's proceedings, which would mention the empire's special interest in Antarctica. Second, a new expedition would be despatched to officially take possession of parts of the proposed AAT that had not been formally claimed. Finally, letters patent would be issued to annex the area and place it under Australia's control.[79] Even after this plan was agreed, though, Australia unsuccessfully urged the British Government to omit the second stage and immediately issue letters patent in 1927 to prevent a Norwegian expedition, funded by whaling magnate Lars Christensen, from claiming any part of the Australian Antarctic.[80] This private concern echoed wider public anxieties. The Queensland Geographical Society publicly called on the Commonwealth to 'secure control of the Antarctic quadrant south of the continent' in 1928.[81] When rumours of a possible American claim, based on recent discoveries by Byrd or historic ones by Wilkes, swirled in 1929–30, an anonymous naval officer angrily told the press that 'Australians have already explored much of this region, and it should belong to Australia!'[82] Continuing reports even prompted backbencher Walter Nairn to raise the issue in parliament, asking prime minister James Scullin whether there were 'steps being taken to claim on behalf of Australia those portions of Antarctica, and the valuable whaling grounds adjacent to them, discovered by the Mawson Expedition?'[83]

It is clear, then, that Australia was no passive recipient of the AAT. The Commonwealth was the driving force behind its annexation, its approach informed by long-held ideas about Australia's self-perceived special interest in the Antarctic; enduring optimism that control of the region would secure unfathomable riches for the nation; a vernacular conception of the territorial rights bestowed by proximity and exploration; an openness to contested legal ideas like the sector principle; and a resurgence in popular and political support for the idea that territorial expansion was essential to ensure Australia's security and protect its interests. Yet efforts to carve out an Australian empire were stymied by continued membership of a British one. Dominion status meant Australia's international legal personality was murky at best, so a defensible Australian sovereignty claim over the AAT in the 1920s would have to rely on British legal instruments, just as it would have done for New Guinea in 1883 or Kerguelen in 1901. Thus, when behind-the-scenes efforts to accelerate the British plan to gradually acquire most of the Antarctic failed, the Commonwealth took the lead in organising an expedition to consolidate its claim.

‹ ›

Despite the three states mentioned in its title, BANZARE was essentially an Australian project. It was announced in February 1929 by Bruce, who told parliament that it was motivated by 'the special interest of the Commonwealth in the Antarctic region lying south of Australia'. More specifically, said Bruce, its primary objectives were to survey the coast of the Australian sector, 'render the region more safe for navigation', and investigate whale populations to determine the Australian sector's economic value and inform the development of whaling regulations 'to conserve them as a permanent source of wealth'.[84] But while this was the public rationale, Bruce privately described the reasons for the undertaking as 'firstly, political; secondly economic and commercial; thirdly, scientific'. By 'political', Bruce meant the proclamation of sovereignty at as many locations as possible between 160°E and 45°E to make the Commonwealth's claim unassailable.[85] The British Government offered the use of *Discovery*, employed since 1925 in cetological research in the Southern Ocean that aimed to provide data to inform whaling regulations, free of charge. The NZ Government offered £2,500 towards the expedition's costs, with Australia covering the remaining £16,000 required, though Bruce hoped to persuade private donors to subsidise this cost. Opposition leader James Scullin offered bipartisan support for an expedition he agreed would 'enable us to plant the Australian flag on new soil', as well as providing significant economic and scientific benefits.[86]

To bring this plan to fruition, Bruce appointed a committee consisting of Senate leader George Pearce, director of the External Affairs Branch Walter Henderson, Council of Scientific and Industrial Research chief executive ACD Rivett, chief of the Australian naval staff William Napier, Treasury secretary HJ Sheehan, and expert advisers Mawson, Masson, David and Davis.[87] The committee's principal task was to develop a program of work for the expedition that provided opportunities to raise the flag and proclaim sovereignty at multiple strategic locations while accounting for *Discovery*'s slow speed and modest coal capacity. The result was a plan to depart from Cape Town in October 1929, take on coal at a Norwegian whaling station on Kerguelen, proceed south to explore the largely unknown Enderby Land, then push as far east along the coast as possible before returning to Australia.[88]

The committee also took charge of financial matters, including securing a £10,000 donation from Melbourne confectionary magnate Macpherson Robertson, who declared that he simply 'wished to promote Australian interests in the Antarctic', but who was also known to be angling for a knighthood.[89] The committee was also responsible for selecting the expedition's staff, settling on a core of Antarctic veterans: Mawson as commander, Davis as *Discovery*'s captain, Morton Moyes as surveyor, Hurley as photographer, and James Marr, who had won a competition to accompany Shackleton's *Quest* expedition as a teenager in 1921 before becoming a krill expert with *Discovery*'s Southern Ocean investigations.[90] Beyond this, most practical arrangements, such as negotiating press rights and outfitting the ship, were handled by Mawson, Davis and the Commonwealth's liaison officer in London, Richard Casey.[91]

The fact that shoring up Australian sovereignty took precedence over scientific and even practical navigation concerns was repeatedly made apparent. Davis, for example, protested that it made no sense to start the coastal surveys at Enderby Land and work eastwards, but was told by Henderson that it was necessary because 'the British title to this region was not very strong at present' and they needed to consolidate British possession before Christensen's Norwegian expedition could claim it.[92] Mawson's sailing orders from Bruce included detailed, prescriptive instructions to visit Enderby, Kemp, Queen Mary and Knox lands, go ashore and raise the flag 'wherever you find it practicable to do so', read a proclamation using the forms provided, place copies of the proclamation form on the flagstaff, make a complete record of each 'act of annexation' using another form, and finally, provide a detailed report of each annexation to the federal government. Yet, in terms of scientific work, the same sailing orders instructed Mawson simply to 'carry out to the best of your ability all scientific work and investigations which it is practicable for you to do', though it did add that information about whales and seals that 'may assist in the future economic exploitation of such fauna' should especially be collected.[93]

The first BANZARE voyage in the summer of 1929–30 was plagued by disputes between Davis and Mawson, as well as *Discovery*'s technical limitations.[94] Mawson was limited to just the two proclamations during this voyage (the ceremony at Proclamation Island and the ad-hoc ritual of hurling a flag from a seaplane), a disappointment he blamed on both conditions and Davis's conservative captaincy.[95] Despite the tensions and disappointments of the first voyage—and the fact that Australia had been plunged into economic depression—Scullin, now prime minister, and Robertson agreed to provide £6,000 each to outfit *Discovery* for a second voyage in the summer of 1930–31.[96] It is perhaps surprising that BANZARE's first voyage was authorised by a Bruce government that was already cutting spending to tackle a ballooning budget deficit, and even more so that the Scullin government agreed to a second voyage at the outset of the Great Depression. Yet these decisions attracted remarkably little criticism. Scullin faced a few gentle queries about the expedition in parliament, but both parliament and the press were largely supportive.[97] An *Argus* editorial, for example, insisted it was 'doubtful whether the Commonwealth will ever again be in such a favourable position to discharge an obligation to science, to the Empire, and to itself by exploring the portion of Antarctic territory which lies to the South of Australia', and urged both the government and private donors to ensure the second voyage went ahead.[98] The Great Depression also failed to dent public enthusiasm for the expedition, and *Discovery*'s reception upon its return to Australia was substantially the same as had occurred for previous expeditions.[99] Scullin insisted when announcing the second voyage that the expedition's work was 'of considerable national interest and importance to the Commonwealth', and this view seems to have been essentially unchallenged.[100]

The second BANZARE voyage involved a cruise to Macquarie Island, Adélie Land and Queen Mary Land, and completing a survey of the newly discovered Mac.Robertson Land. Once again, Mawson discovered new coastlines and performed additional proclamation ceremonies, at Commonwealth Bay, Scullin Monolith and Cape Bruce.[101] While the scientific and geographical results of the expedition were less impressive than those of the AAE, and some of Mawson's discoveries were contested by Christensen's Norwegian expedition, it successfully consolidated British and Australian claims in the Australian sector and provided the legal basis for annexation.[102] The British Government issued an Order in Council on 7 February 1933 asserting sovereignty over the Australian Antarctic Territory and placing it under the administration of the Commonwealth. This was affirmed by the Australian Antarctic Territory Acceptance Act passed by the Australian Parliament in June 1933, coming into force in 1936.[103]

When parliament debated the AAT acceptance Bill in May 1933, the influence of decades of boosterism was readily apparent.

Introducing the Bill, External Affairs minister John Latham stressed that the proposed AAT had 'considerable actual and potential economic importance'. The whaling industry was already firmly established, he argued, pointing to the 263,000 whales killed in the Southern Ocean between 1919 and 1931, and to the thirty-three companies that had deployed Antarctic whaling fleets in the 1930–31 season. Commercial exploitation of other animals and resources in the region was likely. Control of the AAT would allow the Commonwealth to regulate these industries to ensure that the economic development of the Antarctic could continue apace without risking the total extinction of Antarctic fauna. A senior Labor member, Albert Green, responded with wholehearted support. Green argued that 'because Australia is the largest body of land close to the antarctic region, we believe that we are entitled to share in the rich whaling industry carried on in those waters', and felt that taking possession of the AAT could catalyse an Australian Antarctic whaling industry. Richard Casey, a key figure in organising BANZARE and now assistant treasurer in Joseph Lyons's United Australia Party government, noted that he had been constantly approached while serving as Commonwealth liaison officer in London with proposals for 'the exploitation of our sector of the Antarctic', ranging from requests for whaling and sealing licences to more imaginative proposals to try fox farming or exporting penguin eggs. He was therefore confident that 'when the world is restored to some sort of economic sanity, we shall probably be able to begin, without any great delay, the exploitation of the Antarctic'.[104]

When the Bill was introduced for its second reading in the Senate, Pearce called on his colleagues to pass it quickly so that whaling regulations could be imposed before the next whaling season. Pearce declared that it was the government's duty 'to prevent the extinction of these valuable animals', his emphasis on *valuable* animals indicative of how he saw the Commonwealth's duty as preserving whaling as a lucrative industry for the long term.[105] Mawson continued to make the same arguments outside of parliament, calling for new expeditions to explore and prospect for minerals in Mac.

Robertson and Enderby lands, and insisting that Antarctic whaling, sealing, mining and fishing would 'assist in the future prosperity of Australia if she safeguarded her interests in the south'.[106]

Political ideas about Australia's presumed rights in the Antarctic were also evident. Latham noted that the French annexation of Adélie Land had 'called attention to Australia's unsatisfactory position with regard to the Antarctic regions south of this continent', a point reiterated by Pearce in the Senate debates.[107] Latham also warned that 'embarrassing circumstances would arise if any other power assumed the control and administration of the area', pointing to the example of Britain declining to purchase Alaska before it became one of 'the Eldorados of the world'. Casey, meanwhile, emphasised that the annexation was 'the culminating point of twenty years of continuous and concerted effort on the part of Australians to consolidate their interest in the Antarctic'. Casey also recalled discussing the prospect of Australia stretching 'from the tropics to the pole' with the editor of the London *Times* six years earlier. It was, he declared, 'something to be proud of that this day has now arrived'.[108]

The Bill was ultimately passed with bipartisan support. The press, which had played such a key role in shaping and sustaining ideas about Australia and its southern frontier over decades, was overwhelmingly positive about this development. A comment in Melbourne's *Herald* is indicative: 'both on sentimental grounds … and because we do not know what the future may bring forth, there is reason why the Government should take the simple step of proclaiming its interest in these icy lands before other countries supplant us'.[109] *The Sydney Morning Herald* went further, applauding the news that the Australian Antarctic had finally been placed 'as a dependency under the control of the Commonwealth of Australia'. This was a significant moment, the paper argued, for it meant that 'the writ of Australia now runs from the equator to the South Pole'.[110]

‹ ›

The formal acquisition of the AAT in 1933 was a culmination of efforts to better align the territory of the Commonwealth with Australia's presumed sphere of interest. Antarctica and the wider Southern Ocean world had been imagined as a region of incipient riches for over a century, a space to be developed and exploited. Since the 1880s, it had also increasingly been imagined as an *Australian* space—geographical proximity, a history of promoting and supporting the investigation of the Antarctic, and an abiding expectation that the greatest benefits of Antarctic research and industries would flow to Australia, were interpreted as giving Australians a unique interest in the Antarctic. This was part of a wider belief that Australia had a natural sphere of influence extending north and east into the Pacific, west into the Indian Ocean, and south towards the Antarctic. Control of this vast region, or at least the prohibition of other states from acquiring territories within it, was commonly understood as essential to Australia's future security and prosperity. Many efforts to align Australia's territory with its imagined sphere of influence—Queensland's precocious attempt to annex eastern New Guinea in 1883, for instance, or the bid to protest the French annexation of the Crozets and other Southern Ocean islands in 1893, or the aborted campaign to have Kerguelen transferred from France to the Commonwealth in 1901—were clunky and unsuccessful. But the idea that Australia had a right to control and exploit its hinterland, from the equator to the pole, endured.

By the 1920s, when it seemed to many anxious Australians that other states wanted to seize Germany's confiscated colonies in the Pacific just as the wealth of the waters of the Australian Antarctic was being syphoned off by Norwegian whaling firms, the Commonwealth sought to acquire formal title over the region that had long been imagined as Australia's sphere. And by 1933, the Commonwealth's territory stretched from Nauru in the north, just 53 kilometres south of the equator, to the South Pole, and from the newly discovered westernmost slice of Enderby Land at 45°E to Norfolk Island at 167°E. This sprawling network of Australian dependencies straddled shipping routes, created a comforting colonial buffer, and above all was imagined as a site for Australian investment and industry.

CONCLUSION

Exposed Timbers: The Afterlife of the Australian Antarctic

The *Wyatt Earp* was in trouble. Rolling was a routine side effect of several qualities looked for in an Antarctic vessel, but even by these standards the *Wyatt Earp* was a prolific roller. Throughout the night of 19 December 1947, the ship built for the Norwegian herring fishery and repurposed for polar exploration by Lincoln Ellsworth was rolling constantly from 50° on one side of the vertical to 50° on the other in the space of four-and-a-half seconds. Objects—and people—were thrown violently from side to side. Crockery was smashed. Books, cameras and the contents of cupboards were hurled across rooms. Fifteen centimetres of water sloshed around, carrying drenched clothing, dissolving documents and what remained of pots of stew. Many of those on board were to be found gripping grimly to their bunks or debilitated by seasickness. And the ship hadn't even left Bass Strait.[1]

Such were the inauspicious beginnings of the first Australian National Antarctic Research Expedition (ANARE). The federal government had purchased the *Wyatt Earp* from Ellsworth in 1939, largely at the urging of Hubert Wilkins and Douglas Mawson. While there had been no firm plan for the ship, the idea of establishing permanent Antarctic research stations was in the air and it seemed a sensible move to have at least one vessel suited to polar work in the Australian naval fleet.[2] But with the outbreak of World War II, the ship had been pressed into service as a supply transport and guard ship before seeing out the war as a sea scout training vessel in Adelaide. Yet this was also a period of heightened political interest in the Antarctic. Norway, Chile and Argentina had asserted their own sovereignty claims, with the latter two staking claims to territory also claimed by Britain. Britain had responded with Operation Tabarin, a naval expedition to occupy these contested locations, in 1943, while the US Navy launched Operation Highjump to investigate and claim territory from Byrd's old Little America base in 1946–47. It was amidst this rapidly changing geopolitical context that a meeting chaired by External Affairs minister Herbert Evatt recommended, in December 1946, that the Commonwealth immediately despatch a new expedition to recommence the work of exploring and occupying the Australian Antarctic.

When Ellsworth returned from his final Antarctic expedition in 1939, having claimed 207,000 square kilometres of the AAT for the United States, he predicted that his would be the last of the old-style polar expeditions. The world had 'lost much of its romance with radio, planes, cars and so on', Ellsworth said, and Antarctic exploration was changing, becoming mechanised, professionalised, and above all the province more of governments than of private adventurers.[3] Phillip Law, ANARE's chief scientist, similarly observed that Antarctic exploration after World War II 'was of a completely different nature. In place of the privately organised, short-term "amateur" expeditions of the pre-War era, there developed government-financed, highly professional activities.'[4]

While this was certainly true—and became truer as time wore on—ANARE still retained a whiff of the old amateurism. The expedition was thrown together in the space of six months or so. The *Wyatt Earp* was, at Mawson's suggestion, pulled from semi-retirement and overhauled to resume service amidst the ice. Gear was scrounged from leftover military supplies, including khaki coats, submariners' jumpers, and plywood huts designed for tropical conditions. And while Law would eventually oversee the modernisation of the Australian Antarctic Division and its recruitment processes, staff for the first ANARE in 1947 were still selected mainly through old boys' networks and general impressions rather than the qualifications, interviews and psychological evaluations of the truly professional era.

Like the 1929–31 BANZARE that preceded it, the first ANARE was first and foremost a political exercise. Law, seconded from his position as a physics lecturer at Melbourne University, developed an innovative scientific program for the expedition, but soon realised that the organising committee's priorities were primarily 'directed toward the political objectives of establishing stations and making landings'.[5] And while Law was frustrated by decisions that compromised the scientific program, he was nonetheless supportive of the political imperative, remarking that 'no nation can hope to rope off a section of the earth as its property unless it sustains its claim by actively occupying a portion of that area and carrying out useful work there'.[6] The plan for ANARE required the expedition to establish two subantarctic research stations, one on Macquarie Island and the other on Heard Island, which were to be maintained for at least five years, and to scout the AAT's coastline to identify a site for a future continental station. And while an ordinary naval ship could be used to ferry supplies for the subantarctic station, only the *Wyatt Earp*, with its reinforced wooden hull, was deemed suitable for plunging through the icepack.

The shabby old ship did not live up to expectations. After refurbishments in Adelaide, the *Wyatt Earp* departed for Melbourne, where staff and supplies were waiting, on 13 December 1947. Within a day, the ship's main engine and gyrocompass had failed. The next day, it was the steering chain. The day after, a lifeboat davit. To top it off, the ship leaked prolifically throughout this brief trial run. Leaving Williamstown on 19 December, it suffered another mechanical failure and fared poorly in the first storm it faced. After further delays due to engine trouble, the southern voyage finally got properly underway when the vessel sailed out of Hobart on

26 December. Within a week, however, the *Wyatt Earp* was headed back north, having been halted at only 51°S by engine and propeller problems. After another month-long overhaul in a Melbourne drydock, ANARE got underway again on 8 February 1958. But the *Wyatt Earp* was cramped and unpleasant, struggled to punch through pack ice, and still leaked and rolled prolifically, failings which ultimately stymied the southern voyage. While the naval vessel *LST 3501* had successfully landed the staff and supplies needed to commence the effective occupation of Heard and Macquarie islands, the Antarctic party under former BANZARE pilot Stuart Campbell failed in its objectives. Ice prevented them from reaching the mainland, though they did explore the Balleny Islands before returning to Melbourne.[7] Here, they were greeted by a few friends, family members and naval officers on the dockside, but none of the cheering crowds or press that had characterised the comings and goings of Antarctic ships during the 'Heroic Era'. If ANARE's chaotic departure recalled the amateurism of the prewar world, its return offered a glimpse of the future, when the movement of ships to and from Antarctic stations evolved from momentous events to part of the routine functions of a Commonwealth department.

The voyage of the *Wyatt Earp* in 1947–48 was a failure, but it laid the foundation for the occupation of the Australian Antarctic. A permanent Australian Antarctic Division was created within the Department of External Affairs to coordinate the Commonwealth's Antarctic programs, with Law as director. Plans for a continental station were placed on hold until a more suitable ship could be obtained. Finally, in the summer of 1953–54, Law chartered the Danish icebreaker *Kista Dan* to construct Mawson Station, the first permanent research station on the Antarctic continent. A second station, Davis, was constructed in the Vestfold Hills (site of Wilkins and Ellsworth's 1939 battle to bury sovereignty proclamations) in 1957. The Antarctic Division took over a US station, Wilkes, in 1959, eventually replacing it with the current Casey Station in 1969.

‹ ›

The Australian Antarctic Territory occupies a curious position in contemporary Australia. The Commonwealth has a longstanding commitment to the Antarctic Treaty System (ATS), the international governance regime that developed around the 1959 Antarctic Treaty and which designates Antarctica a 'natural reserve, devoted to peace and science'.[8] One of the key principles of this system is an agreement that ratifying the Antarctic Treaty constitutes neither recognition nor renunciation of any state's territorial claims in the Antarctic, and that no activities that take place while the treaty is in force constitute a basis for confirming, refuting or asserting a territorial claim.[9] The ATS has enjoyed bipartisan support in Australia since the Commonwealth negotiated, signed and ratified the Antarctic Treaty, and the most recent articulation of Australia's Antarctic policy, the 2022 update to the *Australian Antarctic Strategy and 20 Year Action Plan*, reaffirms this commitment to a robust ATS.[10] At the same time, the Commonwealth has maintained a commitment to preserving Australian sovereignty over the AAT, its adjacent seas, and the subantarctic Macquarie, Heard and McDonald islands, a position that has also enjoyed longstanding bipartisan support and was reaffirmed in the same 2022 strategic plan. This approach, simultaneously supporting both Australia's claim to sovereignty and a system that effectively places sovereignty claims in suspended animation, has been described as bifocalism.[11] The same idea is evident in, for instance, the idea that Australia aims to both 'foster economic opportunities arising from Antarctica and the Southern Ocean' and uphold the ATS's commitments to robust environmental protections.[12] The AAT is therefore imagined as both national territory and international reserve, and the Commonwealth as both sovereign and custodian.

It is an oft-repeated refrain that Australia and its people have a special interest in the Antarctic, a product of a prominent role within the ATS and a history of Antarctic exploration and research dating back at least to Mawson's AAE in 1912, if not earlier. Yet, while the distinct interest of Australia and Australians in the world to their south is often mentioned, the origins and influence of this belief have seldom been investigated. I argue that this conception of a distinctly Australian connection with the Antarctic comprises three fundamental ideas.

The first is a belief that geographical proximity made the Antarctic a sphere of especial interest to Australia. This notion took many forms. It can be seen, for instance, in the idea that deeper knowledge of the Southern Ocean world—and ideally a greater colonial presence within it—was necessary to improve the safety, reliability and efficiency of Australia's maritime connections with the rest of the world. It can be seen in the assumption that the Antarctic had an enormous influence on Australia's weather and climate, and that an improved understanding of this influence would aid the development of the Australian continent. And it can be seen in anxieties about the presence of foreign states and empires in the lands and seas to Australia's south.

The second fundamental idea is an assumption that Australia's Southern Ocean hinterland was a space of boundless opportunity. While there were of course critics and sceptics, there were also always optimists and boosters ready to argue that there was 'a mine of inexhaustible wealth ... at our very doors' just waiting to be exploited.[13] Whether it was whaling, sealing, penguin oil, mining, iceberg harvesting or tourism, the idea that this region was destined to become a valuable and productive Australian dependency was durable and pervasive. From the 1880s, these ideas about interests and opportunities became entangled with ideas about Australia's right—and perhaps even its destiny—to control a vast region extending far beyond the limits of the Australian continent.

From this entanglement emerged the third fundamental idea: that Australia had a natural right to control the world to its south, whether through an informal 'Australian Monroe Doctrine' that excluded others from Australia's perceived sphere of influence, or through the formal policy of territorial acquisition pursued from the 1920s. The Antarctic came to be imagined not just as proximate to Australia but contiguous with it, a natural extension of Australian territory to the south. As this conception of Australian rights in the Antarctic developed, there was an increasing acceptance that existence of an inchoate right to control Australia's southern frontier also generated obligations and responsibilities—to aid exploration, rescue explorers, and manage resources to ensure their long-term profitability.

Many of the stories told in this book appear to make little sense in isolation. Why did the federal government rush to despatch the first ANARE in 1947, forcing it to make do with a profoundly ill-suited ship that critically hampered the expedition's work? Why did the Commonwealth aggressively pursue the annexation of the AAT in the 1920s and 1930s, including despatching the BANZARE in a context of savage cuts to government spending as the Great Depression took hold? Why were Australians so disproportionately invested in the global appeal to aid the families of Scott and his companions? Why did Australia's first federal Cabinet attempt to urgently acquire the Kerguelen archipelago before the first federal elections had even taken place? Why did a band of Antarctic enthusiasts in Melbourne hold so stubbornly to the dream of organising an Australian Antarctic expedition in the 1880s and 1890s? And why, despite a litany of failed attempts, did the dream of an Australian Antarctic whaling company or a profitable Antarctic tourist industry refuse to die?

The Southern Frontier seeks to reconceptualise and reframe these and other moments in Australia's Antarctic history. Events and decisions that seem odd, perhaps even inexplicable, can instead be understood as logical outcomes of a long genealogy of ideas about Australia and its relationship to the Antarctic. These ideas about Australia's Antarctic interests, opportunities, rights and responsibilities were articulated, debated and invoked across a range of contexts from the early nineteenth century, from lecture halls to legislatures and from business prospectuses to the press. They were shaped and promoted by enthusiasts and boosters, influenced by international developments, and transformed by their entanglement with other ideas and anxieties in Australian intellectual life. Ultimately, these ideas defined what could be imagined as desirable, possible and intolerable on Australia's southern frontier, shaping a mentality that made it possible to imagine a vast sweep of Antarctica and the islands and seas of the Southern Ocean as naturally an Australian space, one destined to both be controlled by the Commonwealth and enhance its security and prosperity.

These ideas are essential to understanding why Australia so aggressively pursued the annexation of the AAT in the 1920s and 1930s, as well as why sovereignty remains a non-negotiable cornerstone of Australian Antarctic policy in the twenty-first century. But they also reveal much about Australia itself. The vision of Australia's future embedded in these ideas is one of an Australian empire stretching from the equator to the South Pole. And by the end of the 1950s, the map of Australia bore a remarkable resemblance to the sprawling sphere of influence imagined since the 1880s. As well as Tasmania and the Australian mainland, the Commonwealth's dominion extended, via an assortment of legal mechanisms and justified in a variety of ways, to Christmas and the Cocos (Keeling) Islands in the north-west, to Papua, New Guinea and Nauru in the north-east, to Norfolk Island in the east, and to the Macquarie, Heard and McDonald islands and the AAT in the south. Importantly, Australia did not, to twist the famous words of JR Seeley, acquire this empire 'in a fit of absence of mind'.[14] The Australian empire was a product of popular ideas, geopolitical anxieties, expansionist policies and relentless political manoeuvring.

Historians of Australia have tended to underestimate the significance of territorial expansion to the nation's history. Many older narratives were, as Miranda Johnson and Cait Storr put it, narratives of internal expansion from colonial bridgeheads 'to the natural limits of the continent'.[15] Accounts of Australia's extracontinental empire are almost exclusively accounts of its *Pacific* empire, and while Australian ambitions and administrations in the Pacific constitute an important field of scholarship, any account of Australian imperialism that examines a single frontier in isolation can only ever be fragmentary.[16] Analysis of Australia's imperial history has also overwhelmingly shied away from the term 'empire' in favour of framing Australia as a 'sub-imperial' actor.[17] This concept of sub-imperialism seeks to recognise that Australia relied on British legal mechanisms to expand its territory, such as the letters patent that transferred the AAT to Commonwealth control. Yet, in trying to emphasise the role of metropolitan oversight, these accounts obscure the expansionist ideas, mentalities and policies that were the true drivers of Australia's territorial expansion. Australia's empire was a product of Australian ambitions.

By approaching Australia's history from the perspective of its southern frontier, this book has sought to recover a vision of Australian imperialism in the Southern Ocean world that has largely been forgotten. Recognising the persistent influence of this vision on Australia's relationship with the Antarctic reveals that the exploration, annexation and occupation of the AAT was a culmination of this way of thinking. This in turn reveals that Australian imperialism in the Pacific, Indian and Southern ocean worlds was a more assertive, more ambitious, more multidirectional, and altogether more influential force in Australia's history than has hitherto been recognised. Historians must therefore engage with Australia not only as an outpost of Britain's empire but as simultaneously the centre of Australia's. The territorial expansion of Australia flowed both inwards and outwards from the continental coast.

This has clear implications for Australian history, but also has significance for the global history of empire. Australia was far from alone in scrambling to assert control of marginal spaces like the AAT. In its efforts to transform such spaces into productive territories, the Commonwealth competed with the likes of Norway, France, the United States and even New Zealand. Attempts to justify Australia's claims were part of, and were in conversation with, wider efforts by states like Argentina, Canada, Chile and Norway to justify territorial claims to equally marginal spaces. Australia was an empire in a world of empires, and the imperialism of small states was, in its own way, as significant as the imperialism of the old powers.

‹ ›

The trouble-plagued trip in the summer of 1947–48 was the final polar voyage of the *Wyatt Earp*. The shabby old ship had proved spectacularly ill-suited to a role as the Commonwealth's dedicated Antarctic vessel, and within a few months of returning from the first ANARE it was sold to a small Melbourne shipping company. The ship that had once been at the heart of the Commonwealth's battle to affirm its sovereignty in the AAT ended its days plying the tramp trade along the Australian coast under the name MV *Natone*. On the night of 23 January 1959, the *Natone* ran aground in cyclonic conditions off the Queensland coast, a few kilometres north of Double Island Point lighthouse, during a voyage from Brisbane to Port Moresby. The crew survived a torrid night as the ship was torn apart by rocks and waves, before using salvaged hatch covers to evacuate to the shore when morning broke. Over the following days, the ship broke apart, leaving bits of wreckage strewn along the coast. Here, on this sunny Queensland beach, a few timbers from the *Wyatt Earp* are exposed from time to time.[18]

In many ways, the fate of the *Wyatt Earp* echoes the fate of the once-influential vision of the Australian Antarctic. From the middle of the nineteenth century to the middle of the twentieth, there was an expectation that the Australian Antarctic would, in time, become a productive and important Australian territory. Precisely what benefits would be derived from control of this region was a matter of debate, but there was increasingly over this period a powerful sense that Australian rights and interests extended south to the Antarctic. This vision of Australia's future, as a multicellular polity with dominion extending over two continents, three oceans, and an assortment of islands stretching from the equator to the South Pole, has faded from memory. Its legacies, however, remain. They can be seen in, for example, Australia's unrelenting commitment to a territorial claim that is recognised by only four other nations. They can be seen in the nation's prominent and influential position in international Antarctic science and governance. And they can be seen in the anxieties that periodically rear their head in relation to the actions of other states, most often China or Russia, within the borders of the AAT.[19] Just as wind, sun and sea expose the timbers of the *Wyatt Earp* on Rainbow Beach, so too do contemporary events and utterances expose occasional glimpses of that older, forgotten vision of the Australian Antarctic.

ACKNOWLEDGEMENTS

This is a book about ideas, their genealogies and their effects, so it is only fitting that I begin with an acknowledgement of the many scholars who inspired, supported and shaped this research long before it was a book. To Alison Bashford, Justine Greenwood, Chris Hilliard, Peter Hobbins, Adrian Howkins, Miranda Johnson, Sophie Loy-Wilson, Mark McKenna, Penny Russell, Glenda Sluga, Koen Stapelbroek, Ryan Tucker Jones, Richard Waterhouse and above all Andrew Fitzmaurice, thank you.

Research for this book was supported by an Australian Postgraduate Award and several postgraduate research schemes at the University of Sydney: the John Frazer Travelling Scholarship, Joan Allsopp Travel Bursary and Australasian Pioneers Club Travel Bursary. It was underpinned, too, by the tireless work of the staff at the myriad archives and libraries cited throughout.

I wrote this book in fits and starts while working many jobs at many universities. I would never have persisted with trying to finish it without the kindness and support shown by Alessandro Antonello, Kate Fullagar, Claire Lowrie and Frances Steel. Thank you for showing me academia at its best. I am likewise grateful to my students at Monash University and the universities of Sydney,

Wollongong and Notre Dame, whose enthusiasm for exploring the past has constantly renewed my own.

I benefited tremendously from the opportunity to write this book in two exceptional research environments. The blueprint for it came together during a postdoc at the Australian National University's Centre for Environmental History in 2022, while the majority of the book was written while working as a lecturer in the History program at Monash University. I am grateful to all my colleagues at both the ANU and Monash for their advice and support, and especially to Julie Kalman, Samson Lim, Paula Michaels, Kate Murphy and Carolyn Strange. A special note of thanks goes to Ruth Morgan, whose intellectual generosity and mentorship made this project possible.

I cannot imagine attempting to write this book without the solidarity and kindness of a remarkable community of early career historians. My thanks go to Michelle Bootcov, Genevieve Dashwood, Jamie Dunk, Nick Ferns, Meg Foster, Jarrod Hore, Amy Jelacic, Liam Kane, James Keating, Bernard Keo, Emma Kluge, Ebony Nilsson, Kate Rivington, Jess Urwin and Amy Way for their incisive comments, relentless encouragement and unparalleled collegiality.

I am enormously grateful to Melbourne University Publishing for their support for this book, especially Duncan Fardon for guiding it expertly to completion. I would also like to thank MUP's anonymous reviewers for commenting so insightfully on the manuscript, Paul Smitz for his exceptional work editing it, and Erin Greb for producing the maps that enhance it.

And finally, thank you to my family and to those whose friendship sustained me through the decade I've spent on this project: Josh, Luke, Georgie, Michael, Brad and Paul. Above all, thank you to Jess (and Asta). Our little family is the circle of light that makes all of this possible.

NOTES

Introduction: Reorienting the Map

1 Lincoln Ellsworth, *Beyond Horizons*, William Heinemann, 1938, pp. 291–5; Archives of the American Geographical Society, AGSNY AC 1/269/3, flight log data and notes compiled during the Ellsworth Trans-Antarctic Flight, 1935, 2.02–2.09, accessed via University of Wisconsin–Milwaukee, https://collections.lib.uwm.edu/digital/collection/agsny/id/68378 (viewed August 2024).

2 See, for example, 'Ellsworth Far in Flight over Unknown Antarctic', *The New York Times*, 24 November 1935, p. 1; 'Anxiety for Polar Flyers', *Daily Mail* (London), 25 November 1935, p. 11; 'Har Ellsworth nødlandet?', *Arbeiderbladet*, 25 November 1935, p. 13; 'Concern over Antarctic Flight Airmen', *The Times of India*, 25 November 1935, p. 9; 'Ellsworth Plane', *The Sydney Morning Herald* (*SMH*), 25 November 1935, p. 9; 'Puzzling Silence', *Evening Post* (Wellington), 25 November 1935, p. 12; 'Ellsworth Lost', *South China Morning Post*, 26 November 1935, p. 10; 'No News of Ellsworth', *The Manchester Guardian*, 27 November 1935, p. 6; 'Ellsworth's Fate Remains Mystery', *Evening Post* (Washington, DC), 29 November 1935, p. A-2; 'Nine Days' Silence', *Evening Post* (Wellington), 5 December 1935, p. 9.

3 National Archives of Australia (NAA), A981, ANT 38, cablegram from Department of External Affairs to Secretary of State for Dominion Affairs, 2 December 1935.

4 NAA, A981, ANT 38, letter from JK Davis to RG Casey, 5 December 1935.

5 Ellsworth, *Beyond Horizons*, p. 333.

6 NAA, A981, ANT 38, report on Ellsworth Antarctic Relief Expedition by Captain LC Hill; 'Explorers Safe', *SMH*, 18 January 1936, p. 17.

7 Ellsworth, *Beyond Horizons*, pp. 291–340; 'Mr. Ellsworth and the Discovery II', *Polar Record*, vol. 2, no. 12, July 1936, pp. 166–72.

8 NAA, A461, P413/6, letter from DM Dow to Prime Minister's Department, 27 January 1936.

9 Ellsworth, *Beyond Horizons*, pp. 333–9.

10 'Mr. Ellsworth's Visit', *The Argus*, 15 February 1936, p. 26; NAA, A461, P413/6.

11 NAA, A461, P413/6, letter from Fox Movietone News to Defence Ministry, 5 February 1936; letter from TW Bearup to R Archdale Parkhill, 7 February 1936. See, for example, 'Discovery II', *The Age*, 12 February

1936, p. 10; 'Ellsworth Returns', *The Argus*, 17 February 1936, p. 10; 'The Great Adventurer', *The Age*, 18 February 1936, p. 13; 'Ellsworth', *The Canberra Times*, 18 February 1936, p. 1; 'Back from the Antarctic', *Mercury*, 18 February 1936, p. 9; 'You Have Found Our Lost Boy', *The Argus*, 19 February 1936, p. 8.

12 'Mr. Ellsworth', *SMH*, 21 February 1936, p. 11.

13 'The Antarctic Rescue', *SMH*, 21 January 1936, p. 10. See also 'Pioneer Spirit', *Mercury*, 19 February 1936, p. 6.

14 Leonard Huxley (ed.), *Scott's Last Expedition*, Smith Elder, 1913, p. 544.

15 NAA, A981, ANT 38. See, for example, cablegram from Dominion Affairs to External Affairs, 3 December 1935; cablegram from prime minister of Australia to prime minister of New Zealand, 16 December 1935; minute paper from Defence to External Affairs, 16 December 1935.

16 Regina Ganter, 'The View from the North', in Martin Lyons and Penny Russell (eds), *Australia's History: Themes and Debates*, UNSW Press, 2005, p. 43.

17 Henry Reynolds, *North of Capricorn: The Untold Story of the People of Australia's North*, Allen & Unwin, 2003; Regina Ganter, 'Turning the Map Upside Down', *History Compass*, vol. 4, no. 1, 2006, pp. 26–35; Julia Martínez and Adrian Vickers, *The Pearl Frontier: Indonesian Labor and Indigenous Encounters in Australia's Northern Trading Network*, University of Hawaii Press, 2015; Russell McGregor, *Environment, Race, and Nationhood in Australia: Revisiting the Empty North*, Palgrave Macmillan, 2016; Mark McKenna, *From the Edge: Australia's Lost Histories*, Melbourne University Publishing, 2016, pp. 64–109.

18 Marilyn Lake, 'Colonial Australia and the Asia-Pacific Region', in Alison Bashford and Stuart Macintyre (eds), *The Cambridge History of Australia*, Cambridge University Press, 2013, pp. 535–59; Marilyn Lake, 'The Australian Dream of an Island Empire: Race, Reputation and Resistance', *Australian Historical Studies*, vol. 46, no. 3, September 2015, pp. 410–24; Katerina Teaiwa, 'Ruining Pacific Islands: Australia's Phosphate Imperialism', *Australian Historical Studies*, vol. 46, no. 3, 2015, pp. 375–91; Cait Storr, *International Status in the Shadow of Empire: Nauru and the Histories of International Law*, Cambridge University Press, 2020; Ian Hoskins, *Australia and the Pacific: A History*, NewSouth, 2021.

19 Philippa Mein Smith, Peter Hempenstall and Shaun Goldfinch (eds), *Remaking the Tasman World*, University of Canterbury Press, 2008; Rachel Standfield, *Race and Identity in the Tasman World*, Routledge, 2012; Ryan Tucker Jones, 'A Whale of a Difference: Southern Right Whale Culture and the Tasman World's Living Terrain of Encounter', *Environment and History*, vol. 25, no. 2, 2019, pp. 185–218; Daniel Davy, *Gold Rush Societies and Migrant Networks in the Tasman World*, Edinburgh University Press, 2021.

20 Charlie Fox, 'The View from the West', in Lyons and Russell, *Australia's History*, pp. 81–97; Ruth A Morgan, 'Western Australia and the Indian Ocean: A Land Looking West?', *Studies in Western Australian History*, vol. 28, 201, pp. 1–12.

21 McKenna, *From the Edge*, p. xvi; Mark McKenna, *Return to Uluru*, Black Inc., 2021.

22 Tom Griffiths, 'Ecology and Empire: Towards an Australian History of the World', in Tom Griffiths and Libby Robin (eds), *Ecology and Empire: Environmental History of Settler Societies*, Edinburgh University Press, 1997, p. 17.

23 Frank Broeze, *Island Nation: A History of Australians and the Sea*, Allen & Unwin, 1998, Introduction.

24 McKenna, *From the Edge*, p. xvi.

25 Brigid Hains, *The Ice and the Inland: Mawson, Flynn, and the Myth of the Frontier*, Melbourne University Press, 2002.

26 Tom Griffiths, *Slicing the Silence: Voyaging to Antarctica*, NewSouth, 2007, p. 3; Tom Griffiths, 'The Breath of Antarctica', *Tasmanian Historical Studies*, vol. 2, 2006, pp. 4–14.

27 Joy McCann, *Wild Sea: A History of the Southern Ocean*, NewSouth, 2018.

28 Lynette Russell, '"A New Holland Half-Caste": Sealer and Whaler Tommy Chaseland', *History Australia*, vol. 5, no. 1, 2008, p. 08.1. See also Lynette Russell, *Roving Mariners: Australian Aboriginal Whalers and Sealers in the Southern Oceans, 1790–1870*, State University of New York Press, 2012.

29 Alessandro Antonello, 'Australia, the International Geophysical Year and the 1959 Antarctic Treaty', *Australian Journal of Politics & History*, vol. 59, no. 4, December 2013, pp. 532 46; Alessandro Antonello, 'The Southern Ocean', in David Armitage, Alison Bashford and Sujit Sivasundaram (eds), *Oceanic Histories*, Cambridge University Press, 2018, pp. 296–318; Alessandro Antonello, *The Greening of Antarctica*, Oxford University Press, 2019; Emma Shortis, '"Who Can Resist This Guy?": Jacques Cousteau, Celebrity Diplomacy, and the Environmental Protection of the Antarctic', *Australian Journal of Politics & History*, vol. 61, no. 3, September 2015, pp. 366–80; Emma Shortis, 'Lessons from the Last Continent: Science, Emotion, and the Relevance of History', *RCC Perspectives: Transformations in Environment and Society*, no. 4, 2019, pp. 53–60.

30 RA Swan, *Australia in the Antarctic: Interest, Activity, and Endeavour*, Melbourne University Press, 1961; Marie Kawaja, 'Australia in Antarctica: Realising an Ambition', *Polar Journal*, vol. 3, no. 1, 2013, pp. 31–52; Joy McCann, *Ice Bound: Australian Stories from Antarctica*, National Library of Australia Publishing, 2022; Marcus Haward and Tom Griffiths (eds), *Australia and the Antarctic Treaty System: 50 Years of Influence*, UNSW Press, 2011.

31 See, for example, Stephen Murray-Smith, *Sitting on Penguins: People and Politics in Australian Antarctica*, Hutchinson, 1988; Philip Ayres, *Mawson: A Life*, Melbourne University Press, 1999; Carolyn Strange and Alison Bashford, *Griffith Taylor: Visionary, Environmentalist, Explorer*, National Library of Australia, 2008.

32 Gillian Triggs, *International Law and Australian Sovereignty in Antarctica*, Legal Books Ltd, 1986; Christy Collis, 'The Proclamation Island Moment: Making Antarctica Australian', *Law Text Culture*, vol. 8, 2004, pp. 1–18; Noel D Barrett, 'Was Australian Antarctica Won Fairly?', *Polar Record*, vol. 45, no. 4, October 2009, pp. 360–7.

33 See, for example, Deborah Gare and David Ritter, *Making Australian History: Perspectives on the Past Since 1788*, Cengage, 2008; Mark Peel and Christina Twomey, *A History of Australia*, Palgrave Macmillan, 2011; Stuart Macintyre, *A Concise History of Australia*, Cambridge University Press, 3rd edn, 2014; Bashford and Macintyre, *The Cambridge History of Australia*.

34 'Annexation of British Islands by France', *The Argus*, 13 August 1892, p. 7.

35 See Tracey Banivanua Mar and Penelope Edmonds, 'Indigenous and Settler Relations', in Bashford and Macintyre, *The Cambridge History of Australia*, vol. 1, pp. 342–66.

36 See Griffiths, 'Ecology and Empire', pp. 1–21; Hains, *The Ice and the Inland*.

37 See Christy Collis, 'The Australian Antarctic Territory: A Man's world?', *Signs: Journal of Women in Culture and Society*, vol. 34, no. 3, spring 2009, pp. 514–19; Lize-Marié van der Watt and Sandra Swart, 'The Whiteness of Antarctica: Race and South Africa's Antarctic History', in Peder Roberts, Lize-Marié van der Watt and Adrian Howkins (eds), *Antarctica and the Humanities*, Palgrave Macmillan, 2016, pp. 125–56; Angela Woollacott, 'Frontier Violence and Settler Manhood', *History Australia*, vol. 6, no. 1, 2009, pp. 11.1–11.15.

38 See Adrian Howkins, *Frozen Empires: An Environmental History of the Antarctic Peninsula*, Oxford University Press, 2016; Shirley V Scott, 'Three Waves of Antarctic Imperialism', in Alan D Hemmings, Klaus Dodds and Peder Roberts (eds), *Handbook on the Politics of Antarctica*, Edward Elgar, 2017, pp. 37–49.

39 See Stephen Howe, *Empire: A Very Short Introduction*, Oxford University Press, 2002; Peter Fibiger Bang, 'Empire—A World History: Anatomy and Concept, Theory and Synthesis', in Peter Fibiger Bang, CA Bayly and Walter Scheidel (eds), *The Oxford World History of Empire: Volume One: The Imperial Experience*, Oxford University Press, 2021.

40 For overviews of this historiography, see Griffiths and Robin, *Ecology and Empire*; William Beinart and Lotte Hughes, *Environment and Empire*, Oxford University Press, 2007; James Beattie, 'Recent Themes in the Environmental History of the British Empire', *History Compass*, vol. 10, no. 2, 2012, pp. 129–39; Eugene Anderson and James Beattie, 'Ecology: Environments

and Empires in World History, 3000 BCE–ca. 1900 CE', in Bang, Bayly and Scheidel, *The Oxford World History of Empire: Volume One*.

41 Beattie, 'Recent Themes in the Environmental History of the British Empire', pp. 129–39; Andrew Fitzmaurice, *Sovereignty, Property, and Empire*, Cambridge University Press, 2014.

42 Alfred Crosby, *Ecological Imperialism: The Biological Expansion of Europe*, Cambridge University, 1986.

43 Corey Ross, *Ecology and Power in the Age of Empire: Europe and the Transformation of the Tropical World*, Oxford University Press, 2017, p. 3.

44 Daniel Immerwahr, 'The Greater United States: Territory and Empire in U.S. History', *Diplomatic History*, vol. 40, no. 3, June 2016, pp. 373–91.

45 Daniel Immerwahr, *How to Hide an Empire: A Short History of the Greater United States*, The Bodley Head, 2019, p. 19.

46 *The Argus*, 15 February 1936, p. 24.

47 Antonello, 'Australia, the International Geophysical Year', pp. 532–46.

48 Anthony Bergin and Marcus Haward, *Frozen Assets: Securing Australia's Antarctic Future*, Australian Strategic Policy Institute, 2007; Australian Government, *Australian Antarctic Strategy and 20 Year Action Plan*, Commonwealth of Australia, 2016; Australian Government, *Maintaining Australia's National Interests in Antarctica*, Inquiry into Australia's Antarctic Territory, Joint Standing Committee on the National Capital and External Territories, Commonwealth of Australia, 2018; Australian Government, *Australian Antarctic Strategy and 20 Year Action Plan: 2022 Update*, Commonwealth of Australia, 2022.

49 See, for example, Haward and Griffiths, *Australia and the Antarctic Treaty System*; Kawaja, 'Australia in Antarctica', pp. 31–52; McCann, *Ice Bound*.

50 'Antarctic Lures Ellsworth Again', *The New York Times*, 6 May 1938, p. 1.

51 'Oil and Minerals in Antarctic', *SMH*, 3 August 1938, p. 15.

52 'Explorers' Plans', *The Argus*, 3 September 1938, p. 7.

53 'Ellsworth Tells Expedition's Plans', *The New York Times*, 25 July 1938, p. 4; NAA, A981, ANT 22, memorandum from F Keith Officer to WR Hodgson, 6 May 1938.

54 'New Antarctic Land', *SMH*, 13 January 1939, p. 11; 'Antarctic Lands', *The West Australian*, 14 January 1939, p. 20.

55 'Antarctic Claim', *SMH*, 7 February 1939, p. 10; 'Australia Claims Princess Elizabeth Land', *The Canberra Times*, 7 February 1939, p. 1.

56 NAA, A981, ANT 22, cablegram from WM Hughes to F Keith Officer, 14 January 1939; cablegram from WM Hughes to Hubert Wilkins, 14 January 1939; NAA, A461, P413/6, cablegram from External Affairs to F Keith Officer, 16 January 1939.

57 NAA, A981, ANT 22, memorandum from WR Hodgson to WM Hughes, 1938; letter from WM Hughes to Hubert Wilkins, 8 September 1939.

58 NAA, A981, ANT 22, Hubert Wilkins, 'Report of the Ellsworth Antarctic Flight Expedition, 1938–39', 6 February 1939.
59 Ibid.
60 Ibid.
61 'Polar Exploration', *The Canberra Times*, 20 January 1939, p. 4; NAA, A981, ANT 22, WM Hughes, Cabinet submission on 'Offer by Ellsworth to Sell his Vessel "Wyatt Earp" to the Commonwealth Government', 27 January 1939; 'Wyatt Earp Is Handed Over', *The Argus*, 14 February 1939, p. 7; NAA, A981, ANT 39, letter from Douglas Mawson to RG Casey, 3 February 1939; memorandum from External Affairs Department for WM Hughes on the Antarctic, 27 February 1939.
62 NAA, A981, ANT 22, telegram from F Keith Officer to WR Hodgson, 28 January 1939; 'Claim of Territory in Antarctic', *SMH*, 8 February 1939, p. 18; 'South Polar Lands', *SMH*, 18 February 1939, p. 10.
63 NAA, A981, ANT 39, letter from F Strahan to FJ McKenna, 2 May 1939; telegram from HS Gullett to Hubert Wilkins, 3 August 1939.
64 'Station at Pole', *The Argus*, 3 March 1939, p. 10. See also 'Polar Station Proposal', *SMH*, 3 March 1939, p. 10.
65 See, for example, 'Antarctic Claims', *SMH*, 17 February 1939, p. 10.

1 'The Memorable First of June'

1 'The Nautical Fete', *Hobart Town Advertiser*, 4 June 1841, p. 2; 'The Ball on Board the Discovery Ships', *The Courier*, 4 June 1841, p. 2; State Library of Tasmania, NS3677/1/1, Box NS5/1, letter from John Franklin to James Ross, 27 May 1841.
2 'Naval Entertainment', *Colonial Times*, 8 June 1841, p. 3.
3 *Report of the Fifth Meeting of the British Association for the Advancement of Science*, John Murray, 1836, p. 21; *Report of the Eighth Meeting of the British Association for the Advancement of Science*, John Murray, 1839, pp. xxi–xxii.
4 For authoritative accounts of the obsession with the science of terrestrial magnetism and the origins of the Ross expedition, see John Cawood, 'The Magnetic Crusade: Science and Politics in Early Victorian Britain', *Isis*, vol. 70, no. 4, 1979, pp. 492–518; Edward J Larson, *An Empire of Ice: Scott, Shackleton, and the Heroic Age of Antarctic Science*, Yale University Press, 2011, pp. 27–59; Matthew Goodman, From 'Magnetic Fever' to 'Magnetical Insanity': Historical Geographies of British Terrestrial Magnetic Research, 1833–1857, PhD thesis, University of Glasgow, 2018, https://theses.gla.ac.uk/30829 (viewed August 2024).
5 Charles Wilkes, *Narrative of the United States Exploring Expedition during the Years 1838–42*, vol. II, Lea & Blanchard, 1845, p. 168; 'Ships in Harbour', *Sydney General Trade List*, 30 November 1839, p. 3.
6 Wilkes, *Narrative*, p. 43; *Sydney Gazette*, 3 December 1838, p. 2.

7 See, for example, 'French Antarctic Voyage', *Sydney Herald*, 10 April 1839, p. 2; 'English Intelligence', *Sydney Gazette*, 27 July 1839, p. 2.
8 For a blow-by-blow account of the US expedition's messy origins, see Alan Gurney, *The Race to the White Continent: Voyages to the Antarctic*, Norton, 2000, pp. 93–128.
9 Wilkes, *Narrative*, pp. 290–2.
10 Ibid., pp. 169–290.
11 'Dinner to the American Squadron', *The Australian*, 14 December 1839, p. 2.
12 'Domestic Intelligence', *Sydney Herald*, 23 December 1839, p. 2; 'American Fleet', *The Colonist*, 14 December 1839, p. 2.
13 'The Americans', *Sydney Herald*, 30 December 1839, p. 2.
14 'Shipping Intelligence', *Sydney Herald*, 27 December 1839, p. 2; 'Shipping Intelligence', *Sydney Gazette*, 28 December 1839, p. 2; 'The Americans', *Sydney Herald*, 30 December 1839, p. 2; 'News of the Day', *Sydney Monitor*, 1 January 1840, p. 2; Wilkes, *Narrative*, 276–7.
15 Wilkes, *Narrative*, pp. 303–7.
16 Ibid., p. 483.
17 Ibid., pp. 315–57.
18 Ibid., p. 384.
19 *Sydney Monitor*, 13 March 1840, p. 2.
20 Wilkes, *Narrative*, pp. xxv–xxxii.
21 *The Australian*, 11 March 1840, p. 2.
22 'Discovery of the Antarctic Continent', *Sydney Herald*, 13 March 1840, p. 2.
23 'The Antarctic Expedition of Discovery', *Sydney Herald*, 20 August 1841, pp. 2–3.
24 'Discovery', *The Colonist*, 18 March 1840, p. 2.
25 'American News', *Sydney Herald*, 8 December 1840, p. 2; 'Antarctic Discovery', *Australasian Chronicle*, 10 December 1840, p. 3.
26 See, for example, 'The Antarctic Continent', *Sydney Herald*, 19 December 1840, p. 2; 'English Extracts', *The Colonist*, 26 December 1840, p. 2; 'Exploring Expedition', *Southern Australian*, 22 December 1840, p. 4; 'The Antarctic Continent', *The Australian*, 22 December 1840, p. 3.
27 'The Southern Exploring Expeditions', *Free Press*, 24 April 1841, p. 2; 'The Antarctic Expedition of Discovery', *Sydney Herald*, 20 August 1841, pp. 2–3; 'The Late Naval Court-Martial', *The Sydney Morning Herald* (*SMH*), 4 May 1843, p. 4; 'The United States Exploring Expedition', *Commercial Journal*, 23 July 1845, p. 1; 'The United States Exploring Expedition', *SMH*, 4 June 1845, p. 3; 'A Run through the Icebergs', *Colonial Times*, 19 June 1846.
28 'Local', *Hobart Town Examiner*, 16 May 1843, p. 2.
29 For excellent accounts of the French expedition, see Janet Martin-Nielsen, *A Few Acres of Ice: Environment, Sovereignty, and 'Grandeur' in the French*

Antarctic, Cornell University Press, 2023, pp. 26–43; Gillen D'Arcy Wood, *Land of Wondrous Cold: The Race to Discover Antarctica and Unlock the Secrets of Its Ice*, Princeton University Press, 2020.

30 James Cook, *A Voyage towards the South Pole, and Round the World*, 3rd edn, W Strahan & T Cadell, 1779, p. 268.

31 See, for example, 'Discovery of a New Continent', *Hobart Town Courier*, 25 January 1839, p. 3; 'Discovery of a New Continent', *The Colonist*, 2 February 1839, p. 3; 'Discovery of a New Continent', *The Australian*, 2 February 1839, p. 2.

32 See, for example, *The Colonist*, 2 February 1839, p. 2; 'French Antarctic Voyage', *Sydney Herald*, 10 April 1839, p. 2; 'French Expedition to the South Polar Seas', *Sydney Gazette*, 18 May 1839, p. 4.

33 *Hobart Town Courier*, 13 December 1839, p. 3; *The Colonist*, 28 December 1839, p. 2.

34 See Edward Duyker, *Dumont d'Urville: Explorer & Polymath*, Otago University Press, 2014, pp. 429–49.

35 Jules Dumont d'Urville, *An Account in Two Volumes of Two Voyages to the South Seas By Captain (later Rear-Admiral) Jules S-C Dumont d'Urville of the French Navy*, vol. 2, ed. and trans. Helen Rosenman, Melbourne University Press, 1987, pp. 446–52.

36 See d'Urville, *An Account in Two Volumes*, pp. 464–92. For a concise overview of these events, see Martin-Nielsen, *A Few Acres of Ice*, pp. 33–7.

37 Wilkes, *Narrative*, pp. 364–5; d'Urville, *An Account in Two Volumes*, pp. 486–7. This event has been thoroughly evaluated by, for example, Martin-Nielsen, *A Few Acres of Ice*, p. 37; D'Arcy Wood, *Land of Wondrous Cold*, p. 188; Gurney, *The Race to the White Continent*, pp. 174–5, 199.

38 *Hobart Town Courier*, 21 February 1840, p. 2.

39 See Ann Moyal, *A Bright & Savage Land: The Science of a New Continent—Australia—Where All Things Were 'Queer and Opposite'*, Penguin, 1986, pp. 72–3; John Lillie, 'Introductory Paper', *Tasmanian Journal*, vol. 1, 1842, pp. 1–12.

40 'To the Editor', *True Colonist*, 10 January 1840, p. 7; 'To the Editor', *Colonial Times*, 14 January 1840, p. 7.

41 Duyker, *Dumont d'Urville*, pp. 444–9.

42 'Expedition', *Hobart Town Advertiser*, 28 February 1840, p. 2.

43 See, for example, 'Van Diemen's Land', *Sydney Gazette*, 14 March 1840, p. 3; 'Van Diemen's Land', *Australasian Chronicle*, 20 March 1840, p. 3; 'Van Diemen's Land', *The Colonist*, 21 March 1840, p. 2; 'The French Discovery Ships', *The Australian*, 21 March 1840, p. 3; 'The French Discovery Ships', *South Australian Register*, 28 March 1840, p. 6; 'Antarctic Discovery', *Sydney Herald*, 15 April 1840, p. 2; 'Ship News', *The Australian*, 16 April 1840, p. 2.

44 Edward Sabine, 'The Magnetic Survey of the British Islands, Reduced to the Epoch 1842–5', *Philosophical Transactions*, vol. 160, 1870, pp. 265–75.

45 Larson, *An Empire of Ice*, pp. 27–39; Edward J Larson, 'Public Science for a Global Empire: The British Quest for the South Magnetic Pole', *Isis*, vol. 102, no. 1, 2011, pp. 34–59.

46 James Clark Ross, *A Voyage of Discovery and Research in the Southern and Antarctic Regions, during the Years 1839–43*, vol. 1, John Murray, 1847, pp. xxii–xlviii.

47 Herman Melville, *Moby Dick*, ed. Tony Tanner, Oxford University Press, 2008, ch. 101.

48 See Rohan Howitt, 'The Company-Microstate: The Auckland Islands and Corporate Colonialism in Global History, 1849–52', *Journal of Global History*, vol. 19, no. 1, 2024, pp. 37–56.

49 On whales resisting whalers, see Ryan Tucker Jones, 'A Whale of a Difference: Southern Right Whale Culture and the Tasman World's Living Terrain of Encounter', *Environment and History*, vol. 25, no. 2, May 2019, pp. 185–218.

50 British Library, MS 15716, 'A Journal of a Voyage towards the South Seas, on Board the brig Tula … from July, 1830, to January, 1833'.

51 Charles Enderby, George Enderby and John Biscoe, 'Recent Discoveries in the Antarctic Ocean', *The Journal of the Royal Geographical Society of London*, vol. 3, 1833, p. 112.

52 'The Journal of John Balleny', in George Murray (ed.), *The Antarctic Manual*, Royal Geographical Society, 1901, pp. 336–45.

53 The loan of Balleny's journal to Ross is explained in a covering letter from Charles and George Enderby to the trustees of the British Museum, dated 23 January 1846, enclosed in the copy of Biscoe's journal presented to the museum by the Enderbys: see British Library, MS 15716.

54 Ross, *A Voyage of Discovery*, vol. 1, pp. 1–108.

55 See, for example, 'Literature and Science', *The Colonist*, 24 February 1838, p. 4; 'English Intelligence', *Sydney Gazette*, 27 July 1839, p. 2; *Hobart Town Courier*, 17 January 1840, p. 2; 'The Antarctic Expedition', *True Colonist*, 17 January 1840, p. 5; 'The Antarctic Expedition', *Hobart Town Courier*, 24 January 1840, p. 4.

56 Andrew Lambert, *The Gates of Hell: Sir John Franklin's Tragic Quest for the North West Passage*, Yale University Press, 2009, pp. 93–140; Kathleen Fitzpatrick, *Sir John Franklin in Tasmania 1837–1843*, Melbourne University Press, 1949, pp. 49–54, 245–9.

57 Ross, *A Voyage of Discovery*, vol. 1, John Murray, 1847, pp. 107–10.

58 Ibid., pp. 109–10; Lambert, *The Gates of Hell*, pp. 115–23.

59 'Local', *Hobart Town Courier*, 16 October 1840, p. 2; 'Letter from Lady Franklin to John Griffin, 7 September 1840', in George Mackaness (ed.),

Some Private Correspondence of Sir John and Lady Jane Franklin, Tasmania, 1837–1845, part 1, DS Ford, 1947, pp. 99–101.

60 'Ball to Captains Ross and Crozier, and Officers of the H.M.S. "Erebus" and "Terror"', *Courier*, 30 October 1840, p. 2.

61 Ross, *A Voyage of Discovery*, vol. 1, pp. 120–5; Jim Endersby, 'Joseph Hooker: The Making of a Botanist', *Endeavour*, vol. 25, no. 1, March 2001, pp. 3–7.

62 Ross, *A Voyage of Discovery*, vol. 1, pp. 123–5.

63 Ibid., pp. 117, 346–52.

64 Ibid., pp. 150–2.

65 Ibid., p. 228.

66 Ibid., pp. 124–6; Ross, *A Voyage of Discovery*, vol. 2, p. 2; Lambert, *The Gates of Hell*, p. 131.

67 *The Courier*, 9 April 1841, p. 2.

68 Ibid.; *The Courier*, 13 April 1841, p. 2.

69 'Theatre', *The Courier*, 4 May 1841, p. 2.

70 'Theatre', *Hobart Town Advertiser*, 7 May 1841, p. 2; 'Theatre', *Colonial Times*, 4 May 1841, pp. 2–3.

71 Ross, *A Voyage of Discovery*, vol. 2, pp. 4–26.

72 *Tasmanian Journal*, vol. 1, 1843, pp. 27–34, 41–54, 124–35, 207–23, 240–6.

73 Ross, *A Voyage of Discovery*, vol. 2, p. 33.

74 'The Antarctic Expedition', *South Australian Chronicle*, 30 May 1891, p. 9.

75 See, for example, 'Antarctic Expedition', *Van Diemen's Land Chronicle*, 27 August 1841, p. 3; 'The Tasmanian Journal No. 4', *True Colonist*, 15 July 1842, p. 4; 'A Sketch of the Antarctic Regions', *The Courier*, 22 July 1842, p. 4; 'The Antarctic Expedition', *Launceston Examiner*, 20 August 1842, p. 3; *Launceston Examiner*, 11 October 1843, p. 2; 'The Antarctic Expedition', *The Courier*, 5 January 1844, p. 4; 'Flora Antarctica', *Launceston Examiner*, 25 September 1844, p. 3; *Launceston Examiner*, 2 January 1847, p. 3; 'Arctic Searching Expedition', *Launceston Examiner*, 19 July 1848, p. 4; 'Obituary', *Launceston Examiner*, 19 June 1862, p. 2.

76 'Memorial to the Late Sir James Ross', *SMH*, 19 October 1869, p. 3. See, for example, 'History of the British Navy', *Empire*, 30 July 1866, p. 2; 'Australian Geography', *Mercury*, 2 April 1867, p. 1; 'Australian Geography', *Mercury*, 3 April 1867, p. 1.

77 'The South Pole Expedition', *The Age*, 24 April 1900, p. 4; 'South Pole Expedition', *Daily Telegraph*, 26 April 1900, p. 5.

78 See, for example, Gurney, *The Race to the White Continent*; David Day, *Antarctica: A Biography*, Knopf, 2012.

79 Martin-Nielsen, *A Few Acres of Ice*, p. 44.

80 DR Hainsworth, 'Exploiting the Pacific Frontier: The New South Wales Sealing Industry 1800–1821', *Journal of Pacific History*, vol. 2, 1967, p. 64.

81 Lynette Russell, *Roving Mariners: Australian Aboriginal Whalers and Sealers in the Southern Oceans, 1790–1870*, State University of New York Press, 2012.

82 Philippa Mein Smith, 'The Sealing Industry and the Architecture of the Tasman World', *Fabrications*, vol. 29, no. 3, 2019, pp. 317–37; Rhys Richards, *Sealing in the Southern Oceans 1788–1833*, Paremata Press, 2010; Hainsworth, 'Exploiting the Pacific Frontier', pp. 59–75.

83 See, for example, 'Southern or Antarctic Continent', *Hobart Town Gazette*, 13 January 1821, p. 2; 'Southern or Antarctic Continent', *Sydney Gazette*, 10 March 1821, p. 2; 'The Antarctic Islands', *Sydney Gazette*, 15 December 1821, p. 2; 'A New Sea Discovered', *Sydney Gazette*, 18 March 1826, p. 3.

84 'The Whale Fishery', *The Australian*, 20 February 1829, p. 3; 'Recent Discoveries in the Antarctic Ocean', *Hobart Town Courier*, 3 January 1834, p. 4.

85 See E Tammiksaar, 'The Russian Antarctic Expedition under the Command of Fabian Gottlieb von Bellingshausen and Its Reception in Russia and the World', *Polar Record*, vol. 52, no. 5, September 2016, pp. 578–600; Rip Bulkeley, *Bellingshausen & the Russian Antarctic Expedition, 1819–21*, Palgrave Macmillan, 2014.

86 *Sydney Gazette*, 15 April 1820, p. 3; *Sydney Gazette*, 13 May 1820, p. 3; *Sydney Gazette*, 20 May 1820, p. 3; *Sydney Gazette*, 30 September 1820, p. 3; *Sydney Gazette*, 11 November 1820, p. 2.

87 *Sydney Gazette*, 8 September 1821, p. 3; *Sydney Gazette*, 8 December 1821, p. 3. See also Michael E Hoare, Science and Scientific Associations in Eastern Australia, 1820–1890, PhD thesis, Australian National University, 1974, pp. 20–38.

88 'The Americans', *Sydney Herald*, 30 December 1839, 2; *Sydney Gazette*, 24 April 1841, p. 2.

2 'The Radius of Their Duty'

1 'Parliament', *The Argus*, 21 May 1873, p. 6.

2 *The Argus*, 21 May 1873, p. 2.

3 *Victorian Parliamentary Debates*, Legislative Council and Legislative Assembly, vol. 16, 1873, pp. 122–3.

4 For example, 'Parliament', *The Argus*, 28 May 1873, p. 6; 'Legislative Assembly', *Geelong Advertiser*, 28 May 1873, p. 3; 'Parliament', *The Age*, 28 May 1873, p. 3; 'Melbourne', *The Sydney Morning Herald* (*SMH*), 28 May 1873, p. 5; *The Argus*, 31 May 1873, p. 5; 'Politics', *Leader*, 31 May 1873, p. 21.

5 *The Argus*, 21 May 1873, p. 5.

6 'Victoria', *South Australian Register*, 7 June 1873, p. 6.

7 See, for example, Robert McCormick, 'Geological Remarks on Kerguelen's Land', *Tasmanian Journal*, vol. 1, no. 1, 1841, pp. 27–34; 'French Antarctic Expedition', *Tasmanian Journal*, vol. 1 no. 1, 1841, 74–5; Joseph Kay, 'Terrestrial Magnetism', *Tasmanian Journal*, vol. 1, no. 2, 1841, pp. 124–35; 'Report of the President and Council of the Royal Society on the Instructions for the Antarctic Expedition', *Tasmanian Journal*, vol. 1, no. 3, 1842, pp. 226–40; Robert McCormick, 'A Sketch of the Antarctic Regions', *Tasmanian Journal*, vol. 1, no. 4, 1842, pp. 241–6; 'Antarctic Discoveries', *Tasmanian Journal*, vol. 1, no. 5, 1842, pp. 409–13; J Robertson, 'A Few General Remarks on the Antarctic Continent', *Tasmanian Journal*, vol. 2, no. 6, 1843, pp. 41–54; 'Natural History of Antarctic Expedition', *Tasmanian Journal*, vol. 2, no. 8, 1844, p. 235; 'Botany of the Antarctic Voyage', *Tasmanian Journal*, vol. 2, no. 8, 1844, pp. 235–6; 'Flora Antarctica', *Tasmanian Journal*, vol. 2, no. 8, 1844, pp. 236–7; Christian Gottfried Ehrenberg, 'On Microscopic Life in the Ocean at the South Pole, and at Considerable Depths', *Tasmanian Journal*, vol. 3, no. 2, 1847, pp. 114–28; Joseph Hooker, 'Notes on Some Marine Animals Brought up By Deep-Sea Dredging', *Tasmanian Journal*, vol. 3, no. 2, 1847, pp. 129–30.

8 See, for example, 'Horticultural Society', *Launceston Examiner*, 9 July 1842, p. 4; 'The Tasmanian Journal No. 4', *True Colonist*, 15 July 1842, p. 4; *Launceston Examiner*, 11 October 1843, p. 2.

9 'Sketch of the Antarctic Regions', *The Courier*, 22 July 1842, p. 4.

10 'Mechanics' Institute Public Lecture', *Colonial Times*, 11 June 1850, p. 2; 'The Sources of the Tides', *Launceston Examiner*, 15 June 1850, p. 6.

11 'School of Arts', *Colonial Times*, 9 July 1850, p. 2.

12 'Magnetic Observations: Are They as Useful as Necessary?', *Illustrated Journal of Australasia*, vol. III, 1857, pp. 145–55.

13 See Tom Griffiths and Libby Robin (eds), *Ecology and Empire: Environmental History of Settler Societies*, Edinburgh University Press, 1997; Michael E Hoare, Science and Scientific Associations in Eastern Australia, 1820–1890, PhD thesis, Australian National University, 1974.

14 There is an extensive body of work on the history of public science in Australia. See, for example, Peter H Hoffenberg, *A Science of Our Own: Exhibitions and the Rise of Australian Public Science*, University of Pittsburgh Press, 2019; Tom Griffiths, *Hunters and Collectors: The Antiquarian Imagination in Australia*, Cambridge University Press, 1996; Hoare, Science and Scientific Associations in Eastern Australia.

15 'Notes and Queries', *The Australasian*, 3 December 1864, p. 9; 'The Low Barometer of the Antarctic Temperate Zone', *The Australasian*, 7 September 1867, p. 6; 'The Low Barometer of the Antarctic Temperate Zone', *The Australasian*, 21 September 1867, p. 8; 'The Mystery at the South Pole', *Empire*, 31 May 1871, p. 4.

16 'To the Editor', *Ballarat Star*, 5 August 1871, p. 3.
17 'Why Is the Weather Wintry?', *Border Watch*, 18 January 1868, p. 2; 'Meteorology', *Border Watch*, 22 January 1868, p. 2.
18 *The Fourth Annual Report of the Acclimatisation Society of Victoria*, Wilson & MacKinnon, 1866, p. 10; 'Acclimatisation Society', *The Age*, 21 December 1865, p. 7.
19 'Notes and Queries', *The Australasian*, 9 December 1865, p. 9; Ferdinand von Mueller, *Select Extra-Tropical Plants Readily Eligible for Industrial Culture or Naturalisation in Victoria*, McCarron, Bird, & Co., 1876, p. 184.
20 'Kerguelen Cabbage', *Empire*, 13 March 1874, p. 4; 'The Grazier', *Australian Town and Country Journal*, 14 March 1874, p. 14; 'The Cultivator', *Australian Town and Country Journal*, 4 April 1874, p. 15; 'Kerguelen Cabbage', *Empire*, 9 April 1874, p. 4; 'The Garden', *Sydney Mail*, 30 May 1874, p. 687; 'The Garden', *Sydney Mail*, 13 March 1875, p. 326.
21 Iain Dawson, *New Salad & Vegetable Crops from Australia's Sub-Antarctic Islands: A Report for the Rural Industries Research and Development Corporation*, Rural Industries Research and Development Corporation, 1998.
22 Jakob B Madsen, 'Australian Economic Growth and Its Drivers since European Settlement', in Simon Ville and Glenn Withers (eds), *The Cambridge Economic History of Australia*, Cambridge University Press, 2014, pp. 34–5; Henry Reynolds, *A History of Tasmania*, Cambridge University Press, 2012, pp. 137–86.
23 *Hobart Courier*, 28 November 1848, p. 2.
24 James Clark Ross, *A Voyage of Discovery and Research in the Southern and Antarctic Regions, during the Years 1839–43*, vol. 1, John Murray, 1847, pp. 191–2.
25 'Whaling', *The Courier*, 2 December 1848, p. 2.
26 'Hobart Town', *Colonial Times*, 19 December 1848, p. 2.
27 'Antarctic Ocean', *The Courier*, 26 January 1850, p. 2.
28 Charles Enderby, *Proposal for Re-Establishing the British Southern Whale Fishery*, Effingham Wilson, 1847; Charles Enderby, *The Auckland Islands: A Short Account of Their Climate, Soil, & Productions*, Pelham Richardson, 1849.
29 See Ross, *A Voyage of Discovery*, vol. 1, pp. 140, 169; Benjamin Morrell, *Narrative of Four Voyages to the South Sea … 1822 to 1831*, Harper & Brothers, 1832, pp. 358, 361.
30 For a full account of the Southern Whale Fishery Company's disastrous attempt at colonising the Auckland Islands, see Rohan Howitt, 'The Company-Microstate: The Auckland Islands and Corporate Colonialism in Global History, 1849–52', *Journal of Global History*, vol. 19, no. 1, 2024, pp. 37–56.
31 'Auckland Islands', *SMH*, 15 January 1850, p. 2; 'The Auckland Islands', *SMH*, 18 January 1850, p. 2; *SMH*, 10 May 1852, p. 2; *The Argus*, 20 May 1852, p. 4.

32 'Auckland Islands', *SMH*, 15 January 1850, p. 2; *The Courier*, 2 February 1850, p. 3; 'Auckland Islands', *SMH*, 25 March 1851, p. 3; 'The Havannah and Fly at the Aucklands', *SMH*, 12 April 1850, p. 2; 'Auckland Islands', *The Courier*, 27 April 1850, p. 3; 'New Zealand and the Auckland Isles', *South Australian Register*, 17 May 1850, p. 2.
33 'Auckland Islands', *SMH*, 2 October 1851, p. 2; 'Auckland Islands', *The Argus*, 9 October 1851, p. 4; 'Auckland Islands', *The Courier*, 15 October 1851, p. 3; 'Auckland Isles', *The Courier*, 19 October 1850, p. 2; 'Multum in Parvo', *SMH*, 22 January 1851, p. 2.
34 Robert James Manne, *The Emigrant's Complete Guide to the United States, Australia, Port Stephens, Van Diemen's Land, New Zealand, the Cape of Good Hope and Natal, Canada, New Brunswick and Nova Scotia, and the Auckland Islands*, William Strange, 1850.
35 Charles Enderby, *Proceedings of a Public Dinner Given to Charles Enderby*, 1849, p. 17.
36 *The Times*, 1 July 1851, p. 6; BI Fotheringham, The Southern Whale Fishery Company, Auckland Islands, MPhil thesis, University of Cambridge, 1995, pp. 52–6.
37 Charles Enderby, *A Statement of Facts Connected with the Failure of the Southern Whale Fishery Company at the Auckland Islands*, Richardson Brothers, 1854.
38 See advertisements in *Empire*, 5 June 1852, p. 4; *Otago Witness*, 21 August 1852, p. 2; *SMH*, 12 October 1852, p. 3; and *The Argus*, 12 November 1852, p. 6.
39 *Standard*, 15 March 1854, p. 2; *Standard*, 30 November 1854, p. 1.
40 See, for example, 'Auckland Islands', *Empire*, 26 April 1852, p. 2; 'Auckland Islands', *The Courier*, 28 April 1853, pp. 2–3; 'Auckland Islands', *The Argus*, 5 May 1852, p. 4; *SMH*, 10 May 1852, p. 2; 'Auckland Islands', *The Argus*, 20 May 1852, p. 4; 'Southern Whale Fishery Company', *The Courier*, 2 June 1853, p. 3; 'Auckland Islands', *Adelaide Observer*, 5 June 1852, p. 3; 'Auckland Islands', *SMH*, 27 June 1853, p. 2.
41 [New Zealand] *Protection of Animals Act, 1872*, sec. 6; [New Zealand] *Seals Fisheries Protection Act, 1878*.
42 'Shipping Intelligence', *The Argus*, 1 April 1858, p. 4.
43 'Herd Island', *Hobart Town Daily Mercury*, 10 July 1858, p. 4.
44 WELH Crowther, 'Captain JW Robinson's Narrative of a Sealing Voyage to Heard Island, 1858–60', *Polar Record*, vol. 15, no. 96, 1970, pp. 301–16; 'The Herd Islands', *Hobart Town Daily Mercury*, 13 January 1860, p. 2; 'Sea Elephant Expedition', *The Age*, 18 January 1860, p. 3.
45 Briton Cooper Busch, *The War against the Seals: A History of the North American Seal Fishery*, McGill-Queen's University Press, 1985, p. 171.

46 'Royal Society', *Mercury*, 2 July 1861, p. 2.
47 'Notes and Queries', *The Australasian*, 24 December 1864, p. 9.
48 *The Australasian*, 6 January 1866, p. 8; *Tasmanian Morning Herald*, 26 January 1866, p. 2; 'Whale Fishery', *South Australian Register*, 3 May 1866, p. 3; 'Whale Fishery', *Adelaide Observer*, 5 May 1866, p. 4.
49 *Brisbane Courier*, 10 August 1874, p. 2.
50 See, for example, 'English Intelligence', *The Courier*, 16 October 1840, p. 4; 'English News', *The Courier*, 27 October 1840, p. 5; *The Australian*, 21 November 1840, p. 2; 'Antarctic Expedition', *Launceston Advertiser*, 26 November 1840, p. 3; 'Shipping Intelligence', *The Courier*, 8 February 1840, p. 2; 'Expedition to the Antarctic Regions', *Colonial Times*, 27 May 1845, p. 2; 'The Late Expedition', *Colonial Times*, 19 May 1846, p. 3.
51 Basil Lubbock, *The Colonial Clippers*, 2nd edn, James Brown, 1921, p. 14.
52 *Report of the Thirtieth Meeting of the British Association for the Advancement of Science*, 1861, p. 45.
53 MF Maury, *The Physical Geography of the Sea, and Its Meteorology*, Sampson, Low, Son & Co., 1860, pp. 442–79; *Report of the Thirtieth Meeting of the British Association for the Advancement of Science*, pp. 44–48. See also Rip Bulkeley, 'To Unbar the Gates of the South: Maury's 1860–1861 Proposals for Antarctic Cooperation', *Polar Record*, vol. 47, no. 4, October 2011, pp. 310–26.
54 *The Age*, 20 November 1860, pp. 4–5.
55 See, for example, *The Argus*, 15 November 1860, p. 5; 'Proposed New Exploring Expedition', *The Mercury*, 29 November 1860, p. 3; *Cornwall Chronicle*, 5 December 1860, p. 5; 'Proposed New Exploring Expedition', *Perth Gazette*, 8 February 1861, p. 4; 'Probability of Land Near the South Pole', *South Australian Advertiser*, 15 February 1861, p. 3.
56 *The Australasian*, 6 January 1866, p. 8.
57 'Antarctic Sea Discoveries', *Brisbane Courier*, 18 January 1866, p. 4; *Tasmanian Morning Herald*, 26 January 1866, p. 2.
58 'Whale Fishery', *South Australian Register*, 3 May 1866, p. 3. See also *The Argus*, 16 July 1866, p. 5.
59 'Proposal for a New Scheme of Exploration', *Leader*, 4 January 1868, pp. 16–17.
60 'Antarctic Exploration', *Leader*, 25 January 1868, p. 17.
61 'Science', *Leader*, 2 January 1869, p. 5; 'Science', *Leader*, 15 March 1873, p. 5.
62 Rear admiral Robert Hall to the secretary of Lloyd's, 10 May 1872, Enclosure No. 2 in 'Her Majesty's Ships Calling at the Islands between the Cape of Good Hope and Australia, Correspondence Relative to', *Appendix to the Journals of the New Zealand House of Representatives*, 1876 Session I, H-32.

63 State Library of New South Wales, B421, James Butters, diary of voyage from Liverpool to Melbourne, 4 January – 7 April 1855, and to Sydney, 14–17 April.

64 *The Argus*, 27 March 1855, p. 4; 'The Ocean Chief', *SMH*, 3 April 1855, p. 4; 'The Ship George Marshall', *SMH*, 11 April 1855, p. 4; *The Argus*, 25 April 1855, p. 4; *The Argus*, 26 April 1855, p. 4; 'Shipping Intelligence', *The Argus*, 17 May 1855, p. 4; 'Ships' Mails', *SMH*, 18 May 1855, p. 4; 'Ships' Mails', *Empire*, 21 June 1855, p. 4; *The Argus*, 27 June 1855, p. 4; 'Emigrant Vessels Wrecked in 1855', *Empire*, 15 September 1856, p. 4.

65 See, for example, 'Collision with an Iceberg', *South Australian Advertiser*, 22 July 1861, p. 3; 'The Marco Polo Migrant Ship', *The Argus*, 21 November 1861, p. 7; 'The Australian Ship Royal Standard', *SMH*, 16 August 1864, p. 4; 'A Ship amongst Icebergs', *Freeman's Journal*, 31 December 1864, p. 2; 'A Fearful Scene at Sea', *Queensland Times*, 10 January 1865, p. 4; 'The George Thompson', *Mercury*, 27 May 1868, p. 2.

66 National Library of Australia (NLA), MS 10721, diary of George Thomson, 1868–1869.

67 'The Throes of Nature', *Evening News*, 12 October 1871, p. 4.

68 Thomas Musgrave, *Castaway on the Auckland Isles: Narrative of the Wreck of the Grafton*, HT Dwight, 1865.

69 'The Wreck of the Grafton', *Sydney Mail*, 7 October 1865, p. 6; 'The Loss of the Invercauld', *The Age*, 14 October 1865, p. 6; 'The Late Shipwreck at the Auckland Islands', *Sydney Mail*, 8 February 1868, p. 7; *The Australasian*, 6 August 1870.

70 'Erroneous Charts', *Sydney Mail*, 17 June 1865, p. 10; 'Erroneous Charts', *SMH*, 19 June 1865, p. 2; 'Erroneous Charts', *SMH*, 30 June 1865, p. 2; 'Steam Communication', *Mercury*, 27 December 1865, p. 3.

71 NLA, MAP RM 1658, ice chart of Southern Hemisphere, 1870.

72 'News and Notes', *Ballarat Star*, 9 April 1873, p. 2; *The Australasian*, 12 April 1873, pp. 17–18; 'Science', *Leader*, 12 April 1873, p. 5; 'The Approaching Transit of Venus', *SMH*, 15 April 1873, p. 3; 'Science', *Australian Town and Country Journal*, 7 June 1873, p. 10; 'Scientific Notes', *Empire*, 9 June 1873, p. 4; 'The Transit of Venus', *SMH*, 15 August 1873, p. 6; 'The Transit of Venus', *SMH*, 10 September 1873, p. 6.

73 'Science', *Leader*, 10 May 1873, p. 5.

74 *Victorian Parliamentary Debates*, Legislative Council and Legislative Assembly, vol. 16, 1873, pp. 122–3.

75 'Royal Society of Victoria', *Argus*, 12 August 1873, p. 6.

76 'Topics of the Week', *Australasian*, 31 May 1873, p. 18.

77 Kathleen Fitzpatrick, 'The Burke and Wills Expedition and the Royal Society of Victoria', *Historical Studies: Australia and New Zealand*, vol. 10, no. 40, 1963, pp. 470–8.

78 'The Antarctic Regions', *Sydney Mail*, 16 October 1880, p. 740; 'Melbourne Review', *Australasian Chronicle*, 16 October 1880, p. 8; 'Melbourne Review', *Argus*, 9 October 1880, p. 9.
79 'The Melbourne Review', *The Argus*, 9 October 1880, p. 9.
80 'Science', *Leader*, 7 May 1881, p. 5.
81 'Proposed Exploration of Antarctic Regions', *Leader*, 10 January 1885, p. 16.
82 *The Argus*, 9 July 1870, p. 6; *Brisbane Courier*, 27 August 1870, p. 6; *The Argus*, 7 December 1870, p. 5; 'Antarctic Expedition', *Empire*, 13 December 1870, p. 2; 'Proposed Expedition to the South Pole', *South Australian Register*, 15 July 1871, p. 5; 'Science', *Leader*, 3 August 1878, p. 5.
83 *The Age*, 27 May 1880, p. 3; *SMH*, 15 January 1881, p. 5; *The Argus*, 20 January 1881, p. 6.
84 See, for example, *The Argus*, 3 June 1880, p. 6; 'The South Pole', *The Argus*, 19 July 1880, p. 7; 'The South Pole', *Evening News*, 21 July 1880, p. 3; 'The South Pole', *Launceston Examiner*, 22 July 1880, p. 3; 'The Explorer', *Australasian Chronicle*, 24 July 1880, p. 7; 'The South Pole', *Sydney Mail*, 24 July 1880, p. 168; *SMH*, 15 September 1880, p. 4; *The Argus*, 3 January 1881, p. 4; 'The Week', *Sydney Mail*, 19 February 1881, p. 303. For an account of the Italian proposal, see Ian R Stone and Piero Bosco, 'Plans for an Italian Antarctic Expedition, 1881', *Polar Record*, vol. 42, no. 223, 2006, pp. 359–63.
85 'Science', *Leader*, 20 November 1880, p. 5.
86 RA Swan, *Australia in the Antarctic: Interest, Activity, and Endeavour*, Melbourne University Press, 1961, p. 32.
87 Joy McCann, *Ice Bound: Australian Stories from Antarctica*, National Library of Australia Publishing, 2022, pp. 27–8; Marie Kawaja, 'Australia in Antarctica: Realising an Ambition', *Polar Journal*, vol. 3, no. 1, 2013, pp. 31–52, see pp. 33–4; Marie Kawaja and Tom Griffiths, '"Our Great Frozen Neighbour': Australia and Antarctica before the Treaty, 1880–1945', in Marcus Haward and Tom Griffiths (eds), *Australia and the Antarctic Treaty System: 50 Years of Influence*, UNSW Press, 2011, pp. 10–12.
88 David Day, *Antarctica: A Biography*, Knopf, 2012, p. 89.
89 Andrew McConville, *In Search of the Last Continent: Australia and Early Antarctic Exploration*, Australian Scholarly Publishing, 2022; RW Home, Sara Maroske, AM Lucas and PJ Lucas, '"Why Explore Antarctica?" Australian Discussions in the 1880s', *Australian Journal of Politics and History*, vol. 38, no. 3, 1992, p. 390.

3 'Destiny'

1 *Victorian Parliamentary Debates*, Legislative Council and Legislative Assembly, vol. 50, 1885, pp. 2344–5; 'Legislative Assembly', *The Herald*, 19 November 1885, p. 1.
2 'Parliament', *The Argus*, 10 December 1885, p. 5.

3 AC Macdonald, JH Maiden and TH Myring (eds), *Special Volume of the Proceedings of the Geographical Society of Australasia*, 1885, pp. 125–33.
4 AC Macdonald, 'Section E: Geography, Address by the President', *Report of the Fifth Meeting of the Australasian Association for the Advancement of Science*, 1894, p. 131.
5 GS Griffiths, 'South Polar Problems, or the Objects and Value of Antarctic Research', *Transactions and Proceedings of the Royal Geographical Society of Australasia: Victorian Branch*, Series 1, vol. IV, 1887, pp. 121–33.
6 Griffiths, 'South Polar Problems', p. 131.
7 See, for example, 'Geographical Society of Australasia', *The Age*, 28 January 1886, p. 5; 'Geographical Society of Australasia', *The Argus*, 28 January 1886, p. 6; 'Geographical Society of Australasia', *Record*, 6 February 1886, p. 5.
8 GS Griffiths, 'Evidences of a Glacial Epoch from Kerguelen's Land', *Transactions and Proceedings of the Royal Society of Victoria*, vol. 23, 1887, pp. 45–9; State Library Victoria (SLV), MS 11663/1/4, *Proceedings of the Royal Society of Victoria*, 13 May 1886.
9 'Royal Geographical Society of Australasia', *The Age*, 22 March 1890, p. 10.
10 David Livingston, *The Geographical Tradition: Episodes in the History of a Contested Enterprise*, Blackwell, 1993, p. 170.
11 Macdonald, Maiden and Myring, *Special Volume*, pp. 1–20.
12 'Expedition to the South Pole', *The Sydney Morning Herald* (*SMH*), 7 February 1881, p. 6.
13 Macdonald, Maiden and Myring, *Special Volume*, pp. 1–20.
14 'Geographical Exploration of Australia', *SMH*, 4 April 1883, p. 7; 'Geographical Society of Australasia', *SMH*, 24 April 1883, p. 4; 'Constitution of the Geographical Society of Australasia', in Macdonald, Maiden and Myring, *Special Volume*, p. 19.
15 Macdonald, Maiden and Myring, *Special Volume*, p. 36; State Library of NSW, MLMSS 7540/1, minutes of Australian Geographical Conference, 1884.
16 HC Everill, *Official Report of Captain HC Everill, Leader of the New Guinea Exploring Expedition*, Royal Geographical Society of Australasia, 1886.
17 See, for example, *The Age*, 14 May 1886, p. 5; *The Australasian*, 15 May 1886, p. 7; *The Age*, 21 May 1886, p. 4; *The Age*, 27 May 1886, p. 4; 'The Explorer', *Weekly Times*, 29 May 1886, p. 4.
18 'The Regions of the South Pole', *The Age*, 22 May 1886, p. 13.
19 'The Antarctic Region', *The Herald*, 27 May 1886, p. 2.
20 'Southward Ho!', *The Age*, 25 May 1866, p. 6.
21 *Transactions and Proceedings of the Royal Society of Victoria*, vol. 23, 1887, pp. 259–60.
22 Ibid., pp. 282–90; Royal History Society of Victoria, PAM205, 'Progress Report of the Antarctic Exploration Committee', 1887.

23 For example, 'The Antarctic Exploration Project', *Daily Telegraph*, 2 July 1886, p. 3; 'Antarctic Exploration', *SMH*, 6 July 1886, p. 3; 'A Memorandum of the Objects to Be Served By Antarctic Research', *Brisbane Courier*, 8 July 1886, p. 3; 'Royal Society of Victoria', *The Argus*, 9 July 1886, p. 6.

24 'Antarctic Exploration', *Daily Telegraph*, 3 July 1886, p. 4.

25 'Royal Society of Victoria', *The Argus*, 9 July 1886, p. 6.

26 See, for example, 'Our Melbourne Letter', *Daily Telegraph*, 16 July 1886, p. 2.

27 'Notes and Comments', *The Argus*, 5 August 1886, p. 7.

28 'Our Melbourne Letter', *Ovens and Murray Advertiser*, 14 August 1886, p. 1.

29 *Transactions and Proceedings of the Royal Geographical Society of Australasia: Victorian Branch*, Series 1, vol. IV, 1887, pp. 135–61; 'Antarctic Exploration', *The Age*, 16 July 1886, p. 5; 'Antarctic Exploration', *Leader*, 17 July 1886, p. 29; 'Geographical Notes', *Scottish Geographical Magazine*, vol. 2, no. 10, 1886, p. 622.

30 SLV, MS11663, minutes of Royal Society of Victoria (RSV) council meeting, 7 April 1887; 'Antarctic Exploration', *The Herald*, 4 August 1886, p. 3; 'Proposed Antarctic Expedition', *The Age*, 5 August 1886, p. 5.

31 SLV, MS 11663, Box 1/4, *Proceedings of the Royal Society of Victoria*, 13 May 1886.

32 SLV, MS 11663, minutes of RSV council meeting, 7 April 1887; 'Antarctic Exploration', *Herald*, 4 August 1886, p. 3.

33 See, for example, *The Argus*, 4 August 1886, p. 5; *The Argus*, 5 August 1886, p. 5; 'The Proposed Antarctic Expedition', *Daily Telegraph*, 5 August 1886, p. 5; 'The Icy South', *Evening News*, 11 August 1886, p. 4; 'The Proposed Antarctic Expedition', *Daily Telegraph*, 14 August 1886, p. 5; *The Argus*, 21 August 1886, p. 5; 'Antarctic Exploration', *SMH*, 26 August 1886, p. 8.

34 *The Argus*, 7 August 1886, p. 9.

35 *Leader*, 14 August 1886, p. 25.

36 SLV, MS11663, minutes of RSV council meeting, 7 April 1887; 'Geographical', *SMH*, 28 July 1886, p. 11.

37 *Proceedings of the Linnaean Society of New South Wales*, Second Series, vol. 1, 1887, p. 856; *Journal and Proceedings of the Royal Society of New South Wales*, 1888, p. 13; SLV, MS 11663, minutes of RSV council meeting, 5 August 1886; minutes of RSV council meeting, 5 May 1887; *Proceedings of the Geographical Society of Australasia: South Australian Branch*, sessions 1886–7 and 1887–8, vol. II, 1890, pp. vi–xii; 'Geographical Society', *Telegraph*, 7 July 1886, p. 5.

38 SLV, MS11663, *Proceedings of the Royal Society of Victoria*, 14 October 1886; SLV, MS13020/5/2, letter from HR Rusden to FR Chapman, 16 April 1887.

39 'Royal Society of Tasmania', *Mercury*, 11 August 1886, p. 3.

40 Charles Sprent, 'Antarctic Exploration', *Papers and Proceedings of the Royal Society of Tasmania*, 1886, p. 154.

41 Ibid., pp. 154–5.

42 'Royal Society of Tasmania', *Mercury*, 14 September 1886, p. 3.

43 RA Swan, *Australia in the Antarctic: Interest, Activity, and Endeavour*, Melbourne University Press, 1961, pp. 57–8; Gillian Triggs, 'Australian Sovereignty in Antarctica Part II', *Melbourne University Law Review*, vol. 13, no. 3, 1982, p. 304; Marie Kawaja and Tom Griffiths, '"Our Great Frozen Neighbour": Australia and Antarctica before the Treaty, 1880–1945', in Marcus Haward and Tom Griffiths (eds), *Australia and the Antarctic Treaty System: 50 Years of Influence*, UNSW Press, 2011, pp. 12–14.

44 Marie Kawaja, 'Australia in Antarctica: Realising an Ambition', *Polar Journal*, vol. 3, no. 1, 2013, pp. 31–52, quote p. 31.

45 See Nicholas Ferns, 'Manifest Desinty Crosses the Pacific: The Utility of American Expansion in Australia, 1850–1901', *Australasian Journal of American Studies*, vol. 34, no. 2, 2015, pp. 28–43.

46 See Alecia Pru Simmonds, 'Cross-Cultural Friendship and Legal Pluralities in the Early Pacific Salt-Pork Trade', *Journal of World History*, vol. 28, no. 2, June 2017, pp. 219–48; DR Hainsworth, 'In Search of a Staple: The Sydney Sandalwood Trade 1804–09', *Australian Economic History Review*, vol. 5, no. 1, 1965, pp. 1–20.

47 See Tracey Banivanua-Mar, *Violence and Colonial Dialogue: The Australian-Pacific Indentured Labor Trade*, University of Hawai'i Press, 2007; Miranda Johnson and Cait Storr, 'Australia as Empire', in Peter Cane, Lisa Ford and Mark McMillan (eds), *The Cambridge Legal History of Australia*, Cambridge University Press, 2022, pp. 258–80.

48 Alexis Bergantz, '"The Scum of France": Australian Anxieties towards French Convicts in the Nineteenth Century', *Australian Historical Studies*, vol. 49, no. 2, 2018, pp. 150–66; Alexis Bergantz, *French Connection: Australia's Cosmopolitan Ambitions*, NewSouth, 2021, pp. 48–62.

49 John Dunmore Lang, *The Coming Event, or, Freedom and Independence for the Seven United Provinces of Australia*, Sampson Low, Son and Marston, 1870, pp. 317–429.

50 'The Fiji Islands', *The Australasian*, 30 September 1870, pp. 16–17.

51 For a thorough account of the early federal movement, see John Hirst, *Sentimental Nation: The Making of the Australian Commonwealth*, Oxford University Press, 2000.

52 National Archives of Australia (NAA), A981, ANT 4 Part 1, 1920–21, *Confidential Memorandum on the Spheres of Interest of Australia and New Zealand*, 6 November 1920.

53 'Monroe Doctrine; December 2 1823', The Avalon Project: Documents in Law, History and Diplomacy, 2008, http://avalon.law.yale.edu/19th_century/monroe.asp (viewed August 2024).

54 See Roger C Thompson, *Australian Imperialism in the Pacific: The Expansionist Era 1820–1920*, Melbourne University Press, 1980; Helen Bones and Nicholas Ferns, 'Pacific Nation or Neighbour: Australia's Relationship with New Zealand, Papua New Guinea, and the Pacific', in Bridget Brooklyn, Benjamin T Jones and Rebecca Strating (eds), *Australia on the World Stage: History, Politics, and International Relations*, Routledge, 2023, pp. 171–84.

55 'Sazerac', 'Pacific Island Problems', *The Age*, 1 September 1900, p. 13.

56 NAA, A981, ANT 4, Part 1, 1920–21, *Confidential Memorandum on the Spheres of Interest of Australia and New Zealand*, 6 November 1920. For an exhaustive account of invocations of the idea of an Australian Monroe doctrine, see Rohan Howitt, Ideological Origins of the Australian Antarctic, 1839–1933, PhD thesis, University of Sydney, 2019, pp. 81–99; Cait Storr, '"Imperium in Imperio": Sub-Imperialism and the Formation of Australia as a Subject of International Law', *Melbourne Journal of International Law*, vol. 19, no. 1, 2018, pp. 335–68.

57 'Pacific Monroe Doctrine', *ANZAC Bulletin*, vol. 81, 26 July 1918, p. 14.

58 'Proposed Exploration of Antarctic Regions', *Leader*, 10 January 1885, p. 16.

59 'The Week', *Leader*, 14 August 1886, p. 25.

60 'Antarctic Exploration', *The Herald*, 5 December 1888, p. 6.

61 'Royal Geographical Society of Australasia', *The Age*, 22 March 1890, p. 10.

62 'Memorandum of the Objects to be Served by Antarctic Research', *Transactions and Proceedings of the Royal Society of Victoria*, vol. 23, 1887, pp. 282–90.

63 'Antarctic Exploration', *The Herald*, 16 July 1886, p. 2.

64 'The Antarctic Regions', *The Bunyip*, 27 August 1886, p. 2.

65 'Talk on Change', *The Australasian*, 9 June 1888, p. 33.

66 See Frederick E Johnson, *New South Wales and How to Get There: An Emigrants Guide to Australia*, James Clarke & Co., 1886, p. 45.

67 'Wreck of the Strathmore', *SMH*, 5 May 1876, p. 4.

68 State Library of Western Australia, BA1116/89, 004911D; 'The Message of the Albatross', *Western Mail*, 26 November 1887, p. 39; 'Search for a Shipwrecked Crew', *The Argus*, 1 December 1887, p. 8; 'The Message from the Sea', *West Australian*, 27 March 1888, p. 3.

69 'The Great Postal Scheme', *South Australian Register*, 20 January 1855, p. 2.

70 See, for example, 'The Crozets and Tristan D'Acunha', *SMH*, 27 April 1876, p. 3; 'The Crozets and Tristan D'Acunha', *The Age*, 6 May 1876, p. 7; 'The Crozets', *SMH*, 1 May 1876, p. 3; 'The Rescue of Shipwrecked Persons', *The Argus*, 12 May 1876, p. 7.

71 'Kerguelen Island', *The Age*, 4 April 1885, p. 13.

72 See, for example, *Victorian Parliamentary Debates*, Legislative Council and Legislative Assembly, Session 1875–76, vol. XXIII, pp. 2331–2; New Zealand Parliamentary Papers, Appendix to the Journals of the House of Representatives, 1877, Session I, 'A–01 Despatches from the Governor of New Zealand to the Secretary of State', p. 2; New Zealand Parliamentary Papers, Appendix to the Journals of the House of Representatives, 1877, Session I, 'A–02b Further Despatches from the Secretary of State to the Governor of New Zealand', pp. 5–9; 'Our Missing Ships', *SMH*, 18 December 1872, p. 2; 'Crozet Islands', *The Argus*, 27 July 1877, p. 6; 'Crozet Islands', *The Argus*, 19 March 1880, p. 7; 'Those Who Go Down to the Sea in Ships', *SMH*, 15 September 1890, p. 6.

73 See, for example, *Black's General Atlas of the World*, Adam & Charles Black, 1860; *The New Atlas of Australia*, John Sands, 1886; *Stanford's London Atlas of Universal Geography*, Edward Stanford, 1887.

74 René E Bossiére, *Notice sur les îles Kerguelen, possession française*, A Challamel, 1893; 'Annexation of British Islands by France', *The Argus*, 13 August 1892, p. 7; 'Kerguelen's Land', *SMH*, 1 March 1893, p. 7.

75 'Kerguelen Land', *Evening News*, 1 March 1893, p. 4.

76 *The Argus*, 30 November 1892, p. 4.

77 'Kerguelen's Island', *West Australian*, 11 April 1893, p. 3.

78 'Annexation by France', *Evening News*, 17 August 1892, p. 5; 'French Annexation in the Indian Ocean', *SMH*, 17 August 1892, p. 5.

79 'French Annexation in the Southern Seas', *Daily News*, 26 November 1892, p. 3; 'France in the Indian Ocean', *The Argus*, 26 November 1892, p. 9; *The Argus*, 28 November 1892, p. 5.

80 See Mark McKenna, *The Captive Republic: A History of Republicanism in Australia 1788–1995*, Cambridge University Press, 1996; Hirst, *Sentimental Nation*; Duncan Bell, *The Idea of Greater Britain: Empire and the Future of World Order, 1860–1900*, Princeton University Press, 2009.

81 'Antarctic Exploration Committee', *Proceedings of the Royal Society of Victoria*, New Series, vol. 3, 1891, pp. 150–1; 'Antarctic Exploration', *Mercury*, 26 April 1887, p. 4.

82 'Progress Report of the Antarctic Exploration Committee', 1887, pp. 286–96; 'Antarctic Exploration', *The Argus*, 11 December 1886, p. 11.

83 'Antarctic Exploration', *The Herald*, 6 January 1887, p. 2.

84 'Progress Report of the Antarctic Exploration Committee', 1887, pp. 276–308; 'The Proposed Exploration of the Antarctic Regions', *The Argus*, 25 November 1886, p. 11; *The Argus*, 1 December 1886, p. 7; 'Antarctic Exploration', *The Argus*, 8 January 1887, p. 10.

85 'Antarctic Exploration', *The Argus*, 23 July 1887, p. 5.

86 *Transactions and Proceedings of the Royal Geographical Society of Australasia: Victorian Branch*, Part I, vol. V, 1888, pp. 44–5, 68–9; *Proceedings of the Geographical Society of Australasia: South Australian Branch*, 1890, p. xii; 'Proposed Antarctic Exploration', *Evening News*, 17 November 1887, p. 5; 'Antarctic Exploration', *The Age*, 21 December 1887, p. 9; 'Antarctic Exploration', *The Age*, 24 December 1887, p. 10; 'The Proposed Antarctic Expedition', *Daily Telegraph*, 26 December 1887, p. 5; 'Australia and Antarctic Exploration', *Daily Telegraph*, 30 December 1887, p. 5.

87 'Antarctic Exploration', *The Age*, 21 December 1887, p. 9.

88 SLV, MS 11663/1, minutes of RSV's annual Conversazione, 26 October 1886.

89 'Steam Whaling from Hobart', *Mercury*, 16 June 1887, p. 4; 'Black Whaling Project', *Mercury*, 5 July 1887, p. 3; 'A Whaling Company to the Antarctic Seas', *Leader*, 9 July 1887, p. 22; *Mercury*, 22 July 1887, p. 2; *Mercury*, 15 March 1888, p. 2.

90 See, for example, 'Antarctic Exploration', *SMH*, 8 November 1887, p. 7; 'Science', *Leader*, 29 December 1888, p. 36; 'The Antarctic Expedition', *SMH*, 1 June 1888, p. 7; 'A German Antarctic Expedition', *Daily Telegraph*, 1 June 1888, p. 5; 'Antarctic Exploration', *Mercury*, 20 July 1888, p. 3.

91 See, for example, 'Antarctic Exploration', *The Argus*, 12 April 1887, p. 5; 'Antarctic Exploration', *Daily Telegraph*, 13 April 1887, p. 5; 'The Proposed Antarctic Expedition', *The Argus*, 14 May 1887, p. 9; 'Proposed Antarctic Expedition', *Daily Telegraph*, 3 June 1887, p. 2; 'Antarctic Exploration', *The Argus*, 11 July 1887, p. 10.

92 'Proposed Antarctic Expedition', *Australian Town and Country Journal*, 21 May 1887, p. 11.

93 'The Antarctic Expedition', *SMH*, 21 January 1888, p. 14.

94 *Report of the Fifty-Sixth Meeting of the British Association for the Advancement of Science*, 1887, pp. 277–8; *Report of the Fifty-Eighth Meeting of the British Association for the Advancement of Science*, 1889, pp. 316–19.

95 *Proceedings of the Linnean Society of New South Wales*, Second Series, vol. II, 1888, pp. 1109–11.

96 *Papers and Proceedings of the Royal Society of Tasmania*, 1886, p. xx.

97 *Evening Journal*, 25 February 1888, p. 4; *Transactions and Proceedings of the Royal Geographical Society of Australasia: Victorian Branch*, Part 1, vol. VII, 1889, p. 32.

98 'Scientific', *Adelaide Observer*, 25 February 1888, p. 42; *The Argus*, 19 April 1888, p. 7.

99 *Brisbane Courier*, 18 June 1888, p. 4.

100 'The Week', *Leader*, 21 April 1888, p. 26.

101 'The Antarctic Expedition', *SMH*, 2 February 1888, p. 9; 'Victorian Items', *Mercury*, 8 February 1888, p. 3.

102 'Royal Geographical Society of Australasia', *Record*, 2 June 1888, p. 4.

103 *The Argus*, 17 April 1888, pp. 5, 7; 'Antarctic Exploration', *Leader*, 21 April 1888, p. 29; 'Antarctic Whaling and Exploration', *Mercury*, 17 May 1888, p. 4.
104 *Geographical Journal*, vol. 7, no. 5, May 1896, pp. 502–21.

4 'Another Klondyke'

1 'The Antarctic Expedition', *Illustrated Australian News*, 1 December 1890, p. 6; 'Gossip', *Sydney Mail*, 6 December 1890, p. 1257; 'The Antarctic Exploration Ball', *The Herald*, 13 December 1890, p. 2; 'Society and Fashion', *The Australasian*, 13 December 1890, p. 23; 'Our Melbourne Message', *Australian Star*, 17 December 1890, p. 6; 'Some Ballroom Sketches', *Melbourne Punch*, 25 December 1890, p. 4; 'The White Ball', *Table Talk*, 26 December 1890, p. 11; 'The Antarctic Ball', *Leader*, 27 December 1890, p. 5.
2 'White, Plain and Character Ball', *The Herald*, 17 November 1840, p. 4.
3 'Fancy Dress Ball', *The Age*, 20 December 1890, p. 10; 'The White Ball', *Table Talk*, 26 December 1890, p. 11; 'Social Notes', *The Australasian*, 27 December 1890, p. 38.
4 'South Polar Exploration', *The Colonist*, 13 December 1890, p. 16.
5 Ibid.
6 ME Hoare, 'The Intercolonial Science Movement in Australasia, 1870–1890', *Historical Records of Australian Science*, pp. 7–28.
7 *Report of the First Meeting of the Australasian Association for the Advancement of Science*, 1889, p. 354.
8 GS Griffiths, 'Antarctic Exploration', *Report of the First Meeting of the Australasian Association for the Advancement of Science*, pp. 413–16.
9 *Report of the First Meeting of the Australasian Association for the Advancement of Science*, p. xxxiv.
10 WH Miskin, 'Presidential Address in Section E', *Report of the Second Meeting of the Australasian Association for the Advancement of Science*, 1890, pp. 110–19.
11 'Australia and the Antarctic', *The Australasian*, 8 September 1888, p. 32. See also *The Sydney Morning Herald* (*SMH*), 3 September 1888, p. 4; 'Antarctic Exploration', *The Herald*, 15 September 1888, p. 5; 'The Duty of Australia', *The Herald*, 9 October 1888, p. 2.
12 'News of the Day', *The Age*, 22 September 1888, p. 11.
13 'Antarctic Exploration', *The Herald*, 5 December 1888, p. 6; 'The Australian Natives Association', *The Argus*, 23 March 1889, p. 7.
14 *Daily Telegraph*, 3 June 1889, p. 4; *The Age*, 31 December 1889, p. 8.
15 See, for example, 'Proposed Antarctic Expedition', *SMH*, 6 March 1889, p. 7; *Australian Town and Country Journal*, 25 May 1889, p. 17; *Leader*, 28 September 1889, p. 38; 'Baron Nordenskjold's Latest Enterprise', *The Age*, 15 June 1889, p. 4; *SMH*, 7 March 1890, p. 6; 'Antarctic Exploration', *The Age*, 16 June 1890, p. 5.

16 'Ice Bound', *Daily Telegraph* (Launceston), 23 February 1889, p. 3; 'The Storyteller', *The Colonist*, 9 March 1889, p. 29; 'The Day Will Come', *The Age*, 27 July 1889, p. 14; Laura J Suisted, 'Adrift in Antarctic Seas', *Leader*, 24 December 1892, p. 1.

17 Royal Historical Society of Victoria (RHSV), LIB005938za, X 919.45 MAC, letter from DG Lindhagen to Carl Lewenhaupt, 10 January 1890; letter from Hans Jørgen Gundersen to Mueller, 24 March 1890, in RW Home, AM Lucas, Sara Maroske, DM Sinkora, JH Voight and Monika Wells (eds), *Regardfully Yours: Selected Correspondence of Ferdinand von Mueller, Volume III: 1876–96*, Peter Lang, 2006, pp. 550–1.

18 RHSV, LIB005938za, X 919.45 MAC, RHSV, cablegram from H Gundersen to Royal Academy of Science, 15 August 1890; letter from HK Rusden to Royal Academy of Science, 5 October 1890.

19 'Antarctic Exploration', *The Age*, 28 August 1890, p. 6; *Proceedings of the Royal Geographical Society of Australasia: Victorian Branch*, Series 2, vol. VIII, 1891, pp. 76–83.

20 RHSV, LIB 005938za, X 919.45 MAC, subscription list; *Papers and Proceedings of the Royal Society of Tasmania*, 1890, pp. xxvi–ix, 260–2; *Proceedings of the Royal Geographical Society of Australasia: Victorian Branch*, Series 2, vol. VIII, 1891, pp. 76–83; *Journal and Proceedings of the Royal Society of New South Wales* (1890), 163; *Proceedings of the Royal Geographical Society of Australasia: South Australian Branch*, Sixth Session, 1890–91, pp. 10–15.

21 'Australian Natives Association', *The Herald*, 20 December 1890, p. 3.

22 RHSV, LIB005938za, X 919.45 MAC, RHSV, subscription list.

23 'Antarctic Exploration', *Mercury*, 18 August 1890, p. 3.

24 *The Age*, 6 September 1890, p. 15; *The Argus*, 3 September 1891, p. 5; *The Argus*, 7 September 1891, p. 7; *The Argus*, 25 November 1890, p. 9.

25 'Antarctic Expedition', *Brisbane Courier*, 18 September 1891, p. 6.

26 William Quinn and John D Turner, *Boom and Bust: A Global History of Financial Bubbles*, Cambridge University Press, 2020, pp. 77–97; Graeme Davison, *The Rise and Fall of Marvellous Melbourne*, 2nd edn, Melbourne University Publishing, 2004.

27 *Report of the Third Meeting of the Australasian Association for the Advancement of Science*, 1891, pp. 232–50.

28 CW Purnell, 'Antarctic Exploration', *Report of the Third Meeting of the Australasian Association for the Advancement of Science*, pp. 253–4.

29 Captain Crutchley, 'Some Notes on the Meteorology and Steam Routes of the Southern Oceans', *Report of the Third Meeting of the Australasian Association for the Advancement of Science*, pp. 277–80.

30 'Report of the Committee Appointed to Consider the Question of Antarctic Exploration', *Report of the Third Meeting of the Australasian*

Association for the Advancement of Science, pp. 546–7; 'The Australasian Science Association', *SMH*, 19 January 1891, p. 5.

31 *Transactions of the Royal Geographical Society of Australasia: Victorian Branch*, Part 1, vol. IX, 1891, pp. 57–60; 'Swedish–Australian Antarctic Expedition', *The Argus*, 28 February 1891, p. 7.

32 'Council Meeting, 29 April 1891', *Transactions of the Royal Geographical Society of Australasia: Victorian Branch*, Part 1, vol. IX, 1891, pp. 36–37, 57–60; 'Antarctic Exploration', *The Argus*, 4 July 1891, p. 12.

33 *Transactions of the Royal Geographical Society of Australasia: Victorian Branch*, Part 1,vol. IX, 1891, pp. 31–40; RHSV, LIB005938za, X 919.45 MAC, RHSV, telegram from AT Magarey to Mueller, 1 June 1891; telegram from Magarey to Mueller, 9 June 1891; telegram from Gundersen to Lewenhaupt, 11 June 1891; telegram from Lewenhaupt to Gundersen, 17 June 1891; letter from Magarey to Mueller, 18 June 1891.

34 'Antarctic Exploration', *The Argus*, 4 July 1891, p. 12.

35 *Proceedings of the Royal Society of Victoria*, New Series, vol. 3, 1891, pp. 150–1.

36 'Swedish–Australasian Antarctic Exploration Fund', *The Age*, 31 October 1891, p. 11; RHSV, LIB005938za, X919.45MAC, RHSV, cablegram from Lewenhaupt to Gundersen, 21 July 1891; cablegram from Gundersen to Lewenhaupt, 26 July 1891; letter from Nordenskiöld to Lindhagen, 7 September 1891; letter from Nordenskiöld to Lewenhaupt, 23 September 1891; letter from Crawford Pasco and HK Rusden to Royal Swedish Academy of Science, 4 August 1891; letter from W Potter to Lindhagen, 25 November 1891.

37 'Report of Committee No. 10, Antarctic Exploration', *Report of the Fourth Meeting of the Australasian Association for the Advancement of Science*, 1892, pp. 236–9.

38 RHSV, LIB 005938za, X919.45MAC, RHSV, letter from AC Macdonald to Magarey, 14 July 1891; letter from Magarey to Macdonald, 16 July 1891; letter from Magarey to Macdonald, 22 July 1891; letter from Thomas Gill to Macdonald, 25 September 1891; letter from Magarey to Macdonald, 29 July 1891; 'Report to the Antarctic Committee', 28 January 1892.

39 'Antarctic Expedition Not Progressing', *Mercury*, 9 December 1891, p. 2; 'Proposed Antarctic Expeditions', *Leader*, 19 December 1891, p. 43; 'The Proposed Antarctic Expedition', *Record*, 26 December 1891, p. 3; 'Antarctic Exploration', *The Argus*, 20 February 1892, p. 11.

40 'The Proposed Australian Antarctic Expedition', *The Times*, 8 December 1891, p. 10.

41 RHSV, LIB005938za, X919.45MAC,letter from Gundersen to Potter, 1 June 1892; letter from Lewenhaupt to Gundersen, 22 April 1892; letter from Oscar Dickson and AE Nordenskiöld to Royal Academy of Science,

February 1892; letter from Dickson and Nordenskiöld to Royal Academy of Science, 13 April 1892.

42 'The Swedish–Australian Antarctic Expedition', *The Argus*, 2 June 1892, p. 10.

43 'Scientific Gossip', *Leader*, 30 July 1892, p. 36.

44 Letter from Potter to Mueller, 10 December 1892, in Home et al., *Regardfully Yours*, pp. 630–2; 'Antarctic Exploration', *Australian Star*, 24 November 1891, p. 8; 'Parliament of New South Wales', *SMH*, 25 November 1891, p. 5.

45 *Daily Telegraph*, 26 October 1892, p. 4; 'Whaling in the Antarctic Regions', *SMH*, 27 October 1892, p. 7.

46 *Report of the Fifth Meeting of the Australasian Association for the Advancement of Science*, 1894, p. 132.

47 HJ Bull, *The Cruise of the 'Antarctic' to the South Polar Regions*, Edward Arnold, 1896, pp. 2–4; 'Whaling and Sealing in the Antarctic', *The Argus*, 28 November 1891, p. 11; 'Whaling and Sealing in the Antarctic', *The Argus*, 1 December 1891, p. 10; 'Whaling and Sealing in the Antarctic', *The Argus*, 27 September 1892, p. 10.

48 Bull, *The Cruise of the 'Antarctic'*, pp. 5–33.

49 Ibid., pp. 79–84; 'Whaling in the South Seas', *The Age*, 26 February 1894, p. 5; 'Chamber of Manufactures', *The Age*, 6 March 1894, p. 6; 'The Whaler Antarctic', *The Age*, 12 March 1894, p. 5; 'Welcome to the Captain and Officers of SS Antarctic', *Record*, 17 March 1894, p. 3.

50 'Whaling and Sealing in the South Pacific', *The Age*, 6 January 1894, p. 2.

51 Bull, *The Cruise of the 'Antarctic'*, pp. 81–105; State Library of Tasmania, TRE1/1/2383, Box TRE1/59, 4640, correspondence from the Treasurer to the Premier re. the Steam Whaler 'Antarctic', New Zealand Parliamentary Papers, 1894, Session I, H-25, *Report on Auckland Campbell and Other Islands and on their Seals and Seal-Rookeries*, p. 1; New Zealand Parliamentary Papers, 1894, Session I, H-18, Marine Department (*Annual Report* for 1893–94), pp. 3–4; New Zealand Parliamentary Papers, 1895, Session I, H-29, Marine Department (*Annual Report* for 1894–95), pp. 3–4; 'Auckland Islands', *Otago Daily Times*, 22 May 1894, p. 2; 'New Zealand and the Norwegian Whaler', *Daily Telegraph*, 28 May 1894, p. 4; 'Mishap to the Whaler Antarctic', *Daily Telegraph*, 23 June 1894, p. 5; 'Cruise of the HMS Rapid', *SMH*, 5 July 1894, p. 4; 'Foreign Whalers', *Australian Star*, 28 September 1894, p. 5.

52 Bull, *The Cruise of the 'Antarctic'*, pp. 105–8.

53 Ibid., pp. 114–28; 'The Southern Islands', *Otago Daily Times*, 9 March 1895, p. 2.

54 Bull, *The Cruise of the 'Antarctic'*, pp. 173–211; 'The Whaler Antarctic', *The Age*, 13 March 1895, p. 6; 'South Polar Exploration', *Evening News*, 25 April 1895, p. 3.

55 Bull, *The Cruise of the 'Antarctic'*, p. 211.

56 'Exploration in the Antarctic', *The Age*, 20 March 1895, p. 7; *The Argus*, 10 April 1895, p. 5; *Leader*, 30 May 1895, p. 8; *Transactions and Proceedings of the Royal Geographical Society of Australasia: Victorian Branch*, Part II, vols XII and XIII, pp. 73–100; 'South Polar Exploration', *Evening News*, 25 April 1895, p. 3; 'Antarctic Exploration', *Australian Star*, 22 April 1895, p. 5; 'Whaling in the Southern Seas', *Australian Star*, 30 April 1895, p. 3; 'Royal Commission on Fisheries', *SMH*, 3 May 1895, p. 3.

57 *Report of the Seventh Meeting of the Australasian Association for the Advancement of Science*, 1898, p. 666.

58 See, for example, 'South Polar Expedition', *Daily Telegraph*, 4 May 1895, p. 3; 'Terra Incognito', *Australian Star*, 6 May 1895, p. 2; 'Whaling in the Antarctic Seas', *SMH*, 18 May 1895, p. 7; *SMH*, 3 August 1895, p. 7; 'Antarctic Exploration', *Advertiser*, 7 August 1895, p. 6.

59 'The Silent South', *Sunday Times*, 28 April 1895, p. 4. Other examples include *Proceedings of the Royal Society of Victoria*, New Series, vol. 8, 1896, pp. 189–90; 'Antarctic Exploration', *The Age*, 3 April 1895, p. 7; Whaling, Past and Present', *Mercury*, 21 June 1895, p. 4; *SMH*, 31 July 1895, p. 4; *Freemans Journal*, 10 August 1895, p. 21; 'Augustan Age of Antarctic Exploration', *The Age*, 7 September 1895, p. 9; 'Antarctic Exploration', *SMH*, 12 September 1895, p. 3.

60 'Royal Commission on Fisheries', *SMH*, 3 May 1895, p. 3.

61 'A Voyage in the Antarctic', *The Age*, 23 March 1895, p. 11; 'Among the Icebergs', *Australian Town and Country Journal*, 11 May 1895, p. 21; 'Mr. Borchgrevink's Last Lecture', *Daily Telegraph*, 15 June 1895, p. 3; 'New Continent', *Evening News*, 5 October 1895, p. 2.

62 Andrew McConville, 'Henrik Bull, the Antarctic Exploration Committee and the First Confirmed Landing on the Antarctic Continent', *Polar Record*, vol. 43, no. 225, 2007, pp. 143–53.

63 CE Borchgrevink, 'Voyage of *Antarctic* to Victoria Land', in *Report of the Sixth International Geographical Congress*, John Murray, 1896, p. 174.

64 'The International Geographical Congress of 1895', *Geographical Journal*, vol. 8, no. 3, 1896, p. 292.

65 Hugh B Evans, 'A Voyage to Kerguelen in the Sealer *Edward* in 1897–98', *Polar Record*, vol. 16, no. 105, September 1973, pp. 789–91; 'Sea Elephants and Science', *The Argus*, 14 March 1898, p. 6; Robert Hall, 'Kerguelen's Land', *Leader*, 21 May 1898, p. 6, 8; 'The Aquarium', *Leader*, 24 December 1898, p. 36; *Proceedings of the Royal Society of Victoria*, New Series, Part I, vol. XI, 1898, pp. 209–13; Robert Hall, 'Field Notes on the Birds of Kerguelen Island', *Ibis*, Seventh Series, no. 41, January 1900, pp. 1–34.

66 See TH Baughman, *Before the Heroes Came: Antarctica in the 1890s*, University of Nebraska Press, 1994, pp. 43–76; Cornelia Lüdecke, 'Scientific

Collaboration in Antarctica (1901–04): A Challenge in Times of Political Rivalry', *Polar Record*, vol. 39, no. 1, January 2003, pp. 35–48.

67 'Antarctic Exploration', *The Argus*, 20 September 1895, p. 6.

68 'Antarctic Exploration', *Telegraph*, 18 December 1895, p. 5; Antarctic Exploration', *Australian Star*, 15 January 1897, p. 4; *Proceedings of the Royal Geographical Society of Australasia: South Australian Branch*, Tenth Session, 1897–98, pp. 104–13; 'Antarctic Exploration', *The Argus*, 19 January 1897, p. 5; 'Antarctic Exploration', *Daily Telegraph*, 30 January 1897, p. 8; 'Antarctic Exploration', *Mercury*, 22 January 1897, p. 3; CE Borchgrevink, 'Antarctic and Arctic Exploration', *Mercury*, 30 January 1897, p. 4; *The Australasian*, 6 February 1897, p. 32; 'Antarctic Exploration', *Telegraph*, 27 March 1897, p. 4; 'Antarctic Exploration', *Daily Telegraph*, 10 April 1897, p. 4; *Brisbane Courier*, 30 April 1897, p. 7.

69 Borchgrevink, 'Antarctic and Arctic Exploration', *Mercury*, 30 January 1897, p. 4; 'Antarctic Exploration', *Daily Telegraph*, 10 April 1897, p. 4.

70 CE Borchgrevink, *First on the Antarctic Continent, Being an Account of the British Antarctic Expedition 1898–1900*, George Newnes, 1901, pp. 7–10.

71 Louis Bernacchi, *To the South Polar Regions: Expedition of 1898–1900*, Hurst & Blackett, 1901, p. 23.

72 *Sydney Mail*, 6 August 1898, p. 312.

73 *Papers and Proceedings of the Royal Society of Tasmania*, 1899, pp. xv–xxiv; RHSV, MS 000688, Box 228/1, RGSAVB Minute Book, 1897–1913; 'Welcome to Mr. Borchgrevink', *The Age*, 10 December 1898, p. 9; *Mercury*, 15 December 1898, p. 2; 'Tasmania', *Daily Telegraph*, 21 December 1898, p. 5; 'The Antarctic Expedition', *Mercury*, 17 December 1898, p. 1; 'Antarctic Exploration', *The Argus*, 17 December 1898, p. 10; Bernacchi, *To the South Polar Regions*, p. 27; 'The Southern Cross', *Mercury*, 19 December 1898, p. 3.

74 'The Southern Cross', *Mercury*, 19 December 1898, p. 3.

75 John Murray, 'The Renewal of Antarctic Exploration', *Geographical Journal*, vol. 3, no. 1, 1894, pp. 1–27.

76 See Clements Markham, *Antarctic Obsession: A Personal Narrative of the Origins of the British National Antarctic Expedition, 1901–1904*, ed. Clive Holland, Bluntisham, 1986.

77 *Report of the Sixth Meeting of the Australasian Association for the Advancement of Science*, 1895, pp. 468–9; 'An Anglo-Australasian Antarctic Conference', *Geographical Journal*, vol. 10, no. 4, October 1897, pp. 374–85; 'Antarctic Exploration', *SMH*, 2 December 1898, p. 7.

78 RHSV, MS000142, Box 50B, letter from J Scott Keltie to AC MacDonald, 13 July 1899; 'Antarctic Exploration Fund', *The Age*, 30 January 1899, p. 3; 'Proposed British National Antarctic Expedition', *The Age*, 12 May 1899, p. 6; AC Macdonald, 'Sixty Years of Geographical Discovery', *Report of the*

Seventh Meeting of the Australasian Association for the Advancement of Science, 1898, pp. 672–82; Robert F Scott, *The Voyage of the Discovery*, Smith Elder, 1905, p. 30; 'National Antarctic Expedition', *Brisbane Courier*, 25 April 1900, p. 4; *SMH*, 10 July 1899, p. 4.

79 Borchgrevink, *First on the Antarctic Continent*, pp. 245–86.

80 'Return of the Antarctic Expedition', *Papers and Proceedings of the Royal Society of Tasmania*, 1900, p. 127.

81 'Departure of Mr Borchgrevink', *Daily Telegraph*, 21 April 1900, p. 4; 'Whaling', *Evening News*, 20 April 1900, p. 4; 'Whaling in Southern Seas', *Advertiser*, 24 April 1900, p. 4.

82 See, for example, 'A Winter in the Antarctic', *The Age*, 25 June – 3 July 1900; 'Amid Antarctic Ice', *Advertiser*, 25 June – 3 July 1900; 'Near the South Pole', *Daily Telegraph*, 26–30 June 1900; 'The Southern Cross Expedition to Antarctic Regions', *Mercury*, 25 June – 4 July 1900, p. 3.

83 *Advertiser*, 25 June 1900, p. 4; 'Amid Antarctic Ice', *Advertiser*, 29 June 1900, p. 5.

84 For example, *The Age*, 28 March 1903, p. 4; *Mercury*, 13 April 1901, p. 2; *Tasmanian News*, 18 April 1901, p. 3; *SMH*, 20 April 1901, p. 4; *Mercury*, 7 May 1901, p. 6; *Freeman's Journal*, 1 June 1901, p. 24.

85 'Books and Bookmen', *Brisbane Courier*, 20 April 1901, p. 15.

86 'Books and Bookishness', *The Clipper*, 20 April 1901, p. 3.

87 See Baughman, *Before the Heroes Came*, pp. 109–13.

5 'The Reading of Yesterday's Menu to a Hungry Man'

1 See John Hirst, *Sentimental Nation: The Making of the Australian Commonwealth*, Oxford University Press, 2000, pp. 274–96; Frank Bongiorno, *Dreamers and Schemers: A Political History of Australia*, Latrobe University Press, 2022, pp. 113–159.

2 Henry Copeland, *Kerguelen Island and Australian Commerce*, John Sands, 1899, pp. 13–26.

3 National Archives of Australia (NAA), A1, 1911/14438, letter from Henry Copeland to Edmund Barton, 1 February 1901.

4 NAA, A1, 1911/14438, minute for the governor-general, 15 April 1901.

5 *Gippsland Times*, 22 April 1901, p. 3.

6 'Kerguelen's Island', *The Sydney Morning Herald* (*SMH*), 16 April 1901, p. 5.

7 *The Argus*, 23 April 1901, p. 4.

8 NAA, A1, 1911/14438, note by RN Custance, 30 January 1901; letter from Evan MacGregor to William Onslow, 15 July 1901; letter from Chamberlain to Lord Hopetoun, 9 August 1901.

9 Marilyn Lake, 'The Australian Dream of an Island Empire: Race, Reputation and Resistance', *Australian Historical Studies*, vol. 46, no. 3, September 2015, pp. 410–24, quote p. 410.

10 *West Australian*, 23 November 1901, p. 6.

11 NAA, A6, 1901/1585, telegram from William Higgins and Clements Markham to Edmund Barton, 15 May 1901; letter from Macdonald to John Forrest, 22 January 1902; letter from Forrest to Barton, 29 January 1902; letter from prime minister's secretary to Macdonald, 19 February 1902.

12 See John Hirst, 'Nation Building, 1901–14', in Alison Bashford and Stuart Macintyre (eds), *The Cambridge History of Australia*, vol. 2, Cambridge University Press, 2013, pp. 15–38.

13 Robert Scott, *The Voyage of the Discovery*, vol. II, Smith Elder, 1905, pp. 330–53; Albert Armitage, *Two Years in the Antarctic: Being a Narrative of the British National Antarctic Expedition*, Edward Arnold, 1905, pp. 271–94.

14 Royal Maritime Museum Greenwich, MSS 80/044, letter from J Wilson and L Mackinnon to R Scott, 3 October 1902.

15 'Literary Gossip', *Leader*, 2 December 1905, p. 31.

16 See, for example, 'A Tale of Antarctica', *Daily Telegraph*, 6 February 1904, p. 10; 'Lost in the Antarctic', *Australian Town and Country Journal*, 9 August 1905, p. 20.

17 See, for example, 'German Antarctic Expedition', *SMH*, 3 June 1903, p. 7; 'From the Antarctic', *Daily Telegraph*, 24 July 1903, p. 3; 'A Lost Expedition', *The Age*, 11 February 1905, p. 13; 'Missing French Antarctic Expedition', *Mercury*, 2 May 1905, p. 8.

18 Scott Polar Research Institute, MS100/13/11–14, letters from WS Bruce to HR Mill; Robert N Rudmose Brown, Robert Mossman and JH Harvey Pirie, *The Voyage of the Scotia, Being the Record of a Voyage of Exploration in Antarctic Seas*, William Blackwood, 1906; WS Bruce, *Polar Exploration*, Williams & Norgate, 1911. See also Peter Speak, 'William Speirs Bruce: Polar Explorer and Scottish Nationalist', *Polar Record*, vol. 28, no. 167, 2009, pp. 285–92.

19 'The Antarctic Regions', *Bunyip*, 27 August 1886, p. 2; *The Voyage of the Scotia*, p. viii.

20 See, for example, *Daily Telegraph*, 10 June 1905, p. 4; 'The Siege of the South Pole', *Leader*, 10 March 1906, p. 28; 'Haunt of the Penguins', *Australian Town and Country Journal*, 2 January 1907, p. 54.

21 'Antarctic Tourists', *Evening News*, 31 October 1907, p. 4; 'The Crusade against Consumption', *SMH*, 20 July 1905, p. 10.

22 'The Australian Natives Exhibition', *Daily Telegraph*, 13 October 1905, p. 3.

23 See, for example, 'To the Pole by Motor-Car', *Brisbane Courier*, 1 January 1906, p. 2; 'Another Antarctic Expedition', *Evening News*, 26 April 1906, p. 4; 'Antarctic Exploration', *The Age*, 13 September 1906, p. 5; 'Antarctic Exploration', *SMH*, 5 February 1907, p. 5.

24 EH Shackleton, 'A New British Antarctic Expedition', *Geographical Journal*, vol. 29, no. 3, March 1907, pp. 329–32. See also Beau Riffenburgh, *Nimrod:*

Ernest Shackleton and the Extraordinary Story of the 1907–09 British Antarctic Expedition, Bloomsbury, 2004; Roland Huntford, *Shackleton*, 2nd edn, Abacus, 1996, pp. 4–157.

25 Royal Geographical Society Archives, MS RFS/4.

26 EH Shackleton, *The Heart of the Antarctic, Being the Story of the British Antarctic Expedition 1907–1909*, Heinemann, 1909, pp. vii–26; Huntford, *Shackleton*, pp. 154–91.

27 'Motors for the Antarctic', *The Argus*, 16 February 1907, p. 7; 'To the Antarctic', *The Argus*, 13 April 1907, p. 5; 'Antarctic Exploration', *SMH*, 23 May 1907, p. 7; 'The New Antarctic Expedition', *Leader*, 21 September 1907, p. 40; 'Antarctic Ship Sails', *The Age*, 9 August 1907, p. 5.

28 See David Branagan, *T.W. Edgeworth David: A Life*, National Library of Australia, 2005.

29 TWE David, WF Smeeth and JA Schoffield, 'Notes on Antarctic Rocks Collected by Mr CE Borchgrevink', *Journal and Proceedings of the Royal Society of New South Wales*, 1896, pp. 461–92; 'Royal Society of New South Wales', *SMH*, 8 August 1895, p. 6.

30 'The Frozen South', *SMH*, 6 September 1907, p. 7.

31 'The Antarctic Expedition', *Sunday Times*, 8 December 1907, p. 7.

32 'Antarctic Expedition', *SMH*, 22 October 1907, p. 7; 'The Frozen South', *Daily Telegraph*, 31 October 1907, 4 p.; *SMH*, 2 December 1907, p. 4.

33 'Antarctic Expedition', *The Herald*, 3 December 1907, p. 3. See also 'Antarctic Exploration', *The Herald*, 26 November 1907, p. 6; Antarctic Expedition', *The Herald*, 30 November 1907, p. 5; 'Through Antarctic Ice', *Advertiser*, 2 December 1907, p. 7; Antarctic Exploration', *Leader*, 7 December 1907, p. 34.

34 'Antarctic Exploration', *The Age*, 4 December 1907, p. 7.

35 Royal Historical Society of Victoria (RHSV), Box 228/1, invitation to special meeting of the RGSAVB, 3 December 1907; 'The Antarctic Expedition', *The Argus*, 4 December 1907, p. 8; 'Entertainments', *SMH*, 11 December 1907, p. 5.

36 'The Antarctic', *The Herald*, 11 December 1907, p. 2; 'Antarctic Expedition', *The Age*, 16 December 1907, p. 5.

37 'To the Frozen South', *Evening News*, 5 December 1907, p. 7; 'The Antarctic Expedition', *Evening News*, 7 December 1907, p. 2.

38 'Frost and Finance', *SMH*, 7 December 1907, p. 13.

39 'An Appeal to Australia', *SMH*, 14 December 1907, p. 13.

40 'To the Frozen South', *Evening News*, 5 December 1907, p. 7; 'The Dash for the Pole', *SMH*, 6 December 1907, p. 7; 'Seals for the Zoo', *Daily Telegraph*, 9 December 1907, p. 4.

41 'The Nimrod Expedition', *SMH*, 5 December 1907, p. 6.

42 'Antarctic Fund', *SMH*, 21 December 1907, p. 13.

43 NAA, A2, 1909/2497, cablegram from Edgeworth David to Alfred Deakin, 14 December 1907; letter from David to William Lyne, 16 December 1907.

44 *Commonwealth Parliamentary Debates*, House of Representatives, no. 50, 13 December 1907, pp. 7491–3.

45 Ibid.; NAA, A2, 1909/2497, cablegram from Deakin to Shackleton, 18 December 1907.

46 'Cost of the Polar Expedition', *Daily Telegraph*, 16 December 1907, p. 6.

47 Shackleton, *The Heart of the Antarctic*, pp. 10–38; State Library Victoria (SLV), MS8311, Box 323/2, New Zealand Short Waybill.

48 See Rohan Howitt, 'Antarctica and the Stratigraphy of International Memory', in Glenda Sluga, Kate Darian-Smith and Madeleine Herren (eds), *Sites of International Memory*, University of Pennsylvania Press, 2023, pp. 115–40.

49 'The Nimrod Sets Out', *The Argus*, 2 January 1908, p. 5; 'Antarctic Exploration', *Sunday Times*, 5 January 1908, p. 12; 'Off to the Pole', *Daily Telegraph*, 8 January 1908, p. 10; Sydney University Museums, Macleay Collection, HP88.47.03, HP88.47.15, HP88.47.28.

50 'Among Icebergs', *SMH*, 23 January 1908, p. 7.

51 'Professor David in Antarctica', *Daily Telegraph*, 31 January 1908, p. 6.

52 'With the Nimrod', *SMH*, 9 January 1908, p. 6; 'The Antarctic Expedition', *Mercury*, 20 January 1908, p. 3.

53 University of Sydney Archives (USA), P11:7, letter from acting registrar to Edgeworth David, 3 March 1908; 'The British Antarctic Expedition, 1907', *Daily Telegraph*, 21 March – 3 April 1908, p. 9; 'With Shackleton for the South Pole', *SMH*, 21 March – 4 April 1908, p. 7.

54 See, for example, 'Trouble with Nimrod's Crew', *Daily Telegraph*, 21 March 1908, p. 9; 'Along Antarctic Ice', *SMH*, 13 April 1908, p. 7; 'The Antarctic Expedition', *SMH*, 27 April 1908, p. 8; 'South Pole Expedition', *Daily Telegraph*, 12 June 1908, p. 7; 'To the Antarctic again', *The Argus*, 14 September 1908, p. 4; 'Shackleton Expedition', *SMH*, 31 October 1908, p. 12; 'Dash for the Pole', *SMH*, 11 November 1908, p. 13; *Australasian*, 28 November 1908, p. 39; 'Winter with the Bears and Penguins', *Daily Telegraph*, 2 December 1908, pp. 9–10; 'Meteorology in Australia', *Daily Telegraph*, 21 December 1908, p. 6.

55 'Welcome Home!', *Evening News*, 30 March 1909, p. 7.

56 'Scientists at Sea', *Advertiser*, 27 March 1908, p. 4; 'Students' Saturnalia', *SMH*, 4 May 1908, p. 7.

57 'Southern Seas', *Daily Telegraph*, 13 June 1908, p. 12.

58 NAA, A2, 1909/2497, cablegram from Shackleton to Andrew Fisher, 26 March 1909; memorandum from Fisher to Shackleton, 31 March 1909;

'Gift to Commonwealth', *SMH*, 27 March 1909, p. 13; *SMH*, 27 March 1909, p. 13.

59 'The Professor at the Antarctic', *Sydney Mail*, 11 May 1921, pp. 8–9, 33.

60 *Evening News*, 30 March 1909, pp. 7–8; 'Professor David', *SMH*, 31 March 1909, p. 8; 'Woodford', *Blue Mountain Echo*, 3 April 1909, p. 10; 'Welcome to Professor David', *Sydney Mail*, 7 April 1909, p. 30.

61 'Back from the Antarctic', *Sydney Mail*, 7 April 1909, p. 20; 'Welcome to Professor David', *Evening News*, 29 March 1909, p. 4; 'Professor David', *SMH*, 1 April 1909, p. 6.

62 'South Pole Expedition', *The Argus*, 8 April 1909, p. 6.

63 'Shares Honours with Shackleton', *Sydney Mail*, 31 March 1909, p. 1.

64 'The Antarctic Expedition', *SMH*, 28 May 1909, p. 4; USA, P11:6.7, prospectus for one, two or three lectures on the British Antarctic Expedition of 1907–09; *SMH*, 2 July 1910, p. 12; *SMH*, 5 July 1910, p. 9; *SMH*, 8 July 1910, p. 6; 'Professor David's Lectures', *SMH*, 8 July 1910, p. 10; 'Professor David's Lecture', *SMH*, 21 July 1910, p. 8.

65 See, for example, USA, P11:6.8; 'Professor David's Lectures', *Evening News*, 23 June 1909, p. 9.

66 'Polar Observatory', *SMH*, 19 April 1909, p. 7; 'Radium in Antarctica', *SMH*, 4 May 1909, p. 7; 'Fishing in the Frozen South', *Evening News*, 12 May 1909, p. 9.

67 'The Nimrod Expedition', *Daily Telegraph*, 6 April 1909, p. 4; 'The Nimrod Expedition', *Evening News*, 14 April 1909, p. 10; 'Welcome to Mr Mawson', *Evening News*, 15 April 1909, p. 2; *Evening News*, 20 April 1909, p. 5; 'Lieutenant Shackleton', *Evening News*, 21 April 1909, p. 5; 'The Antarctic Expedition', *Advertiser*, 22 April 1909, p. 8; 'Back from the South Pole', *Sydney Mail*, 28 April 1909, pp. 30–4; 'Royal Society', *SMH*, 28 April 1909, p. 10; *Table Talk*, 6 May 1909, p. 31; 'The Nimrodders', *Daily Telegraph*, 6 May 1909, p. 3; *Blue Mountains Echo*, 8 May 1909, p. 8.

68 'Lieutenant Shackleton as Lecturer', *SMH*, 27 March 1909, p. 13; 'Lieutenant Shackleton's Intentions', *SMH*, 1 April 1909, p. 6; 'Lieutenant Shackleton', *SMH*, 17 April 1909, p. 13; 'The Shackleton Lecture', *Daily Telegraph*, 23 April 1909, p. 5.

69 'Farthest South', *SMH*, 1 May 1909, p. 13.

70 See, for example, RHSV, MS 000142, Box 50B; 'Lieutenant Shackleton's Lecture', *The Argus*, 29 April 1909, p. 7; 'Lieutenant Shackleton's Lecture', *The Age*, 5 May 1909, p. 6; 'Antarctic Exploration', *The Argus*, 8 May 1909, p. 21; 'The Shackleton Lectures', *Evening Journal*, 10 May 1909, p. 2; 'Lieut. Shackleton's Lecture', *West Australian*, 15 May 1909, p. 12; 'Lieutenant Shackleton's Visit', *West Australian*, 26 May 1909, p. 9.

71 'Lieut. Shackleton as Lecturer', *Western Mail*, 22 May 1909, p. 42; 'Lieutenant Shackleton's Lecture', *Daily News*, 18 May 1909, p. 4.

72 'Name the Capital', *Star*, 10 April 1909, p. 28.

73 NAA, Sydney, P1132/9, NN, register of ships fees, 3 January 1906 – 31 December 1912; 'Arrival of the Nimrod', *Daily Telegraph*, 21 April 1909, p. 9.

74 'Nimrod in Sydney', *SMH*, 21 April 1909, p. 10; 'Visit to the Nimrod', *SMH*, 22 April 1909, p. 9.

75 'Visits to the Nimrod', *SMH*, 3 May 1909, p. 7; 'The Nimrod', *Argus*, 5 May 1909, p. 4; *Evening News*, 5 May 1909, p. 1; 'Nimrod Thrown Open', *SMH*, 4 May 1909, p. 7; *Daily Telegraph*, 5 May 1909, p. 9.

76 'The Professor at the Antarctic', *Sydney Mail*, 11 May 1921, pp. 8–9, 33.

77 SLV, M231/3, letter from Shackleton to JK Davis, 4 May 1909; letter from Davis to Shackleton, 7 May 1909; 'Professor David's Dog', *Star*, 22 April 1909, p. 8; 'The "Nimrodders"', *DT*, 6 May 1909, p. 3.

78 'Nimrod at Circular Quay', *Evening News*, 3 May 1909, p. 3; 'Theft from the Nimrod', *The Age*, 4 May 1909, p. 5; *Sydney Mail*, 12 May 1909, p. 9.

79 'The Nimrod', *Evening News*, 13 April 1909, p. 6; 'Search for Islands', *The Argus*, 24 April 1909, p. 21; 'Nimrod's Future Work', *Mercury*, 4 May 1909, p. 2; 'Departure of the Nimrod', *Daily Telegraph*, 10 May 1909, p. 8; 'Royal Company Islands', *The Argus*, 13 August 1909, p. 5.

80 See, for example, 'Professor David', *SMH*, 31 March 1909, p. 8; 'Back from the Ice', *SMH*, 24 March 1909, p. 9; 'Seeking the Pole', *Daily Telegraph*, 22 October 1907, p. 8; 'Radium in Antarctica', *SMH*, 4 May 1909, p. 7.

81 *Evening News*, 29 March 1909, p. 4.

82 'Welcome Home!', *Evening News*, 30 March 1909, p. 7.

83 *British Antarctic Expedition 1907–09: Reports on the Scientific Investigations*, William Heinemann, 1910–16; USA, P11:7.2, P11:6:2.

6 'A Golden El Dorado Down South'

1 'Mawson Expedition', *The Sydney Morning Herald* (*SMH*), 14 June 1911, p. 14.

2 Tom Griffiths, 'A Polar Drama: The Australasian Antarctic Expedition of 1911–14', in Martin Thomas (ed.), *Expedition into Empire: Exploratory Journeys and the Making of the Modern World*, Routledge, 2015, p. 173.

3 State Library Victoria, MS 3231/3, letter from Shackleton to editor of the *Daily Mail*, 17 September 1909; Royal Geographic Society (RGS), MS RFS/4 c., letter from J Scott Keltie to Scott, 9 February 1910; Scott Polar Research Institute (SPRI), MS 100/13/16–18, MS 101/23/1; 'The South Pole', *Leader*, 5 February 1910, p. 22; 'A New British Antarctic Expedition', *Geographical Journal*, vol. 34, no. 4, October 1909, pp. 361–3; RGS, MS RFS/4, MS RFS/4c.

4 SPRI, MS 1175;D, abbreviated log, 7 December 1909 to 28 September 1912; MS 1453/13.

5 National Archives of Australia (NAA), A1, 1911–177, cablegrams between Muirhead Collins and Atlee Hunt, 7–13 October 1909; A1, 1911/177, letter from Scott to Charles Wade, 28 January 1910; letter from Wade to Andrew Fisher, 15 March 1910; letter from Fisher to Wade, 15 June 1910; 'To the Pole', *The Herald*, 30 August 1910, p. 1.
6 'Captain Scott's Expedition', *The Age*, 3 May 1911, p. 9; 'For the Antarctic', *Daily Telegraph*, 3 June 1910, p. 7; 'Antarctic Research', *Daily Telegraph*, 4 August 1910, p. 7; 'Farthest South', *Argus*, 4 October 1910, p. 7; 'Straight for the Pole', *SMH*, 8 October 1910, p. 15.
7 'The Scott Expedition', *SMH*, 10 October 1910, p. 8.
8 NAA, A1, 1911/177; 'Federal Government Asked for £5,000', *Daily Telegraph*, 8 October 1910, p. 13.
9 NAA, A1, 1911/177, letter from Hughes to Maiden, 19 October 1910; 'Government Grant of £2,500', *The Age*, 14 October 1910, p. 7.
10 *The Argus*, 15 October 1910, p. 18.
11 NAA, A1, 1911/177, letter from Allen Taylor to WM Hughes, 19 October 1910; letter from Hughes to Taylor, 22 October 1910; 'Captain Scott's Antarctic Expedition', *Evening News*, 17 October 1910, p. 4.
12 'New South Wales Timber', *Sun*, 29 October 1910, p. 9.
13 'British Expedition to the Antarctic', *Daily Telegraph*, 17 October 1910, p. 13; 'Captain Scott's Lecture', *Evening News*, 20 October 1910, p. 8; 'British Cheers', *The Sun*, 21 October 1910, p. 4; 'Off to the Unknown', *Daily Telegraph*, 21 October 1910, p. 10; SPRI, MS 1517/4/2;D, letter from Scott to Edgar Speyer, 10 December 1910.
14 'To the Pole!', *SMH*, 19 October 1910, p. 11.
15 'To the Antarctic', *SMH*, 15 April – 17 May 1911.
16 Roald Amundsen, *To the South Pole: An Account of the Norwegian Antarctic Expedition in the Fram 1910–1912*, vol. 1, trans. AG Chater, John Murray, 1912, pp. 42–54.
17 'Scott's Expedition', *SMH*, 26 October 1910, p. 9.
18 'Scott or Amundsen', *Evening News*, 17 April 1911, p. 6. See, for example, 'Antarctic Expedition', *The Argus*, 26 October 1910, p. 12; 'The Hardest Nut in Norway', *The Age*, 30 March 1911, p. 7; 'Captain Amundsen's Intentions', *The Age*, 12 April 1911, p. 9; 'The Antarctic Race', *Daily Telegraph*, 27 April 1911, p. 8.
19 'To the Pole!', *Daily Telegraph*, 29 March 1911, p. 9.
20 On the idea of 'Australian Britons', see Carl Bridge, 'Australia, Britain and the British Commonwealth', in Alison Bashford and Stuart Macintyre (eds), *The Cambridge History of Australia*, Cambridge University Press, 2013, pp. 518–36.
21 Nobu Shirase, *The Japanese South Polar Expedition 1910–12: A Record of Antarctica*, trans. Lara Dagnell and Hilary Shibata, Erskine Press, 2011,

pp. 1–54; William R Stevenson, 'Science, the South Pole and the Japanese Expedition of 1910–1912', *Endeavour*, vol. 35, no. 4, 2011, pp. 160–8.

22 'Antarctic Exploration', *SMH*, 9 January 1911, p. 7. See also 'Japanese Expedition', *SMH*, 1 December 1910, p. 9; 'Romance of the Antarctic', *SMH*, 12 January 1911, p. 10; 'The Mawson Expedition', *Australasian*, 21 January 1911, p. 42.

23 Shirase, *The Japanese South Polar Expedition*, p. 83.

24 NAA (Sydney), A1026, Whole Series; 'Letter from S Mills to Consul-General for Japan, 5 May 1911', in Shirase, *The Japanese South Polar Expedition*, pp. 83–4.

25 Shirase, *The Japanese South Polar Expedition*, pp. 84–90; 'Our Japanese Visitors', *SMH*, 15 May 1911, p. 9; 'The Mysterious Japs', *The Sun*, 15 May 1911, p. 1.

26 For a complete analysis of the JAE's time in Sydney, see Rohan Howitt, 'The Japanese Antarctic Expedition and the Idea of White Australia', *Australian Historical Studies*, vol. 49, no. 4, 2018, pp. 510–26.

27 'Mysterious Japs', *Sun*, 15 May 1911. See also Woollahra Local History Centre (WLHC), Vaucluse Municipal Council Minute Books, Book 10, 12–19 May 1911; 'Our Japanese Visitors', *SMH*, 15 May 1911, p. 9; 'Guards Turn Out', *Evening News*, 15 May 1911, p. 7; 'The Japanese Camp', *Evening News*, 23 May 1911, p. 10.

28 Dot Miller, 'Shirase Expedition Autograph Album', Australian Museum, http://australianmuseum.net.au/blogpost/museullaneous/a-dear-friend-by-the-strange-shore (viewed August 2024).

29 'Japanese Pole-Seekers', *Sunday Times*, 18 June 1911, p. 12.

30 WLHC, Oral History Library, Robert Hilliar, interviewed by Jane Britten, 16 June 1993; 'The Departing Japs', *The Sun*, 25 July 1911, p. 6.

31 'Japan and the Empire', *SMH*, 23 June 1911, p. 11; 'With the Japanese at Parsley Bay', *SMH*, 26 June 1911, p. 8; 'A Japanese Lecture', *The Sun*, 27 June 1911, p. 6.

32 See David Branagan, *T.W. Edgeworth David: A Life*, National Library of Australia, 2005, pp. 232–4; Shirase, *The Japanese South Polar Expedition*, pp. 88–90; *SMH*, 24 June 1911, p. 2; *SMH*, 28 June 1911, p. 2; 'I Think So', *SMH*, 5 October 1911, p. 8.

33 Shirase, *The Japanese South Polar Expedition*, pp. 92–95; 'Japan and the Pole', *SMH*, 20 November 1911, p. 9; 'The Great Cold Land', *Evening News*, 20 November 1911, p. 10.

34 RGS, MS RFS/4 c, letter from Keltie to Scott, 19 September 1912.

35 See Shirley V Scott, 'Japan's Renunciation of Territorial Rights in Antarctica and Australian Diplomacy', *Polar Record*, vol. 35, no. 193, 1999, pp. 99–106.

36 'Scott and the Pole', *Daily Telegraph*, 8 March 1912, p. 9; 'Back from the Antarctic', *The Sun*, 7 March 1912, p. 7; 'Antarctic Exploration', *Mercury*, 8 March 1912, p. 5.

37 'Seeking the Antarctic Pole', *Daily News*, 9 March 1912, p. 7.
38 See, for example, 'Race to the South Pole', *The Age*, 8 March 1912, p. 7; 'South Pole', *Telegraph* (Brisbane), 8 March 1912, p. 6; 'Scott Has Discovered the Pole', *West Australian*, 8 March 1912, p. 7.
39 'The Conquest', *Daily Telegraph*, 11 March 1912, p. 7.
40 'Antarctic Research', *SMH*, 8 March 1912, p. 8.
41 'The Antarctic Explorers', *Brisbane Courier*, 3 April 1912, p. 4.
42 *Mercury*, 16 March 1912, p. 6. See also 'Hobart and the Antarctic', *Mercury*, 13 March 1912, p. 4; 'Question of Public Reception', *Mercury*, 19 March 1912, pp. 5–6; 'Welcome to Capt. Amundsen', *Mercury*, 19 March 1912, p. 6; *Mercury*, 23 March 1912, p. 6; 'Honour to Amundsen', *Mercury*, 30 March 1912, p. 8; *Proceedings of the Royal Society of Tasmania*, 1912, pp. xii–xv.
43 'Honour to Amundsen', *Mercury*, 30 March 1912, p. 8.
44 'The Two Expeditions', *Mercury*, 14 March 1912, p. 5.
45 'Captain Amundsen and Charity', *Mercury*, 19 March 1912, p. 6; *Mercury*, 20 March 1912, p. 4.
46 'Antarctic Lectures', *SMH*, 4 January 1912, p. 7; 'Captain Amundsen's Story', *The Age*, 9 March 1912, p. 13.
47 'Antarctic Exploration', *The Argus*, 20 March 1912, p. 12.
48 SPRI, MS 1453/125;D; 'The South Pole', *The Argus*, 30 March 1912, p. 20; 'Amundsen's Lecture', *SMH*, 3 April 1912, p. 22.
49 SPRI, MS 1175;D, abbreviated log 7 December 1909 – 28 September 1912.
50 'To the Antarctic', *SMH*, 14 June 1910, p. 7.
51 'The Unknown Land', *The Argus*, 17 June 1910, p. 6.
52 'Antarctic Research, *Daily Telegraph*, 14 June 1910, p. 9.
53 'To the Antarctic', *Daily Telegraph*, 17 June 1910, p. 9.
54 'Antarctic Exploration', *Advertiser*, 16 July 1910, p. 18; 'Life in the Antarctic', *Advertiser*, 27 July 1910, p. 11; SPRI, MS 1175;D, abbreviated log.
55 'Antarctic Exploration', *SMH*, 9 January 1911, p. 7; 'Australia in the South', *Daily Telegraph*, 9 January 1911, p. 9; 'Dr. Mawson's Antarctic Expedition', *Daily Telegraph*, 9 January 1911, p. 9; 'Antarctic Exploration', *Daily Telegraph*, 19 December 1910, p. 6.
56 'Mawson Expedition', *SMH*, 12 January 1911, p. 8; 'Antarctica', *The Sun*, 11 January 1911, p. 8.
57 Douglas Mawson, 'Australian Antarctic Expedition', *Report of the Meeting of the Australasian Association for the Advancement of Science held at Sydney, 1911*, 1912, pp. 398–400.
58 'Mawson Expedition', *SMH*, 12 January 1911, p. 8.
59 'Australia's Antarctica', *Daily Telegraph*, 12 January 1911, p. 6.
60 'Antarctic Exploration', *Mercury*, 13 January 1911, p. 4.
61 'Science Congress', *The Argus*, 12 January 1911, p. 9; 'To Explore Antarctica', *The Sun*, 16 January 1911, p. 6.

62 'Antarctic Exploration', *The Argus*, 17 January 1911, p. 7; 'Generous Mr. Hordern', *Evening News*, 18 January 1911, p. 9; 'The Far South', *The Sun*, 19 January 1911, p. 5.
63 NAA, A1, 1915/5159, report of deputation 23rd March, 1911; letter from GF Pearce to Fisher, 19 January 1911.
64 'Antarctic Exploration', *The Argus*, 19 January 1911, p. 7; 'Minerals in Antarctica', *SMH*, 31 March 1911, p. 8.
65 See SPRI, MS1175;D, MS996/2, MS101/61/2–6; University of Sydney Archives (USA), P11:8:2, list of subscribers; Douglas Mawson, *The Home of the Blizzard, Being the Story of the Australasian Antarctic Expedition 1911–1914*, vol. 2, Heinemann, 1915, pp. 311–12; 'Antarctic', *The Argus*, 10 May 1911, p. 14.
66 For example, 'Australasian Antarctic Expedition', *SMH*, 22 April 1911, p. 9; 'The Antarctic', *Advertiser*, 4 May 1911, p. 7; 'Australasian Antarctic Expedition', *West Australian*, 11 May 1911, p. 4; 'Dr Mawson and the South', *Daily Telegraph*, 5 June 1911, p. 7; 'Dr Mawson's Expedition', *SMH*, 10 July 1911, p. 8; 'Children and the Mawson Expedition', *Daily Telegraph*, 7 October 1911, p. 6; 'Children and the Mawson Expedition', *Daily Telegraph*, 12 October 1911, p. 5; 'The Mawson Expedition', *Evening News*, 29 June 1911, p. 2; 'Helping Mawson', *Freeman's Journal*, 13 July 1911, p. 31.
67 See Jessica Urwin, 'The Radioactive Dr Mawson: Douglas Mawson and the Quest for Australia's Radium Riches, 1904–58', *Australian Historical Studies*, vol. 53, no. 1, 2021, pp. 26–42; Peter D Shaughnessy and Mark Pharaoh, 'Mawson's Views on Use of Natural Resources in the Antarctic and Sub-Antarctic', *Polar Record*, vol. 57, 2021, e31.
68 NAA, A1, 1915/5159, letter from Mawson to External Affairs, 13 October 1911
69 'The Mystic South', *Daily News*, 18 July 1911, p. 4; 'Antarctic Expedition', *SMH*, 19 July 1911, p. 16.
70 'Mawson Expedition', *Argus*, 28 August 1911, p. 7.
71 'Australasian Antarctic Expedition', *Mercury*, 3 November 1911, p. 6; The Far South', *Sydney Mail*, 13 September 1911, p. 9.
72 'Coal From Antarctica', *West Australian*, 15 October 1912, p. 7.
73 See Andrew Fitzmaurice, *Sovereignty, Property, and Empire, 1500–2000*, Cambridge University Press, 2014, pp. 215–334.
74 'The Mawson Expedition', *Daily Telegraph*, 8 August 1911, p. 7; 'Dr. Mawson's Expedition', *Evening News*, 12 September 1911, p. 4; *Commonwealth Parliamentary Debates*, House of Representatives, no. 37, 13 September 1911, pp. 423–4; 'State Cabinet', *The Argus*, 19 September 1911, p. 6.
75 'The Antarctic Expedition', *Mercury*, 9 November 1911, p. 3; 'Southward Bound', *The Sun*, 10 November 1911, p. 5; 'Building the Portable Hut for Dr. Mawson's Expedition', *Evening News*, 20 November 1911, p. 10.

76 'Wireless in Antarctica', *Daily Telegraph*, 1 November 1910, p. 6.
77 'Links with the Antarctic', *Daily Telegraph*, 27 October 1911, p. 11; 'The Antarctic Expedition', *Mercury*, 23 November 1911, p. 6; 'The Antarctic Expedition', *Mercury*, 25 November 1911, p. 8.
78 For example, 'Southward Ho!', *Daily Telegraph*, 27 December 1911, pp. 9–10; 'All Well', *SMH*, 13 March 1912, p. 19; 'With Dr. Mawson in Antarctica', *Daily Telegraph*, 16 March 1912, p. 15; 'Antarctic Research', *The Argus*, 19 March 1912, p. 7; 'The Icy South', *SMH*, 27 May 1912, p. 9; 'The Mawson Expedition', *Mercury*, 1 June 1912, p. 2.
79 'Right Wales', *The Sun*, 1 April 1912, p. 6; 'Aurora in Dock', *SMH*, 18 April 1912, p. 10; 'Lower Prices for Whale Oil', *SMH* 16 April 1912, p. 11; 'The Whaling Industry', *Daily Telegraph*, 18 April 1912, p. 5; 'The Whaling Industry', *Mercury*, 27 April 1912, p. 16.
80 'Antarctica', *SMH*, 9 April 1912, p. 4; 'Inspection of the Aurora', *SMH*, 5 April 1912, p. 6.
81 See, for example, 'Other Entertainments', *SMH*, 8 May 1912, p. 9; 'At the Lyceum', *The Sun*, 14 May 1912, p. 2; 'Antarctica', *Daily Telegraph* 14 May 1912, p. 15; 'Dr. Mawson's Antarctic Expedition', *Mercury*, 22 June 1912, p. 6; 'His Majesty's Theatre', *Mercury*, 1 July 1912, p. 8; 'Spencer's', *The Herald*, 17 August 1912, p. 7.
82 Robert Dixon, *Photography, Early Cinema and Colonial Modernity: Frank Hurley's Synchronized Lecture Entertainments*, Anthem Press, 2012.
83 'Message from Mawson', *Evening News*, 27 May 1912, p. 3.
84 USA, P11:7:3, letter from Conrad Eitel to Edgeworth David, 6 February 1912.
85 Mawson, *The Home of the Blizzard*, pp. 149–50.
86 'The Mawson Expedition', *Advertiser*, 14 March 1912, p. 10; 'Wireless and Dr. Mawson', *Daily Telegraph*, 11 September 1912, p. 8; 'Mawson and Wireless', *The Argus*, 1 October 1912, p. 6.
87 USA, P11:7:3, letter from Eitel to David, 6 February 1912; letter from Masson to Eitel, 5 November 1912; 'Mawson Expedition', *Mercury*, 5 November 1912, p. 5.
88 'Mawson's Antarctic Expedition', *Mercury*, 24 December 1912, p. 4.
89 Mawson, *The Home of the Blizzard*, pp. 239–72.
90 For example, 'The Pitiless Antarctic', *Evening News*, 25 February 1913, p. 7; 'Is It Worth While?', *Brisbane Courier*, 27 February 1913, p. 7.

7 'Unfair Advantage'

1 Scott Polar Research Institute (SPRI), MS 1537/2/33/1;D.
2 National Archives of Australia (NAA), A2, 1920/656, report from the Joint Committee of Public Accounts; 'To Antarctic', *Evening News*, 16 December 1914, p. 6.

3 See, for example, 'Terra Nova Returns', *The Sun*, 1 April 1912, p. 7; 'Captain Scott in the Antarctic', *Daily Telegraph*, 2 April 1912, p. 8; 'No Race for the Pole', *Daily Telegraph*, 9 April 1912, p. 9; 'Scott's Hope', *The Sydney Morning Herald* (*SMH*), 13 April 1912, p. 17; 'Winds of Antarctica', *Daily Telegraph*, 17 April 1912, p. 11; 'Back from the Antarctic', *The Age*, 25 April 1912, p. 11; 'Antarctic Charms', *Daily Telegraph*, 9 May 1912, p. 10; 'Discoveries in the Antarctic', *Leader*, 1 June 1912; 'The Antarctic', *Daily Telegraph*, 28 December 1912, p. 6.

4 See, for example. *Daily Telegraph*, 16 March 1912, p. 10; *SMH*, 1 April 1912, p. 4; 'Cinematograph in the Antarctic', *The Age*, 16 May 1912, p. 10; 'Antarctic Exploration', *The Age*, 22 May 1912, p. 10; *The Herald*, 10 June 1912, p. 7; *The Herald*, 7 December 1912, p. 2; 'With Scott to the South', *Evening News*, 13 February 1913, p. 8.

5 See, for example, 'Antarctic Research', *The Argus*, 29 February 1912, p. 7; 'Where Is Scott?', *Daily Telegraph*, 3 April 1912, p. 19; 'Last Man to See Scott', *SMH*, 9 May 1912, p. 9; 'Antarctic Explorers', *The Argus*, 11 September 1912, p. 13.

6 See SPRI, MS559/164; 'Captain Scott', *Evening News*, 10 February 1913, p. 7.

7 'The Antarctic', *SMH*, 11 February 1913, p. 8. See also 'Back from the Antarctic', *The Argus*, 11 February 1913, p. 7; 'Return of the Terranova', *The Sun*, 10 February 1913, p. 8.

8 'Tragedy of the South', *The Age*, 11 February 1913, p. 7.

9 *The Herald*, 11 February 1913, p. 4.

10 'Scott's Glorious Sacrifice', *The Sun*, 12 February 1913, p. 8; 'How They Died', *Evening News*, 12 February 1913, p. 10; Scott's Conquest', *Daily Telegraph*, 14 February 1913, p. 9; 'Everlasting Snows', *SMH*, 26 February 1913, p. 14; 'Silence Broken', *Daily Telegraph*, 19 March 1913, p. 12; 'Personal Recollections', *Daily Telegraph*, 12 February 1913, pp. 9–10; 'As Beloved as He Was Brave', *Daily Telegraph*, 13 February 1913, p. 7; 'Expedition Member's Eulogy', *West Australian*, 13 February 1913, p. 7.

11 See, for example, 'Deathless Heroes', *Daily Telegraph*, 12 February 1913, p. 9; 'Impressive Service at St. Paul's', *The Age*, 17 February 1913, p. 9; 'Scott Memorial Service', *Register*, 18 February 1913, p. 9; 'Memorial Services in Perth', *Geraldton Express*, 17 February 1913, p. 3; 'In Memoriam Service', *Brisbane Courier*, 17 February 1913, p. 5; 'Memorial Service in Bendigo', *Bendigo Independent*, 15 February 1913, p. 5; 'Polar Tragedy', *Benalla Standard*, 18 February 1913, p. 3; 'Services in Queensland', *Brisbane Courier*, 18 February 1913, p. 8; 'Memorial Services', *Nowra Leader*, 21 February 1913, p. 8; 'Ceremony in Sydney Schools', *The Age*, 18 February 1913, p. 7; 'The Antarctic Disaster', *Border Watch*, 15 February 1913, p. 2; 'Tennyson's Lines', *Daily Telegraph*, 12 February 1913, p. 10.

12 'St. Paul's', *Daily Telegraph*, 13 February 1913, p. 7; 'St. Paul's', *Daily Telegraph*, 15 February 1913, p. 14; 'To Bring Back the Bodies', *The Sun*, 18 February 1913, p. 5; 'Antarctic Explorers', *The Argus*, 28 February 1913, p. 7; 'Captain Scott's Last Wish', *Advertiser*, 28 February 1913, p. 9.

13 'For the Federal Capital', *Brisbane Courier*, 10 March 1913, p. 7; 'Federal Territory', *The Herald*, 20 February 1913, p. 8; 'Captain Scott', *SMH*, 28 February 1913, p. 10.

14 RF Scott, *Scott's Last Expedition*, vol. 1, Smith Elder, 1913, p. 607.

15 'Chamber of Commerce Appeal', *Daily Telegraph*, 13 February 1913, p. 7; 'Surely They Will Care!', *The Sun*, 17 February 1913, p. 1; 'The Scott Appeal', *Daily Telegraph*, 11 March 1913, p. 6; 'Antarctic Disaster Fund', *SMH*, 21 March 1913, p. 5.

16 'She Must Not Suffer', *The Sun*, 13 February 1913, p. 7.

17 'Surely They Will Care!', *The Sun*, 14 February 1913, p. 1; 'Surely They Will Care!', *The Sun*, 16 February 1913, p. 5.

18 See 'Surely They Will Care!', *The Sun*, 17 February – 13 March 1913, p. 1; 'Scott Shilling Fund', *The Sun*, 19 March 1913, p. 1.

19 See, for example, 'Petty-Officer Evans', *The Sun*, 25 February 1913, p. 1; 'Antarctic Disaster Fund', *SMH*, 25 February 1913, p. 10; 'Lord Mayor's Fund', *Daily Telegraph*, 3 March 1913, p. 8; 'The Scott Fund', *SMH*, 10 March 1913, p. 4; 'The Scott Appeal', *Daily Telegraph*, 20 March 1913, p. 8; 'Antarctic Disaster Fund', *SMH*, 21 March 1913, p. 5; 'The Antarctic Fund', *Daily Telegraph*, 26 March 1913, p. 8; 'The Scott Fund', *The Sun*, 17 April 1913, p. 8.

20 'The Children's Pennies', *Daily Telegraph*, 15 February 1913, p. 12; 'Benefit at the Alhambra', *Daily Telegraph*, 17 February 1913, p. 8; 'Picture Showmen's Gift', *Evening News*, 26 February 1913, p. 10; 'Scott Fund Concert', *Evening News*, 10 April 1913, p. 12.

21 'Amusements', *SMH*, 28 February 1913, p. 5; 'The Scott Memorial Concert', *Daily Telegraph*, 1 March 1913, p. 13; 'Memorial Concert', *The Sun*, 2 March 11913, p. 10.

22 'A Widespread Campaign', *SMH*, 13 February 1913, p. 10; Antarctic Disaster Fund', *SMH*, 25 February 1913, p. 10.

23 'The Scott Fund', *Daily Telegraph*, 3 June 1913, p. 10; 'Scott Memorial Fund', *The Sun*, 15 July 1913, p. 1.

24 'Correspondence', *Bathurst Times*, 21 February 1913, p. 2; 'To the Editor', *Daily Telegraph*, 26 February 1913, p. 10; 'Scott's Dying Appeal', *The Sun*, 18 February 1913, p. 5; 'The Scott Fund', *The Sun*, 25 March 1913, p. 6.

25 'Why Not a Memorial?', *SMH*, 18 February 1913, p. 10; Mount Lyell and the Antarctic', *Daily Telegraph*, 21 March 1913, p. 9.

26 Royal Society Archives, MS/594/19, MS/595/9; SPRI, MS 1464/5.

27 SPRI, MS 1464/24;D; 'The Antarctic Tragedy', *Daily Telegraph*, 14 October 1913, p. 9; 'Scott Memorial', *Daily Telegraph*, 31 March 1913, p. 8; 'The Scott Memorial', *The Age*, 3 March 1913, p. 9.

28 'For the Federal Capital', *Brisbane Courier*, 10 March 1913, p. 7; 'Federal Territory', *Herald*, 20 February 1913, p. 8; 'Proposed Memorial', *Daily Telegraph*, 12 March 1913, p. 8.

29 Max Jones, *The Last Great Quest: Captain Scott's Antarctic Sacrifice*, Oxford University Press, 2004, pp. 193–226; Stephanie Barczewski, *Heroic Failure and the British*, Yale University Press, 2016, pp. 193–219.

30 'Defence Minister's Tribute', *Daily Telegraph*, 19 February 1913, p. 10; 'The Lesson of the Antarctic Tragedy', *Daily Telegraph*, 13 February 1913, p. 6.

31 'Memorial Cross', *Daily Telegraph*, 19 February 1913, p. 10.

32 'The Return of Captain Scott', *Daily Telegraph*, 11 February 1913, p. 6; 'Notes', *Evening News*, 11 February 1913, p. 6.

33 'The Mawson Antarctic Expedition', *Daily Telegraph*, 25 March 1913, p. 11.

34 'The Antarctic Fund', *Daily Telegraph*, 26 March 1913, p. 8.

35 University of Sydney Archives (USA), P11:7:4, letter from Eitel to David, 25 August 1913; 'When Mawson Calls for Aid'.

36 USA, P11:7:4, P11:7:6; NAA, A2911, 1109/1911, letter from George Reid to Lewis Harcourt, 13 June 1913; letter from Henry Lambert to Muirhead Collins, 1 July 1913; Douglas Mawson, *The Home of the Blizzard, Being the Story of the Australasian Antarctic Expedition 1911–1914*, vol. 2, Heinemann, 1915, pp. 311–12; 'Mawson Relief Fund', *The Argus*, 8 July 1913, p. 7; 'Mawson Expedition', *SMH*, 19 July 1913, p. 19; 'Dr Mawson and His Comrades', *Daily Telegraph*, 2 August 1913, p. 13.

37 'Mawson Expedition', *Telegraph* (Brisbane), 5 April 1913, p. 5; 'Mawson Relief', *Evening News*, 10 July 1913, p. 4.

38 USA, P11:7:4, letter from Cook to David, 11 September 1913; *Commonwealth Parliamentary Debates*, House of Representatives, no. 40, 2 October 1913, p. 1794.

39 'Mawson Party', *SMH*, 28 February 1914, p. 21.

40 'Back From Antarctic Ice', *Advertiser*, 27 February 1914, p. 15; 'Welcome Home', *Advertiser*, 3 March 1914, p. 9; 'Civic Welcome', *Advertiser*, 4 March 1914, p. 16; 'Aurora Open for Inspection', *Register*, 4 March 1914, p. 12; 'The Aurora', *Register*, 9 March 1914, p. 6.

41 'The Frozen South', *The Age*, 6 March 1914, p. 6; 'Mawson Arrives', *The Sun*, 12 March 1914, p. 7; 'Dr. Mawson', *SMH*, 13 March 1914, p. 9.

42 See, for example, 'Dr Mawson', *The Argus*, 17 March 1914, p. 9; 'Dr Mawson', *The Argus*, 18 March 1914, p. 15; 'The Royal Society', *Daily Telegraph*, 18 March 1914, p. 11.

43 'Antarctic Coal', *The Sun*, 18 March 1914, p. 12; 'Antarctic Coal', *Evening News*, 18 March 1914, p. 10.

44 'Dr Mawson', *Advertiser*, 13 March 1914, p. 8.

45 USA, P11:7:5, letter from Masson to David, 19 April 1914; letter from Masson to David, 23 April 1914; letter from Masson to David, 11 May 1914.

46 See Phillip Ayres, *Mawson: A Life*, Melbourne University Press, 1999, pp. 84–5.

47 See, for example, USA, P11:7:5, letter from Mawson to David, 18 December 1914; 'Mawson Lecture', *The Sun*, 27 August 1914, p. 6; 'Antarctic Adventure', *The Argus*, 27 August 1914, p. 10; 'Out on the Ice', *Daily Telegraph*, 31 August 1914, p. 8; 'The Mawson Lectures', *Telegraph*, 17 September 1914, p. 7; 'Antarctica', *Mercury*, 29 September 1914, p. 7.

48 'The Frozen South', *The Age*, 6 March 1914, p. 6.

49 'Out on the Ice', *Daily Telegraph*, 31 August 1914, p. 8.

50 'Gold in the Antarctic', *The Sun*, 10 February 1914, p. 5; 'Antarctic Coal', *The Sun*, 18 March 1914, p. 12; 'The Weather Theory', *Mercury*, 27 Match 1914, p. 6.

51 *West Australian*, 9 April 1914, p. 6; 'The Mawson Antarctic Expedition', *Advertiser*, 11 September 1914, p. 11.

52 USA, P11:7:6, letter from David to Davis, 24 October 1913; letter from David to Masson, 27 October 1913; NAA, A2, 1920/656, Ross Sea Relief Expedition report of Australian Advisory Committee, 31 January 1917.

53 'Antarctica', *SMH*, 9 October 1914, p. 6.

54 RW Richards, *The Ross Sea Shore Party 1914–17*, Erskine, 2003; NAA, A2, 1920/656, report from the Joint Committee of Public Accounts; Royal Geographical Society Archives, SSC/132/1; *Mercury*, 21 October 1914, p. 4; 'Antarctic Exploration', *Mercury*, 24 October 1914, p. 8; 'Antarctica', *SMH*, 5 December 1914, p. 13; 'Wireless for the Aurora', *Daily Telegraph*, 5 December 1914, p. 12; 'Imperial Trans-Antarctic Expedition', *SMH*, 8 December 1914, p. 10.

55 NAA, A2, 1920/656, report from the Joint Committee of Public Accounts.

56 'The South Pole', *SMH*, 29 March 1916, p. 11; 'The Antarctic Expedition', *SMH*, 1 April 1916, p. 16; 'Aurora', *SMH*, 5 April 1916, p. 13.

57 Richards, *The Ross Sea Shore Party*; Ernest Shackleton, *South: The Story of Shackleton's Last Expedition 1914–1917*, Heinemann, 1919; Ernest E Mills Joyce, *The South Polar Trail: The Log of the Imperial Trans-Antarctic Expedition*, Duckworth, 1929.

58 SPRI, MS 1537/2/36/1-2, letter from Emily Shackleton to Andrew Fisher, 17 April 1916; letter from Fisher to Emily Shackleton, 25 April 1916; SPRI, MS 1537/2/32/17;D, proposals of the Endurance Relief Committee, May

1916; SPRI, MS1537/2/36/3;D, letter from Mawson to Emily Shackleton, 14 June 1916; NAA, A2, 1920/656, cablegram from colonial secretary to Prime Minister's Department, 3 May 1916; minute on Relief Expedition to Antarctic; memorandum from WR Creswell, 5 May 1916; memorandum from JH Starling to secretary to the governor-general, 8 May 1916.

59 NAA, A2, 1920/656, Ross Sea Relief Expedition report of Australian Advisory Committee, 31 January 1917; letter from Ronald Munro Ferguson to Earl of Liverpool, 24 October 1917; letter from Ferguson to Liverpool, 5 March 1918; State Library Victoria, MS 8311-3234/9, JK Davis, *Report to the Australian Aurora Relief Committee*.

8 'The Equator to the Pole'

1 Fred Jacka and Eleanor Jacka (eds), *Mawson's Antarctic Diaries*, Allen & Unwin, 2008, pp. 313–26; A Grenfell Price, *The Winning of Australian Antarctica: Mawson's BANZARE Voyages 1929–31*, Angus & Robertson, 1962, pp. 57–83; Harold Fletcher, *Antarctic Days with Mawson: A Personal Account of the British, Australian, and New Zealand Antarctic Research Expedition of 1929–31*, Angus & Robertson, 1984; State Library Victoria (SLV), MS 8311 Box 3237/1, JK Davis, *Journal of a Voyage with* Discovery, *1929–30*; National Archives of Australia (NAA), A461, A413/4, BANZARE report 1929–30; NAA, A461, C413/6, letter from Mawson to Frank Strahan, 22 November 1930; University of Sydney Archives (USA), P11/7/8, P11/7/9.

2 Edward J Larson, *An Empire of Ice: Scott, Shackleton, and the Heroic Age of Antarctic Science*, Yale University Press, 2011, pp. 158, 170.

3 Tom Griffiths, *Slicing the Silence: Voyaging to Antarctica*, UNSW Press, 2007, pp. 111, 121.

4 For example, 'Shackleton Expedition', *The Argus*, 29 December 1915, p. 6; 'Antarctica', *The Sydney Morning Herald (SMH)*, 29 December 1915, p. 9; 'Social Gossip', *The Sun*, 11 March 1917, p. 15.

5 State Library of New South Wales, 2416960, *Shackleton's Call to Australia!*, 1917.

6 RF Scott, *Scott's Last Expedition*, Smith Elder, 1913; Douglas Mawson, *The Home of the Blizzard, Being the Story of the Australasian Antarctic Expedition 1911–1914*, Heinemann, 1915; Ernest Shackleton, *South: The Story of Shackleton's Last Expedition 1914–1917*, Heinemann, 1919; Griffith Taylor, *With Scott: The Silver Lining*, Smith Elder, 1916; Griffith Taylor, *Antarctic Adventure and Research*, Appleton, 1930; Herbert Ponting, *The Great White South*, Gerald Duckworth, 1921; Edward RGR Evans, *South with Scott*, Collins, 1921; Apsley Cherry-Garrard, *The Worst Journey in the World*, Constable, 1922; Gerald S Doorly, *The Voyages of the Morning*, Smith Elder, 1916; JK Davis, *With the 'Aurora' in the Antarctic*, A Melrose, 1919; Frank Hurley, *Argonauts of the South*, Putnam, 1925; JWS Marr, *Into the Frozen*

South, Cassell, 1923; Hugh Robert Mill, *The Life of Sir Ernest Shackleton*, William Heinemann, 1923; J Gordon Hayes, *Antarctica: A Treatise on the Southern Continent*, Richards Press, 1928; J Gordon Hayes, *The Conquest of the South Pole: Antarctic Exploration, 1906–1931*, Butterworth, 1932.

7 See, for example, USA, P11:7:10, *Siege of the South* bookings; letter from Douglas Mawson to F Strahan, 20 April 1933; USA, P11:8:2, Mawson Antarctic film; Scott Polar Research Institute (SPRI), MS 964/7/1-37;D, letter from HG Ponting to JG Hayes, 16 December 1933; 'Siege of the South', *The Sun*, 4 March 1932, p. 14; 'With Mawson to Antarctica', *Education: Journal of the NSW Public School Teachers Federation*, vol. 11, no. 10, 15 August 1930, p. 333.

8 See, for example, 'Shackleton's Polar Expedition', *Daily Telegraph*, 24 November 1919, p. 3; 'Shackleton Antarctic Pictures', *Telegraph*, 5 December 1919, p. 3l; 'Antarctic Heroes', *Newcastle Sun*, 12 December 1919, p. 4; 'Hardships of the Antarctic', *Advertiser*, 22 December 1919, p. 9. Also see Robert Dixon, *Photography, Early Cinema and Colonial Modernity: Frank Hurley's Synchronized Lecture Entertainments*, Anthem Press, 2012, pp. 1–146.

9 See, for example, 'Antarctic Animal Life', *Mercury*, 30 September 1919, p. 7; 'Antarctic', *SMH*, 29 August 1923, p. 14; 'Life and Scenery in the Antarctic', *Advertiser*, 22 June 1922, p. 11.

10 'Lecture on Antarctic', *The Argus*, 4 July 1927, p. 14; 'Tonight's Antarctic Lecture', *Herald*, 5 July 1927, p. 17.

11 'Antarctic Regions', *Mercury*, 17 February 1922, p. 8; 'The Antarctic', *Brisbane Courier*, 25 September 1929, p. 18.

12 See, for example, 'Scott's Last Expedition', *SMH*, 6 December 1929, p. 14; 'Lecture on Antarctic Expedition', *Brisbane Courier*, 28 July 1930, p. 8; 'Antarctic Experiences', *Telegraph*, 1 August 1930, p. 19; 'Antarctic Expedition', *SMH*, 27 November 1930, p. 16; 'Capt. Scott's Expedition', *Mercury*, 6 March 1931, p. 7; 'Antarctic Expedition', *The Age*, 11 November 1929, p. 10; 'Land of Ice and Blizzards', *Kyogle Examiner*, 6 September 1924, p. 1; 'The Antarctic', *Daily Telegraphs*, 24 November 1925, p. 2; 'University Extension', *Newcastle Morning Herald*, 14 July 1926, p. 8; *Mercury*, 3 October 1924, p. 4; 'Antarctic Regions', *Mercury*, 17 February 1922, p. 8; 'The Antarctic', *Brisbane Courier*, 25 September 1929, p. 18.

13 'Whaling in the Antarctic', *Mercury*, 27 August 1924, p. 3. See, for example, 'Arctic and Antarctic', *Telegraph*, 19 April 1923, p. 3; 'Sir H Wilkins to Lecture', *Herald*, 27 May 1933, p. 10; 'Explorer's Tour Postponed', *The Herald*, 17 August 1933, p. 25; 'Rymill's Polar Work', *The Age*, 22 June 1938, p. 8; 'Boy Scout Association', *Advertiser*, 29 June 1938, p. 12; 'Antarctic Explorer to Give Free Public Lecture', *Advertiser*, 30 June 1938, p. 17; 'Lecture by John Rymill', *Advertiser*, 5 July 1938, p. 20; 'Mr. John Rymill Tells of

Antarctic Experiences', *Advertiser*, 6 July 1938, p. 19; *Advertiser*, 13 July 1938, p. 26.

14 See, for example, 'Shackleton Again', *The Sun*, 30 June 1921, p. 1; *The Sun*, 30 January 1922, pp. 7–8; 'In Antarctica', *SMH*, 31 January 1922, p. 10; 'Sad Ceremony on Poop', *The Sun*, 2 February 1922, p. 1; 'The Passing Show', *The Argus*, 4 February 1922, p. 7; 'Shackleton's Memory', *The Sun*, 29 May 1922, p. 1; 'Antarctic Exploration', *The Age*, 19 June 1922, p. 9; 'Island of Storm', *The Sun*, 25 June 1922, p. 13.

15 Richard E Byrd, *Little America: Aerial Exploration in the Antarctic the Flight to the South Pole*, GP Putnam, 1930; Richard E Byrd, *Discovery: The Story of the Second Byrd Antarctic Expedition*, GP Putnam, 1935; Richard E Byrd, *Alone*, GP Putnam, 1938. See, for example, 'Antarctic Discovery', *The Argus*, 30 May-19 September 1936.

16 'Ellsworth Antarctic Expedition, 1935–36', *Polar Record*, vol. 2, no. 10, January 1936, pp. 129–30; 'Ellsworth Antarctic Expedition, 1935–36', *Polar Record*, vol. 2, no. 11, January 1936, pp. 101–3; 'Ellsworth Antarctic Expedition, 1935–36', *Polar Record*, vol. 2, no. 12, July 1936, pp. 156–60; 'Ellsworth Antarctic Expedition, 1938–39', *Polar Record*, vol. 2, no. 14, July 1937, p. 169; 'Ellsworth Antarctic Expedition, 1938–39', *Polar Record*, vol. 2, no. 16, July 1938, p. 120; 'Ellsworth Antarctic Expedition, 1938–39', *Polar Record*, vol. 3, no. 17, January 1939, pp. 76–7; 'Ellsworth Antarctic Expedition, 1938–39', *Polar Record*, vol. 3, no. 18, July 1939, pp. 174–5; 'Lincoln Ellsworth's Antarctic Expedition, 1938–39', *Polar Record*, vol. 4, no. 27, January 1944, p. 114.

17 Hubert Wilkins, 'The Wilkins-Hearst Antarctic Expedition, 1928–1929', *Geographical Review*, vol. 19, no. 3, July 1929, pp. 353–76.

18 Royal Geographical Society Archives, SSC/132, British Imperial Antarctic Expedition Prospectus.

19 SPRI, MS 932/9/1;D, letter from J Scott Keltie to HR Mill, 2 April 1919.

20 Thomas Wyatt Bagshawe, *Two Men in the Antarctic: An Expedition to Graham Land, 1920–1922*, Cambridge University Press, 1939.

21 'Antarctica', *SMH*, 11 August 1919, p. 6.

22 'South Pole', *The Sun*, 12 October 1919, p. 1; 'Antarctic Wealth', *The Sun*, 29 December 1919, p. 6.

23 'Minerals in the Antarctic', *The Age*, 12 August 1919, p. 6.

24 'Antarctic Wealth', *The Sun*, 31 December 1919, p. 5; 'To Antarctica By Air', *The Herald*, 1 January 1920, p. 5. On Taylor's unpopular environmental determinism, see Carolyn Strange and Alison Bashford, *Griffith Taylor: Visionary, Environmentalist, Explorer*, National Library of Australia, 2008.

25 See, for example, 'Antarctica', *SMH*, 11 August 1919, p. 6; 'South Pole', *The Sun*, 12 October 1919, p. 1; 'Captain Wilkins', *The Sun*, 3 November 1919,

p. 5; 'Antarctic Wealth', *The Sun*, 29 December 1919, p. 6; 'Cope's Polar Expedition', *The Age*, 26 January 1920, p. 5; 'The Cope Expedition', *The Herald*, 26 April 1920, p. 9.

26 SPRI, MS 964/7/1-37;D, letter from Ponting to Hayes, 12 August 1930; letter from Ponting to Hayes, 16 August 1930; 'Antarctic Cruises', *The Age*, 19 February 1930, p. 12; 'The Antarctic', *SMH*, 19 February 1930, p. 15; 'Antarctic', *Mercury*, 19 February 1930, p. 9; 'To Tour Antarctica', *The Sun*, 18 February 1930, p. 10; 'Cruises to Antarctic', *The Argus*, 19 February 1930, p. 7; 'Visits to Antarctica', *Brisbane Courier*, 19 February 1930, p. 16; 'Tourist Cruise in Antarctic', *The Herald*, 5 March 1930; 'Holidaying in Antarctica', *The Herald*, 10 May 1930, p. 17; 'Pleasure Tour in South', *The Herald*, 24 October 1930, p. 5; 'First Antarctic Holiday', *The Sun*, 26 October 1930, p. 4; 'Don and "Smithy" for Antarctic Stunts?', *Daily Pictorial*, 26 October 1930, p. 5; 'Antarctic Tourists', *Daily Telegraph*, 17 October 1931, p. 5; 'Antarctic Cruiser', *SMH*, 19 October 1931, p. 10; 'The South Pole', *Mercury*, 19 September 1931, p. 2.

27 SLV, MS 8311, Box 3251/5, letter from Ninnis to Mawson, 2 April 1928.

28 Ibid.

29 See Rohan Howitt, 'Oil from Penguins: Extraction and Empire in the Southern Ocean World, 1890–1917', *International Review of Environmental History*, vol. 9, no. 2, 2023, pp. 51–76.

30 USA, P11:7:4, P11:7:6.

31 State Library of Tasmania (SLT), G093/1/1, Macquarie Island Weather Bureau officer's report, 1916.

32 SLT, G093/1/1, memorandum by Allardyce, 17 June 1920.

33 SLT, G093/1/1, letter from Ernest Clerk to acting premier, 20 August 1935; report of interview between Clerk and treasurer, 17 December 1937; letter from Clerk to premier, 23 December 1937; letter from Clerk to treasurer, 19 February 1939.

34 See, for example, 'Life and Scenery in the Antarctic', *Advertiser*, 22 June 1922, p. 11; 'Antarctic Continent', *The Argus*, 6 July 1927, p. 22; SLT, G093/1/1, memorandum for Government House private secretary, 25 August 1933.

35 SLT, G093/1/1, report of interview between Clerk and treasurer, 17 December 1937.

36 See Marie Kawaja, 'Australia in Antarctica: Realising an Ambition', *Polar Journal*, vol. 3, no. 1, 2013, pp. 31–52; Marie Kawaja and Tom Griffiths, '"Our Great Frozen Neighbour" Australia and Antarctica before the Treaty, 1880–1945', in Marcus Haward and Tom Griffiths (eds), *Australia and the Antarctic Treaty System: 50 Years of Influence*, UNSW Press, 2011, pp. 9–47; Marie Kawaja, The Politics and Diplomacy of the Australian Antarctic,

PhD thesis, Australian National University, 2010; RA Swan, *Australia in the Antarctic: Interest, Activity, and Endeavour*, Melbourne University Press, 1961.

37 Robert K Headland, *The Island of South Georgia*, Cambridge University Press, 1984, app. 2; Ian B Hart, *Whaling in the Falkland Islands Dependencies 1904–1931: A History of Shore and Bay-Based Whaling in the Antarctic*, Pequena, 2006; JN Tønnessen and AO Johnsen, *The History of Modern Whaling*, trans. RI Christophersen, C Hurst, 1982, pp. 157–201.

38 NAA, A981, ANT 4, Part 2, copy of indenture for whaling in the Ross Sea, 5 September 1922; memorandum on British policy in the Antarctic; The National Archives of the United Kingdom (TNA), ADM 116/2386, order in council, 30 July 1923; Tønnessen and Johnsen, *History of Modern Whaling*, pp. 347–413.

39 Tønnessen and Johnsen, *History of Modern Whaling*, pp. 352–3; Bjørn L Basberg and Bryan Lintott, 'Perspectives on the Economic and Political History of the Ross Sea', *Polar Record*, vol. 13, no. 2, 2023, pp. 288–311; SLV, MS 8311, Box 3251/6, extract from *Annual Report* of Marine Department NZ for 1929–30.

40 SLV, MS 8311, Box 3252/1, letter from Davis to Kinsey, undated.

41 Ibid., cablegram from Page to Bruce, 10 December 1923.

42 NAA, A981, ANT 4, Part 2, memorandum on control of Ross Sea area.

43 Ibid., memorandum from comptroller-general to Prime Minister's Department, 27 February 1924.

44 'Antarctic', *Mercury*, 15 February 1929, p. 8.

45 USA, P11:7:8, minutes of Antarctic Committee meeting 18 March 1929; TNA, CO 78/183/7.

46 'Antarctic Whaling', *The Argus*, 28 September 1920, p. 8.

47 'Whaling Industry', *SMH*, 29 November 1928, p. 13.

48 *Mercury*, 8 March 1929, p. 5; *Telegraph* (Brisbane), 3 June 1930, p. 17; *Mercury*, 6 July 1931, p. 6.

49 'The Future of Whaling', *The Age*, 9 May 1931, p. 9.

50 'Whaling Wealth at Our Back Door', *Daily News* 18 February 1933, p. 15.

51 'Whales', *The Sun*, 21 April 1929, p. 2.

52 'Australian Whaling Company Limited', *West Australian*, 24 August 1929, p. 18.

53 SLV, MS 8311, Box 3251/7; SPRI, MS100/75/11; 'Australian Whaling Co', *SMH*, 29 July 1929, p. 13; 'Whaling Company', *West Australian*, 13 August 1929, p. 15; 'Revival of Whaling', *The Age*, 30 January 1933, p. 6; 'Whaling Possibilities', *SMH*, 16 February 1933, p. 8.

54 'To Enable Australia to Share in the Huge Profits of Whaling', *Mercury*, 27 August 1929, p. 6; 'Big Whaling Company', *West Australian*, 15 August 1929, p. 17; 'Pacific and Ross Sea Whaling Company', *Daily News*,

28 August 1929, p. 2; University of Melbourne Archives (UMA), 80/80 105/54, Box 1/3, letter from Flora Masson to Orme Masson, 24 September 1929.

55 See Cait Storr, '"Imperium in Imperio": Sub-Imperialism and the Formation of Australia as a Subject of International Law', *Melbourne Journal of International Law*, vol. 19, no. 1, 2018, pp. 335–68.

56 'Pacific Islands', *The Sun*, 15 April 1919, p. 1.

57 'Monroe Doctrine', *The Sun*, 8 February 1919, p. 3. See also E George Marks, *Watch the Pacific: Defenceless Australia*, Coles Book Arcade, 1924; E George Marks, *Pacific Peril, or Menace of Japan's Mandated Islands*, Wynyard Book Arcade, 1933.

58 'Australia and the Pacific Islands', *Daily Telegraph*, 4 February 1919, p. 4.

59 'Australia and Pacific Islands', *Sunday Times*, 2 February 1919, p. 4; 'Pacific Islands', *The Sun*, 14 October 1919, p. 7.

60 See Storr, '"Imperium in Imperio"'; Susan Pedersen, *The Guardians: The League of Nations and the Crisis of Empire*, Oxford University Press, 2015.

61 See Helen Bones and Nicholas Ferns, 'Pacific Nation or Neighbour: Australia's Relationship with New Zealand, Papua New Guinea, and the Pacific', in Bridget Brooklyn, Benjamin T Jones and Rebecca Strating (eds), *Australia on the World Stage: History, Politics, and International Relations*, Routledge, 2023, pp. 171–84.

62 'Antarctica', *The Argus*, 30 April 1919, p. 9; 'Antarctic', *SMH*, 30 April 1919, p. 10.

63 NAA, CP359/2, 9, claim to Antarctic lands.

64 David Hunter Miller, 'National Rights in the Antarctic', *Foreign Affairs*, vol. 5, no. 3, April, 1927, p. 508; TNA, ADM 1/8565/226, letter from H Lambert to secretary of the Admiralty, 28 July 1919.

65 TNA, ADM 1/8565/226, letter from Lambert to under secretary of state, Foreign Office, 5 December 1919.

66 NAA, A4311, 362/6, Leo Amery to Ronald Munro Ferguson, 6 February 1920; NAA, MP1185/9, 453/204/938, memorandum from Edward Millen to Naval Department, 20 May 1921.

67 SLV, MS 8311, Box 3232/1, letter from Davis to EL Piesse, undated.

68 NAA, MP1185/9, 453/204/938, letter from David to Malcolm Shepherd, 29 November 1920; letter from Mawson re future policy in Antarctic regions.

69 NAA, MP1185/9, 453/204/938, letter from Mawson re future policy in Antarctic regions; SLV, MS 8311, Box 3232/1, letter from Davis to Piesse, undated.

70 TNA, ADM 116/2386, memorandum on control of the Antarctic; NAA, A981, ANT 4, Part 2, memorandum on control of Ross Sea area; TNA, T 161/186/3, telegram from WM Hughes to Winston Churchill, 15 July 1922.

71 NAA, A981, ANT 4, Part 2, memorandum from VW Bradbury to Australian Navy Board, 10 October 1924.

72 See, for example, 'Antarctic', *SMH*, 11 February 1925, p. 18; 'The Value of Adelie Land', *The Herald*, 5 March 1925, p. 8; 'Adelie Land', *The Argus*, 6 March 1925, p. 12; 'Adelie Land', *Mercury*, 6 July 1925, p. 2; 'Adelie Land', *The Argus*, 28 August 1925, p. 11.

73 TNA, ADM 116/2386, telegram from Henry Forster to Amery, 4 December 1924.

74 NAA, A981, ANT 4, Part 3, memorandum on Australian sector of the Antarctic and recent French claim to administer Adelie Land.

75 See Gillian Triggs, 'Australian Sovereignty in Antarctica, Part I', *Melbourne University Law Review*, vol. 13, no. 2, 1981, pp. 123–58.

76 'Adelie Land', *Mercury*, 4 July 1925, p. 9; 'Adelie Land', *The Argus*, 4 July 1925, p. 31; 'Adelie Land', *SMH*, 4 July 1925, p. 15.

77 NAA, A981, ANT 4, Part 3, despatch from Forster to Amery, 16 September 1925.

78 TNA, ADM 116/2386, Committee of Imperial Defence—British Policy in the Antarctic, May 1926.

79 TNA, CAB 32/51, minutes of first meeting of Committee on British Policy in the Antarctic, 10 November 1926; minutes of second meeting, 17 November 1926; minutes of third meeting, 18 November 1926; report of Committee on British Policy in the Antarctic.

80 NAA, A461, I413/1, Australia to D.C. letter of 22 December 1927.

81 'The Antarctic', *Brisbane Courier*, 11 February 1928, p. 18.

82 'America's Claims in Antarctic', *Daily Telegraph*, 10 Aril 1929, p. 8.

83 *Commonwealth Parliamentary Debates*, House of Representatives, no. 27, 4 July 1930, p. 3718. For rumours of an American claim, see 'Britain's Blunder in the Antarctic', *The Sun*, 7 January 1930, p. 1; 'The Antarctic', *SMH*, 4 April 1930; 'America's Claim', *The Canberra Times*, 21 June 1930, p. 4; 'U.S. Claim', *The Sun*, 6 July 1930, p. 2; SPRI, MS100/75/9, Mawson Collection, letter from Douglas Mawson to Mill, 3 February 1929.

84 *Commonwealth Parliamentary Debates*, House of Representatives, no. 8, 21 February 1929, pp. 461–2.

85 USA, P11:7:6, minutes of Antarctic Committee meeting, 12 March 1929.

86 *Commonwealth Parliamentary Debates*, House of Representatives, no. 12, 22 March 1929, pp. 1747–9.

87 USA, P11:7:8, letter from Bruce to David, 18 March 1929; minutes of Antarctic Committee meeting, 27 March 1929.

88 USA, P11:7:8, minutes of Antarctic Committee meeting, 12 March 1929; minutes of Antarctic Committee meeting, 27 March 1929; letter from Henderson to David, 30 August 1929.

89 USA, P11:7:8, minutes of Antarctic Committee meeting, 15 June 1929; UMA, 80/80 105/54, Box 1/3, letter from Rosaline Masson to Orme Masson, 1 May 1929.

90 USA, P11:7:8, cablegram from Richard Casey to Henderson, 4 May 1929; minutes of Antarctic Committee meeting, 13 May 1929; minutes of Antarctic Committee meeting, 15 June 1929.

91 See, for example, USA, P11:7:8, minutes of Antarctic Committee meeting, 27 March 1929; minutes of Antarctic Committee meeting, 13 May 1929; SLV, MS 8311, Box 3237/1, JK Davis, *Journal of a Voyage with* Discovery*, 1929–30.*

92 USA, P11:7:8, minutes of Antarctic Committee meeting, 12 March 1929.

93 NAA, A461, N413/1, sailing orders, 30 October 1930; USA, P11:7:8, letter from Henderson to David, 30 August 1929; form of proclamation of an annexation.

94 SLV, MS 8311, Box 3237/8, Davis, *Journal of a Voyage with* Discovery; letter from Davis to Henderson, 27 May 1930; SPRI, MS100/75/13-14, letter from Mawson to Mill, 18 June 1930; letter from Mawson to Mill, 15 December 1930.

95 NAA, A461, A413/4, BANZ Antarctic Research Expedition 1929–30; NAA, A461, C413/6, letter from Mawson to Strahan, 22 November 1930; Price, *The Winning of Australian Antarctica*, pp. 57–83.

96 USA, P11:7:10, letter from Strahan to David, 20 March 1931; *Commonwealth Parliamentary Debates*, House of Representatives, no. 21, 22 May 1930, p. 2044.

97 *Commonwealth Parliamentary Debates*, House of Representatives, no. 18, 1 May 1930, p. 1331; *Commonwealth Parliamentary Debates*, House of Representatives, no. 31, 29 July 1931, p. 4623.

98 *The Argus*, 14 April 1930, p. 6.

99 SLV, MS 8311, Box 3237/1, Davis, *Journal of a Voyage with* Discovery; SLT, CRO1/1/464, letter from Kenneth McKenzie to Wm Lodewyk Crowther, 11 April 1931.

100 *Commonwealth Parliamentary Debates*, House of Representatives, no. 21, 22 May 1930, p. 2044.

101 NAA, A461, A413/4, BANZ Antarctic Research Expedition 1930–31 season; Douglas Mawson, 'The B.A.N.Z. Antarctic Research Expedition 1929–31', *Geographical Journal*, vol. 80, no. 2, August 1932, pp. 101–31.

102 See Christy Collis, 'The Proclamation Island Moment: Making Antarctica Australian', *Law Text Culture*, vol. 8, 2004, pp. 1–18; Noel D Barrett, 'Was Australian Antarctica Won Fairly?', *Polar Record*, vol. 45, no. 4, October 2009, pp. 360–7.

103 'Proclamation', *Commonwealth of Australia Gazette*, 24 August 1936, p. 1553.

104 *Commonwealth Parliamentary Debates*, House of Representatives, no. 21, 26 May 1933, pp. 1949–58.

105 *Commonwealth Parliamentary Debates*, Senate, no. 22, 1 June 1933, pp. 2017–18.
106 'Antarctic as Source of Wealth', *Advertiser*, 31 July 1933, p. 8.
107 *Commonwealth Parliamentary Debates*, House of Representatives, no. 21, 26 May 1933, pp. 1951–3; *Commonwealth Parliamentary Debates*, Senate, no. 22, 1 June 1933, pp. 2017–18.
108 *Commonwealth Parliamentary Debates*, House of Representatives, no. 21, 26 May 1933, pp. 1955–6.
109 'Australia Looks Southward', *The Herald*, 15 February 1933, p. 6.
110 'Conquest of the Antarctic', *SMH*, 26 December 1933, p. 6.

Conclusion: Exposed Timbers—The Afterlife of the Australian Antarctic

1 Phillip Law, *The Antarctic Voyage of HMAS Wyatt Earp*, Allen & Unwin, 1995, pp. 51–4.
2 NAA, A981, ANT 39, 172734, memorandum from WM Hughes on utilisation of *Wyatt Earp* and employment of Sir Hubert Wilkins, undated.
3 'Ellsworth Sighs for Romance of Polar Dog Teams', *The Argus*, 4 March 1939, p. 1.
4 Law, *The Antarctic Voyage*, p. 5.
5 Ibid., p. 72.
6 NLA, MS 9458.4.003, Phillip Law, untitled lecture to Legacy Club, 1949.
7 See Law, *The Antarctic Voyage*; Tim Bowden, *The Silence Calling: Australians in Antarctica 1947–97*, Allen & Unwin, 1997.
8 Protocol on Environmental Protection to the Antarctic Treaty (1991); Antarctic Treaty (1959).
9 Antarctic Treaty (1959), Article IV.
10 Marcus Haward and Nicholas Cooper, 'Australian Interests, Bifocalism, Bipartisanship, and the Antarctic Treaty System', *Polar Record*, vol. 50, no. 1, 2012, pp. 60–71; *Australian Antarctic Strategy and 20 Year Action Plan: 2022 Update*, Commonwealth of Australia, 2022.
11 Haward and Cooper, 'Australian Interests', pp. 60–71; Daniel Bray, 'The Geopolitics of Antarctic Governance: Sovereignty and Strategic Denial in Australia's Antarctic Policy', *Australian Journal of International Affairs*, vol. 70, no. 3, 2016, pp. 256–74.
12 *Australian Antarctic Strategy and 20 Year Action Plan: 2022 Update*, Commonwealth of Australia, 2022.
13 *Colonial Times*, 19 December 1848, p. 2.
14 JR Seeley, *The Expansion of England*, Macmillan, 1883, p. 8.
15 Miranda Johnson and Cait Storr, 'Australia as Empire', in Peter Cane, Lisa Ford and Mark McMillan (eds), *The Cambridge Legal History of Australia*, Cambridge University Press, 2022, pp. 258–80, quote p. 258.

16 See, for example, Cait Storr, '"Imperium in Imperio": Sub-Imperialism and the Formation of Australia as a Subject of International Law', *Melbourne Journal of International Law*, vol. 19, no. 1, 2018, pp. 335–68; Christopher Waters, 'The Last of Australian Imperial Dreams for the Southwest Pacific: Paul Hasluck, the Department of Territories and a Greater Melanesia in 1960', *Journal of Pacific History*, vol. 51, no. 2, 2016, pp. 169–85; Marilyn Lake, 'The Australian Dream of an Island Empire: Race, Reputation and Resistance', *Australian Historical Studies*, vol. 46, no. 3, September 2015, pp. 410–24; Roger C Thompson, *Australian Imperialism in the Pacific: The Expansionist Era 1820–1920*, Melbourne University Press, 1980.

17 See, for example, Helen Bones and Nicholas Ferns, 'Pacific Nation or Neighbour: Australia's Relationship with New Zealand, Papua New Guinea, and the Pacific', in Bridget Brooklyn, Benjamin T Jones and Rebecca Strating (eds), *Australia on the World Stage: History, Politics, and International Relations*, Routledge, 2023, pp. 171–84; Storr, '"Imperium in Imperio"'; Stuart Ward, 'Security: Defending Australia's Empire', in Deryck Schreuder and Stuart Ward (eds), *Australia's Empire*, Oxford University Press, 2008, pp. 232–58; Luke Trainor, *British Imperialism and Australian Nationalism: Manipulation, Conflict and Compromise in the Late Nineteenth Century*, Cambridge University Press, 1994.

18 'Violent Seas Wreck Former Wyatt Earp', *The Canberra Times*, 26 January 1959, p. 1; Law, *The Antarctic Voyage*, p. 124; James Hunter, 'HMAS Wyatt Earp', *Signals*, vol. 121, December 2017.

19 See, for example, Elizabeth Buchanan, 'The (Other) Continent We Can't Defend', *The Interpreter*, 13 August 2019.

INDEX